Why Some Politicians Are More Dangerous than Others

James Gilligan, MD

WHY SOME POLITICIANS ARE MORE DANGEROUS THAN OTHERS

polity

First published in 2011 by Polity Press

Polity Press
65 Bridge Street
Cambridge CB2 1UR, UK

Polity Press
350 Main Street
Malden, MA 02148, USA

ISBN-13: 978–0–7456–4981–8

A catalogue record for this book is available from the British Library.

Typeset in 11 on 14 pt Sabon
by Servis Filmsetting Ltd, Stockport, Cheshire
Printed and bound by the MPG Printgroup, UK

The publisher has used its best endeavours to ensure that the URLs for external websites referred to in this book are correct and active at the time of going to press. However, the publisher has no responsibility for the websites and can make no guarantee that a site will remain live or that the content is or will remain appropriate.

Every effort has been made to trace all copyright holders, but if any have been inadvertently overlooked the publisher will be pleased to include any necessary credits in any subsequent reprint or edition.

For further information on Polity, visit our website: www.politybooks.com

Dedicated to
Bernard Lown, MD

Everyone is entitled to his own opinion, but not his own facts.

Daniel Patrick Moynihan

In analyzing history, do not be too profound, for often the causes are quite simple.

Ralph Waldo Emerson, *Journals*

Contents

Acknowledgements

I would like to express my deep gratitude to my long-time research associate, Dr Bandy Lee, for performing the most complicated statistical analyses of the data in this book, in association with her colleague on the Yale University faculty, Rani Desai, of the Department of Statistics and Epidemiology, I also am indebted to Dr Lee and her colleague in the Department of Psychiatry, Dr Bruce Wexler, for valuable editorial suggestions, John Thompson has also made very helpful editorial suggestions, as has my wife, Carol.

Introduction: Murder Mysteries

This book is a murder mystery in that it presents a mystery about murder. Or, to be more exact, a series of mysteries concerning murder, including "self-murder" or suicide. Right at the start, two unanswered questions begin the series of mysteries I will attempt to solve. First, why do rates of homicide and suicide tend to increase and decrease together (which they do) – given that we commonly think of people who commit murder as very different from those who kill themselves (which they usually are – though not always)? The second mystery is: why do these rates of murder and suicide fluctuate so enormously – sometimes more than doubling and at other times dropping to less than half – within the population of the US over a time period too brief to allow for significant changes in the individuals composing the population?

As a psychiatrist, I have worked as a clinician with murderers in prisons and also with both prisoners and private patients who were struggling with suicidal impulses. My question was not "Who done it?" or, in

1

the case of suicide, who was tempted or attempting to do it (that mystery had already been solved), but rather, "Why?" I had also been called upon to deal with epidemics of violence within the Massachusetts prisons, at a time when rates of homicide and suicide had skyrocketed. In doing so, I discovered that epidemics of violence can be brought under control.

Nothing prepared me, however, for the discovery of an epidemic of another sort. As someone interested in the causes and prevention of violence, I had been following suicide and homicide rates as reported from one year to the next in the US and around the world. I noticed that these rates increased sharply at certain times and decreased equally dramatically at other times. Suicide and homicide rates have been reported on a yearly basis in the US since 1900. I was intrigued by the fact that suicide and homicide rates tend to rise and fall together, which suggested the possibility that whatever was causing a rise in the one might be causing a rise in the other. But my eye was also caught by what looked like a pattern of peaks and valleys. Tracking rates of suicide and homicide for over a century, from 1900 through 2007 (the last year for which we have comparable data), I saw three large, sudden, and prolonged increases and decreases in these measures of lethal violence, which reached a peak and were then followed by equally dramatic decreases. Both the increases and the decreases were steep and consistent (that is, they continued without interruption for several years and then the rates fluctuated within an unusually high or low range for several more years or decades), so that a graph of these death rates looks like a profile of mountain peaks or mountain ranges interspersed with valleys. Indeed, the difference between the mountains and the valleys was sufficiently great – with the peaks themselves at times more than twice as high as the valleys – for it to become clear to me that I was seeing a map showing epidemics of lethal violence, interspersed with periods of return to more "normal" or endemic rates.

I had puzzled over these epidemics for years without a clue as to what was causing them. And then one day I noticed that all three of the epidemics of lethal violence corresponded with the presidential election cycle. Specifically, rates of suicide and homicide began rising to epidemic levels only after a Republican was elected president, and remained within that range throughout the time Republicans occupied the White House. The increase began during their first year or years in office, and peaked in their last year or years. They did not reverse direction and fall below epidemic levels until after Democrats took office, with the fall occurring within the first year or two of the new Democratic administration, and the rates usually reaching their lowest point during the last year or years in which a Democratic president occupied the White House. When I subjected these yearly changes to a statistical analysis, I found that in all three cases – for suicide, for homicide, and for total lethal violence (meaning suicide and homicide rates combined) – the association between political party and lethal violence rates was statistically significant. Suicide and homicide increased when Republicans were in the White House and decreased under Democratic administrations, with a magnitude and consistency that could not be attributed to chance alone.

My first thought was: how can this be? Surely, it can't be that simple. And of course it is not that simple. It cannot be simply the political label of the party of the president that raises or lowers violent death rates. If there is a causal relationship between party and violent death, rather than a chance correlation, then it would seem almost self-evident that it must lie in the differences between the policies and achievements of the two parties, and the effect that those differences have on people's behavior. But are there such differences, and can they be demonstrated to have that effect on violent death rates?

And why do suicide and homicide rates parallel each other? The statistics, no matter how significant, fly in the face of common assumptions made about violent behavior. People who commit suicide are generally considered to be either sad or mad; they are patients usually seen in a psychiatric office or hospital. People who commit homicide are usually seen as criminals and considered to be bad. They are commonly regarded as needing not treatment but punishment, and they are found, for the most part, in prisons, not mental hospitals or private offices. Similarly, the causes of suicidal and homicidal behavior are commonly viewed as residing within the individual. We expect people who kill themselves to have a history of depression, a genetic predisposition to depression, or some other psychiatric illness, or to have suffered from extreme trauma or physical illness, such as terminal cancer. People who kill others, by contrast, are usually regarded as moral monsters – sociopaths, criminals, "bad seeds," or just plain "evil." Even though the statistics show that suicide

4

and homicide rates parallel each other and that both are associated with the presidential election cycle, and these data are compiled by civil servants, trained epidemiologists, and statisticians employed by the National Center for Health Statistics of the US Public Health Service, it is hard to believe these statistics without reconsidering most of the assumptions we have been accustomed to making about who commits suicide and homicide and why.

So, in fact, the matter is not simple, and the mystery deepens. It is true that a correlation, no matter how unlikely it is to be due to chance, does not prove causation. Remember the tongue-in-cheek claim that the stock market declines after a team from the American Football Conference wins the Super Bowl, and soars when a team from the National Conference wins? Apparently this has been true 33 out of 41 years, a success rate of 80%![1] Sometimes, as in this instance, correlations simply result from meaningless coincidences, with no plausible causal mechanism connecting the two.

Or a correlation may be due to some third factor with which both of the phenomena in question are related. If heart attack rates are correlated with the rate of telephone ownership in a society, that is almost certainly due to the fact that both of those variables – heart attacks and telephone ownership – are associated with the degree of economic development in the society, and that variable is actually causing the increase in heart attacks (by several causal mechanisms, including

---

[1] Downloaded from Snopes.com/business . . . superbowl.asp on 10/8/2010.

greater longevity, which brings a larger proportion of the population into the age range in which heart attacks are more likely; less frequent exercise, because people are more likely to drive to work than to walk; a richer diet with more animal fat and cholesterol; and so on) – whereas no causal mechanism has even been hypothesized that could support the notion that simply buying a telephone, in and of itself, causes you to have a heart attack.

But what about the correlation between political parties and rates of lethal violence? This is the mystery I have set out to solve. As a psychoanalytically oriented psychiatrist, my training and most of my experience as a therapist had led me to seek the sources of psychological suffering or character disorders in the vicissitudes of people's personal lives, not in political events. As a reader of literature, I was familiar with Dr. Johnson's assertion, "How small, of all that human hearts endure, / That part which laws and kings can cause or cure." Yet here was evidence staring me in the face indicating that laws and kings may subject human hearts to the unendurable, or have an equally powerful effect in the opposite direction. To solve the mystery of the correlation between political parties in power and violent deaths, it would be necessary to discover the causal mechanisms by which a change in the party of the president can lead more people to kill themselves or others, or, conversely, can reduce the incidence of lethal violence. How could this be so?

In the first chapter, "A Matter of Life and Death," I present the data – not mine but those compiled by the US government. They show: (1) the rise and fall of rates of homicide and suicide from 1900 through 2007; (2) the three periods during which these rates of lethal violence reached epidemic levels and then declined to non-epidemic ones; (3) the association of these periods of epidemic rates of lethal violence with Republican administrations and of non-epidemic levels with Democratic administrations; and (4) that the year-to-year changes in both suicide and homicide rates showed net cumulative increases during the 59 years in which Republicans were in power (following the baseline year, 1900), and equally large decreases during the 48 years of Democratic administrations. (By "net cumulative" increases or decreases I mean the sum of the year-to-year increases and decreases that occurred during the years the two parties were in power. From 1900 through 2007, there were 107 years in which the violent death rates either increased or decreased from what they had been during the previous year. During 59 of those years, Republicans were in power, and during 48, Democrats. For example, the lethal violence rate in the US was 15.6 per 100,000 people in 1900, and 17 in 1901: an increase of 1.4. In 1902 it decreased to 15.7, a decrease of 1.3, so that during that two-year period, the calendar years 1901 and 1902, there was a net cumulative increase of 0.1 [i.e., 1.4 minus 1.3, or, in other words, 15.7 minus 15.6] during those years of Republican governance. During the entire 107-year period, there was a net cumulative increase of 19.9 violent deaths per 100,000 population during the 59 years Republicans were in power, and an almost exactly equal net decrease of 18.3 during the 48 years of Democratic administrations.)

Examining the data, I conclude that, however I slice and dice them – for example, confining the study to the period before the Great Depression, or before World War II, or after World War II, in order to rule out the possibility that some great but unique historical event, rather than the party in power at the time, could have skewed the data – one finding remains constant: rates of lethal violence (suicide and homicide) rose to epidemic levels *only* during Republican administrations, and decreased below those levels *only* under Democrats. As a consequence of that, the sum of year-to-year changes showed a net *increase* in both suicide and homicide under Republicans, and a net *decrease* under Democrats, even during these shorter time periods. Given the stability of that correlation between the political parties and the violent death rates, and my inability to disconfirm it, the question that remains is: what does it mean? Why is it occurring, and doing so repeatedly? As a physician, my interest has always been in matters of life and death, not politics, and this foray into politics because of a chance discovery that implicated political actors only happened because of my attempt to learn what was causing these deaths and how we could save lives.

In chapter 2, "What Kind of a Man Are You?" I ask: are there other changes in the social environment, besides the change in the political party of the president, that also correlate with changes in violent death rates – for example, changes in the rate and duration of unemployment; in the frequency, depth, and duration of recessions and depressions; or changes in the degree of social and economic inequality? Could changes in these economic measures be among the causal mechanisms that increase or decrease people's motivation to kill themselves or others?

In chapter 3, "Nothing Succeeds Like Failure," I extend my investigation to ask whether the economic conditions identified in chapter 2 increase or decrease depending upon which party is in power. In doing so, I come upon a paradox that constitutes a new mystery: why is the party that proclaims itself to be the party of prosperity and economic growth, and of public safety and "law and order," the party that mounted the "wars" on crime and drugs, associated with higher rates of lethal violence and of poverty, unemployment, and recession? And if one party is consistently inflicting a greater degree of economic stress and distress upon the American public and achieving a lower level of prosperity and economic security than the other party is, and in that sense achieving economic failure rather than success, how could it continue to win elections and remain a viable party?

In chapter 4, "The Shame of It All," I come to the heart of the mystery: the emotion that motivates aggressive impulses to kill others, and the emotional forces that motivate redirecting that aggression onto the self, as in suicide. In *Violence: Reflections on a National Epidemic*, I identified shame as the proximal cause of violence, the necessary – although not sufficient – motive for violent behavior.[2]

---

[2] James Gilligan, *Violence: Reflections on a National Epidemic*, New York: Vintage Books, 1997. Originally published as *Violence: Our Deadly Epidemic and Its Causes*, New York: Grosset/Putnam, 1996. See also James Gilligan, "Shame, Guilt and Violence," *Social Research*, 70(4): 1149–80, 2003.

In chapter 5, "Who Wants To Be Redundant?," I ask whether unemployment, relative poverty, and the sudden loss of social and economic status have been observed to increase the intensity of the emotion of shame. If they do, this could bridge the gap between political and economic events and individual behavior. Although we know on an anecdotal level that people may kill themselves when they become ruined financially, we still resist thinking of these tragic instances as part of an epidemic of violence. We've all heard of "trickle-down" theories of economics, but what about trickle-down theories of violence, affecting both the sad or mad and the evil or bad alike?

In chapter 6, "Red States, Blue States: Honor vs. Guilt," I shift gears. Instead of examining how one population (that of the US) changes over time, I will investigate how distinct populations (of the Red vs. the Blue States, i.e., those with Republican vs. those with Democratic voting majorities) differ from each other at the same time – in the year 2000, and again in 2004. In doing so, I will examine cultural differences between these two groups of states and also personality differences between Republican and Democratic voters. Then, in the final chapter, "The Mystery Solved: What Is To Be Done?," I will solve the mystery of why violent death rates increase under Republicans and decrease under Democrats, and consider the implications this has for the way we think about politics, economics, and violence.

1

A Matter of Life and Death

For the first 13 years of the twentieth century, from 1900 through 1912, the presidents of the US were Republicans: McKinley, Teddy Roosevelt, and Taft. In 1913, Woodrow Wilson, a Democrat, took office and held it for the following eight years, through 1920. The graph in figure 1.1, illustrating the rate of lethal violence in the US from 1900 to 2007, shows a line beginning in 1900, at which time the violent death rate (the sum of suicide and homicide rates) was 15.6 for every 100,000 people per year. It is important to add at this point that these violent death rates are "age adjusted," meaning that the proportion of people in different age groups is held constant because mortality rates are so influenced by age, with homicide rates being commonest among young adults and suicide rates highest among the elderly. Age adjusting is a means of holding the age distribution within the population constant, so that variations in death rates are not merely an artifact of changes in the proportion of the population that falls within the most vulnerable age groups. This

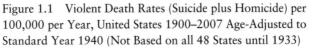

Figure 1.1   Violent Death Rates (Suicide plus Homicide) per
100,000 per Year, United States 1900–2007 Age-Adjusted to
Standard Year 1940 (Not Based on all 48 States until 1933)

Sources: D.L. Eckberg, "Estimates of Early Twentieth-century U.S. Homicide
Rates: An Econometric Forecasting Approach," *Demography*, 32: 1–16,
1995; Paul C. Holinger, *Violent Deaths in the United States*, New York:
Guilford Press, 1987.

is important in vital statistics for the same reason that holding the value of the dollar constant so as to adjust for inflation is important in economic statistics. It means that the changes in the vital statistics that are shown on the graph are not simply artifacts, or side-effects, of the post-World War II "baby boom," for example.

To return to the graph, the line, beginning at 15.6 in 1900, then rises in a steep, upward slope, increasingly steadily, making an especially large jump after the (financial) Panic of 1907, and by 1908 and 1911 reaches peaks of 22.6 violent deaths per 100,000, 50 percent higher than where it began in 1900. Thus we see that during the period 1900–12, when Republicans occupied the White House, lethal violence escalated from non-epidemic to epidemic levels. To make it clear what we are talking about, each one point increase in lethal violence signifies 3,000 additional deaths at today's US population level of approximately 300 million, so an increase from 15.6 to 21.9 between 1900 and 1912 corresponds to what today would be an increase of about 18,900 additional violent deaths – per year.

Following Woodrow Wilson's accession to office in March 1913, the rate continued at its epidemic level for the first year, peaking at 23.3 in 1914, his second year in office, and then began an abrupt, steep, and consistent year-by-year decline throughout the last six years of his presidency (well before, during, and after America's brief participation in World War I), until it bottomed out at a rate of 17.4 by Wilson's last full year in office (1920). In short, the years of Republican presidents were associated with a rise in lethal violence to epidemic levels, and the switch to a Democratic president was associated with a reversal of this trend, ending the epidemic.

But the reversal was short-lived. For the next twelve years, Republican presidents (Harding, Coolidge, and Hoover) occupied the White House, and, as figure 1.1 shows, the violent death rate escalated into the epidemic range again, beginning in the first year of Harding's administration, and remained in a "mountain (epidemic) range" for the entire 12 years the Republicans occupied the White House, with increases almost every year after 1923, their third year in power. That steep upward climb continued until it peaked at the record high of 26.5 violent deaths per 100,000 by 1932, the last full year in which Republicans were in office. It is worth noting that the upward climb began long before the onset of the Great Depression in 1930. The violent death rate had already increased from the low of 17.4, which the Republicans inherited from Wilson's last year in office, to 22.3 by 1929. It continued to rise further, and even more steeply, during the first (and worst) years of the Depression, finally peaking at the record high of 26.5 – a full 9.1 more violent deaths per year for every 100,000 people than during Wilson's last year in office. To give you a sense of the magnitude of that increase, at today's population level, this would amount to an increase of 27,300 additional suicides and homicides per year. Thus the second epidemic of lethal violence also occurred following the election of a Republican to the presidency, and continually increased in magnitude from that time, 1920, through 1932, the last year of Republican hegemony before they were replaced by a Democrat.

In 1933, Franklin Roosevelt began the first of what would become twenty uninterrupted years of Democratic presidents. In 1945, Truman succeeded Roosevelt, remaining in office through 1952. In fact, Democrats controlled the White House for 28 of the 36 years from 1933 through 1968, with Kennedy and Johnson in power during the last 8 of these years. Only one Republican president, Eisenhower, occupied the White House (from 1953 through 1960) during that period. Although Eisenhower was a Republican, he is the only Republican president who did not increase violent death rates significantly after coming to office. Essentially, they remained at the same level as they had been under the Democrats who preceded him.

What is most remarkable about this period from the standpoint of our mystery, is that the 20 years – and even the 36 years – following Roosevelt's election to office ushered in the longest "valley" – the longest uninterrupted period of freedom from epidemic levels of violence in the twentieth century. As you can see from the graph, the violent death rate began an abrupt, steep, and almost uninterrupted decline, beginning in Roosevelt's first year in office (1933), starting from the level of 26.5 violent deaths per 100,000 population that he inherited from his Republican predecessors and by 1941, the last year before America entered World War II, dropping below the epidemic floor of 19 to a rate of 18.8. From 1941 through 1969, the violent death rate did not once climb back into the epidemic range of 19–20 or more. Indeed, for a full quarter of a century, from 1942 through 1967, it did not reach as high as 18 again.

To clarify how I am using the term "epidemic," I calculated both the mean and the median of the violent death rates throughout the past century, which were 19.4 and 20 respectively, and I use the term "epidemic" to refer to death rates that are unusually high, or in other words above the average (mean or median) level. Thus when I speak of epidemics I will mean those violent death rates that fall within the range of 19.4 or 20 to 26.5, the latter being the highest level reached over the past century. Non-epidemic rates, conversely, will mean those that range from 11 to 19.4. (Almost all of these rates have remained well above 20 during the periods I am calling epidemics, and well below 19.4 during the period I am calling "normal," so it makes little difference whether we consider 19.4 or 20 to be the approximate point of transition between the "mountain range" and the "valley.")

To summarize thus far, the three Republican presidents who preceded Roosevelt presided over an epidemic of lethal violence, just as Wilson's three Republican predecessors had. Roosevelt, like Wilson, ended the epidemic; and violent death rates continued to remain below the epidemic range under his Democratic successors.

Let me take a moment to emphasize again that, although the numbers themselves may appear small (an increase in a death rate from, say, 15 to 20 per 100,000 people per year, or even from 18 to 19, may sound like an increase of only 1 death, or 5), at today's US population level of 300 million people, each single digit increase in the death rate signifies 3,000 additional violent deaths per year. When one considers that that is almost exactly the same as the number of people who were killed on 9/11/2001, and that those 3,000 deaths changed history, becoming the rationale for two wars in which the United States is still engaged, these figures are not trivial.

So far, then, we have covered the first two of the three epidemics of lethal violence that occurred between 1900 and 2007. We noted that both began during Republican presidencies and ended during Democratic ones. The first epidemic began in 1905, in the middle of Teddy Roosevelt's presidency – during and following which the death rate increased from 15.6 to 21.9 – and ended when Wilson came to power in 1913, reaching a low of 17.4 by his last year in office. Another twelve years of Republican presidents, beginning in 1921, witnessed steep year-to-year increases in the death rate, which reached a new and record-high epidemic level of 26.5 by 1932 – the highest of the century, in fact. This was then reduced under Roosevelt to 15 by 1944, showed a brief uptick (though still well below epidemic levels) after the end of the war, as usually happens when major wars end (as I will discuss below), and then resumed its decline back to its 1944 level of 15 by 1951 and 1952, Truman's last two years in office. The violent death rate remained below epidemic levels not only throughout Franklin Delano Roosevelt's last two terms in office, but also during the entire administrations of Truman, Eisenhower, Kennedy, and Johnson.

However, once Johnson was replaced by the Republican Nixon in 1969, the rate quickly climbed again into the epidemic stratosphere for the third time in the century. It began increasing from the first year of the

Nixon administration; rose above the epidemic "floor" by his second year in office, 1970, when it reached 19.9; and continued increasing year after year to 23.2 by 1975. It remained in the epidemic range of 21.9–22.9 during the Democrat Carter's four years in office, 1977–80, and continued at epidemic levels of 19.9–22.4 under the Republicans Reagan and Bush Sr., from 1981 through 1992.

When Clinton took office in 1993, having inherited a violent death rate of 21.7 from his Republican predecessor, the first President Bush, the violent death rate began a steep and consistent decline year after year, dropping below epidemic levels (to 18.3) by 1997, the first year of his second four-year term in office, until by his last year in office (2000) it had fallen to 16. Republicans had been in power during 20 of the 24 years between 1969 and 1993. And it was not until a Democrat, President Clinton, became elected for two terms in office that the third and longest lethal violence epidemic of the twentieth century, one that lasted for 28 years (1970–97), finally ended.

The moment a Republican president, George Bush Jr., succeeded Clinton in 2001, the dramatic decline in lethal violence that had occurred under Clinton abruptly ended and reversed itself as the death rate began drifting upward again. By 2007, the last year for which there are comparable data, it had reached 17.2.

To sum up: as the graph in figure 1.1 shows, there were three epidemics of lethal violence in the twentieth century, all of which began under Republicans and all of which ended under Democrats. It took them a while, even with steady, uninterrupted declines year after year, but Democrats ended these epidemics by 1918, 1941, and 1997. The epidemics lasted from 1904 to 1917, 1921 to 1940, and 1970 to 1996, a total of 61 years. And there were three periods during which violence resided in the "valley" range, below epidemic levels, 1918–20, 1941–69, and 1997–2007, all of which began under Democrats (in 1918, 1941, and 1997) and lasted a total of 43 years. The first two of those non-epidemic ranges ended once Republicans returned to power. It is too early at this point to say whether the current non-epidemic violent death range will have ended by the last year of Bush Jr.'s administration in 2008, since we do not yet have comparable data beyond the year 2007. What we do know is that both violent death rates, suicide and homicide, abruptly discontinued the year-by-year decline they had shown under Clinton, and once again began increasing as soon as Bush took office.

Although the violent death rate in America continued falling after the US entered the Second World War[1] in the

---

[1] For a review of the mixed effects of wars on homicide rates (but not suicide), see "Violent Acts and Violent Times," ch. 4 in Dane Archer and Rosemary Gartner, *Violence and Crime in Cross-National Perspective,* New Haven, CT: Yale University Press, 1984, pp. 63–97. They found evidence of prolonged post-war increases in homicide rates in most nations. That is clearly not what occurred in the United States following World War II, however, for these rates increased only twice, in 1945 and 1946, going from 5 in 1944 to 6.4 in 1946, but then immediately began a consistent year-by-year decrease the following year. By 1951 it had reached 4.9, lower even than its lowest level during the war, and remained below 5 from 1953 to 1964. It did not reach epidemic levels again until 1970, shortly after the Republicans returned to power in 1969, and then remained within the epidemic range until Democrats returned to power under Clinton. Suicide rates before, during, and after World War II followed essentially the same pattern as the homicide rates just described – as they did, indeed, during the entire time period being studied here.

closing days of 1941, the decline had begun long before that, descending from 26.5 in 1932, the Republicans' last year in office, to 18.8 by 1941, and had thus fallen below epidemic levels before the US had entered the war. The rate of lethal violence (homicide and suicide), then continued to fall during the war years, reaching a low of 15 by 1944, at the height of the war. But it then remained within roughly that same range or lower, from 14.3 to 15.9, for 14 post-war years (1951–64), during the presidencies of Truman, Eisenhower, Kennedy, and Johnson. Thus the war itself neither ended the epidemic levels of violence that Roosevelt had inherited from his Republican predecessors – they had already ended before the war began – nor led to either a major or a prolonged increase in lethal violence during the post-war years. Although there was a brief uptick in lethal violence rates following the end of the war, in 1945 and 1946, to as high as 16.9 (still well below epidemic levels), they then began falling again the following year, reaching lows of 15.3 and 15.2 by 1951–2, the last years of Truman's presidency, thus returning to the same level as their lowest point during the war. They remained in this same low range during the next 12 years, reaching a record low of 14.3 in 1957.

Except for under Eisenhower, violent death rates during all Republican administrations either rose sub-stantially above those inherited from their predecessors or remained within an inherited epidemic range. While this single exception distinguishes Eisenhower's presi-dency (1953–60) from those of the 11 other Republican presidents since 1900, it does not contradict the general observation that rates of lethal violence rise to epidemic levels only under Republican presidents. With Ike, they did not rise but remained in roughly the same range as during Truman's last year in office, from slightly below to slightly above 15, and ended only insignificantly (0.1) higher than they had been under Truman.

Death rates from suicide and homicide ranged from 15.1 to 15.9 through Kennedy's three years in office and Johnson's first year. There was then a rise, although not to epidemic levels, during the last three years of the Johnson administration, with the lethal violence rate reaching 18 during Johnson's last year in office (1968) for the first time since 1941. From the point of view of the mysterious association between epidemics of lethal violence and Republicans in the White House, the most relevant point about that increase is that the rate of lethal violence under Johnson, even at its highest, remained below the epidemic levels that followed once this 36-year Democratic-dominated period of relative non-violence ended and was replaced by 27 Republican-dominated years marked by an uninterrupted epidemic of violence (1970 through 1996).

The 1968 election constituted one of the major electoral realignments of the twentieth century, comparable to the 1920 (post-World War I) election that led to 12 years of Republican presidencies which culminated in the Great Depression and the highest lethal violence rates of the century, and to the 1932 election that led to 36 years of what has been called the New Deal Agenda (to which the nominally Republican President Eisenhower subscribed whole-heartedly). The year 1968 was the one in which the Republicans' "Southern strategy" – i.e., the appeal to white racial prejudice and the white backlash against the gains of the civil rights movement – resulted in the radical transformation of the 11 former Confederate southern states and two border states (Kentucky and Oklahoma) from almost uniformly Democratic to almost uniformly Republican in their political affiliations and voting patterns. This in turn brought the Republican party back into control of the White House for 20 of the next 24 years. What followed was the longest epidemic of lethal violence in the history of the past 107 years, lasting for 27 years from 1970 through 1996. The rates of suicide and homicide increased steadily during every year of Nixon's 6-year presidency, crossing the threshold into epidemic levels by his second year in office, when they reached 19.9, and continuing to a high of 23.2 by Ford's first year as president.

Another Democrat, Jimmy Carter, who succeeded Ford in 1977, was the only one of the seven Democratic presidents of the twentieth century under whom an inherited epidemic of lethal violence did not fall below epidemic levels. Instead, the epidemic levels of suicide and homicide he inherited from his Republican predecessors were basically unaffected one way or the other by his presidency, with both rates remaining at epidemic levels during his term in office, just as they had under Nixon and Ford. It is important for our purposes here to stress that the Carter administration did not initiate an epidemic level of lethal violence (no Democrat ever has), but he was alone among Democrats in not reversing the epidemic he inherited. The fact that he was in the White House for only four years does not alone explain the persistence of the epidemic under his administration since all of his Democratic predecessors (like Clinton later in the century) began reversing the epidemics they had inherited from their Republican predecessors early in or at the very start of their first terms in office – with lethal violence rates then declining consistently year by year. During the administrations of the two Republicans who followed Carter, Reagan and Bush Sr., violent death rates, although they fluctuated up and down from 19.9 to 22.4, never dropped below epidemic or mountain range levels during this 12-year period (1981–92).

To recapitulate, when Bill Clinton assumed power in 1993, he inherited a violent death rate of 21.7 from the first President Bush. During Clinton's first year in office, violent death rates began a steep and steady year-by-year decline, finally reaching a level that was below the epidemic floor of 19 by the beginning of his second term in 1997. In other words, it took four years of continuous declines to end the epidemic levels of violence inherited from the Republicans. Following that, the death rates continued to drop, reaching a low of 16 by 2000, his last year in office. The moment Bush Jr. took office in 2001, this dramatic decline abruptly stopped and reversed direction, beginning a slow and fluctuating upward climb. Since we have definitive data only through 2007, we cannot yet assess the full effect of the Bush presidency on rates of lethal violence in the US. At the moment, all we can say is that the violent death rate had risen from 16 to 17.2 by 2007, which translates into an increase of 3,600 violent deaths a year compared with Clinton's last year in office. By comparing Bush's record with that of Clinton, we can observe that, if violent death rates had continued the same decline after 2000 as they had shown under Clinton, the rate of murder, rather than increasing to 6.8 per 100,000 as it did under Bush, would have declined to 2.9 by 2007, and the 2007 suicide rate, instead of increasing to 10.4, would have dropped to 8.9. The point of calculating those numbers is not to say that these changes necessarily would have happened, but simply to indicate how substantial the differences were between the pattern of changes in death rates that actually did occur under each president.

What can be said with certainty of both Eisenhower and Carter is that neither of them represents an exception to our more general finding that rates of lethal violence increase from non-epidemic levels to epidemic ones *only* under Republicans, and recover from epidemics *only* under Democrats. What this suggests is that it is necessary, but not sufficient, to have a Republican president in order for an epidemic of violence to start, and that it is necessary, but not sufficient, to have a Democratic president in order for an epidemic to end.

To summarize, then, the overall differences in violent death rates under Republican and Democratic presidents are statistically significant (that is, they cannot be explained as a function of chance alone). The correlation is strong enough to override both historical vagaries (the Great Depression, World War II) and individual differences (Eisenhower, Carter). Hence, the mystery: why do rates of lethal violence increase to epidemic levels only during Republican administrations, and decline to "normal" or non-epidemic levels only under Democratic presidencies?

Another way of looking at the same data leads to

the observation that rates of both suicide and homicide often fluctuate, sometimes increasing and sometimes decreasing from one year to the next, under both Republicans and Democrats. However, as we already know from having seen the steep increases that lead from valleys to mountain peaks under Republicans, and the steep decreases that lead from mountain peaks to valleys under Democrats, rate increases from one year to the next occur more often, and also tend to be larger when they do occur, under Republicans than under Democrats. And the opposite is true: rate decreases are both more frequent, and larger when they do occur, under Democrats than under Republicans.

When we add together the sum of all the year-to-year increases and decreases that occurred under each party, we find that the Republican presidencies showed a net cumulative increase in suicide rates of 14.5 suicides per 100,000 population per year from 1900 through 2007. And the Democrats showed an almost exactly equal net decrease of 13.3 suicides per 100,000 per year during their years in office from 1913 through 2000. Similarly, the Republican administrations witnessed a net increase of 5.4 in the homicide rate and the Democrats a net decrease of 5. Thus the total net increase in rates of lethal violence under Republicans is 19.9 (the sum of 14.5 and 5.4), and the total net decrease under Democrats, 18.3 (the sum of 13.3 and 5). There is less than 1 chance in 1,000 that any of these correlations between political party in power and rates of suicide, homicide, and total lethal violence (suicide plus homicide) could have happened simply by chance.

The higher the dose, the greater the response: risk factors vs. protective factors

An important concept in medical research is called the "dose-response curve." For example, the more cigarettes people smoke per day, the more likely they are to develop lung cancer: the higher the dose, the greater the response. And the greater the number of years they do so, the more likely they are to get lung cancer: again, the greater the cumulative dose, the larger the response. This provides powerful support for the hypothesis that cigarette smoking is a "risk factor" for lung cancer. Conversely, the more that people exercise regularly (within reasonable limits), the less likely they are to have a heart attack: again, a dose-response curve. The higher the dose of exercise, the greater the protection from heart attacks. So regular exercise is a "protective factor" against heart attacks.

Dose-response curves are one of the "gold standards" in medical research. They do not in and of themselves prove a causal relationship between the postulated causal agent (whose "dose" is being measured) and the response (the effect). But the failure to demonstrate a dose-response curve can under most circumstances be taken as evidence against causality. And when there is other evidence that is consistent with the same causal hypothesis, the existence of such a curve can reinforce the likelihood that one has discovered a variable that can make a difference to people's health.

By analogy, we can ask, could Republican administrations be risk factors for lethal violence, and Democratic administrations protective factors? One way to test that hypothesis would be to ask: is there a higher cumulative increase in rates of lethal violence the more years Republicans are in power? And is there a higher cumulative decrease in these rates the longer Democrats are in power? The answer to both questions is yes. Just as with cigarette smoking and regular exercise, the greater the dose of Republican administrations, the greater the violent response, and the greater the dose of Democratic administrations, the greater the reduction in violence.

In order to simplify this discussion, I will combine both of those responses into a single number, namely, the net difference in violent death rates between the two parties. For example, if the Republicans over the past 100 years presided over a net increase of 15 deaths per 100,000 per year, and the Democrats, a net decrease of 15, then the difference in death rates between the two parties would be 30. All that means is that the Republicans brought about a cumulative increase of 30 more violent deaths per 100,000 per year than the Democrats did, during the time period being studied; or, to say the same thing another way, that the Democratic administrations resulted in 30 fewer such deaths per year than the Republican ones did.

And if there is a dose-response curve at work here, we might expect that, if we studied a smaller number of years, then the net difference between the two parties would be correspondingly smaller: over 50 years, the net difference would be smaller than it was for 100 years; over 25 years, smaller still, etc. And that is exactly what we find when we compare the difference between the two parties' effects on violent death rates.

We can also compare each party with itself alone, and when we do that, we find that the more years the Republicans were in power, the greater the net increase that occurred in violent death rates, and the fewer years, the smaller the increase; and similarly for the decreases that occurred under the Democrats. We find these dose-response curves for both parties for both forms of lethal violence (homicide and suicide) and for the sum of the two (the total lethal violence rate). The consistency of these relationships across different periods of history and different lengths of time, especially given the number of random adventitious events that could conceivably skew the results in one direction or another, increase the likelihood that there may be a powerful and quite specific causal relationship between the political parties in power and the violent death rates, not just a coincidental correlation. That is, given the sheer amount of "noise" or "static" in a study of this magnitude, what is most surprising, and most difficult to explain away, is the fact that the "signal" comes through so loud and clear – and consistently.

For example, there was a net cumulative total of 38.2 more deaths per 100,000 per year under Republicans than under Democrats over the 108 years from 1900 through 2007. Or, to say the same thing another way, the difference between the changes in death rates under the two parties represents 38.2 *fewer* deaths under the Democrats than under the Republicans. At today's population level, that amounts to a difference in death rates representing roughly 114,600 fewer violent deaths per year under Democrats than under Republicans.

If we look at the net difference between the two parties during successively smaller periods of time, we find that during the years 1912 through 2007, 96 years, the net cumulative difference in death rates between the two parties was smaller than from 1900 to 2007, only 31.9. During the 88 years from 1920 through 2007, it was smaller still, only 27.4; and so on: the fewer the number of years, the smaller the net difference between the two parties' death rates.

If one is looking for evidence of a causal relationship that is responsible for a correlation, this is an important point to discover. Nevertheless, it is true that even this does not prove that these correlations show causation. What is true is that the *failure* to find a dose-response curve would make it less likely that there was a causal relationship between the two variables that were correlated with each other.

Another fact that the dose-response curves reveal is how consistent, reliable, durable, and unchanging the correlations between these two parties and the rates of violent death have been throughout the entire 108 years for which we have data, in their respective (and diametrically opposite) directions – with death rates increasing so regularly and continuously under Republicans, and decreasing just as consistently under Democrats, from the beginning of the period right up to the most recent set of comparisons of the two parties with each other (1992–2007) or of one party with itself (2000–7). That does not mean that every Republican administration attained an absolute increase, or every Democratic one an absolute decrease, during its time in office. What it does mean is that even when slight fluctuations occurred under each party, no net decrease under a Republican administration that was already in the "mountain range" of epidemic levels was ever sufficient to bring it below that to the "valley" of non-epidemic rates. And no Democratic administration's random increases were ever sufficient to bring it from a "valley" into a "mountain range." For example, during the Kennedy–Johnson years, 1961–8, lethal violence rates increased from 15.3 per 100,000 to 18 (and in fact were just below 17 during all but the last two of those years); yet, even at their highest, they never came close to breaking through the epidemic "floor" of 19.4–20. Likewise, during the Reagan – Bush Sr. years, these rates decreased slightly, from 22.5 to 21.7, yet never approached the "floor" of 19.4–20.

It is not as though the Republican party experienced an epidemic of violent death during one period and then showed a recovery from an epidemic at another time, or that the Democratic party initiated an epidemic at one time and a recovery from one at another. And it is not that either party showed a positive or negative correlation with death rates only in conjunction with a unique and unrepeated national crisis such as either of the two world wars, the Great Depression, the Cold War, or the civil rights revolution, so that that crisis, rather than the political party that happened by chance to be in power at the time of the crisis, might have been the actual cause of the increase or decrease in the lethal violence rates. For both parties, their characteristic correlations with violent death rates are long-term and repeat themselves from 1900 to the last period for which we have comparable data, 2000–7, with the same pattern continuing through all the historical crises that occurred during this time period.

What may be most significant about the comparison between the violent death rates under Republican administrations and those that occurred during Democratic ones is this: it is not the case that the Republicans have a higher net increase in violent death rates and the Democrats a lower net increase, or that the Democrats have a larger net decrease and the Republicans a smaller one. In other words, it is not that one party is bringing about smaller changes in the death rates and the other higher ones, but all in the same direction. Rather, the *direction* of change under the two parties is *opposite*. The net changes are *only increases* under Republicans and *only decreases* under Democrats.

To make these facts and their implications clearer, let me make an analogy between the long-term effect of these year-to-year changes in death rates, and a different set of year-to-year changes with which most people are likely to be more familiar: the fluctuations of the stock market. Suppose your family had asked the trust departments of two different banks to each invest $10,000 of the family's money, beginning in 1900, and that agreement continued unchanged until you inherited the trust in 2007. So naturally, you then inquired at each bank how much money was in each of the trusts. Suppose that you then discovered that the first bank had been able to increase the initial investment from $10,000 to $35,000 (in constant dollars), but the money invested by the second bank had not done nearly as well; in fact it had declined to zero by 1941. And suppose you also found that the second bank's inferiority in investment results, relative to the first bank, was not simply confined to the period between 1900 and 1941, but had continued from 1941 through 2007, during which time it continued to lose money for its clients. Finally, suppose that you were then going to decide which bank to choose to manage some additional funds that you had to invest. Which bank would you choose?

In this fictional analogy, I have compared changes in something on which people place a positive value (money), not something on which they place a negative value (violence). But if you adjust for that change, you can see that the difference in financial results between the two banks corresponds exactly to the difference in lethal violence results between the two political parties. Just as the second bank brought about both long-term and continuing, recent declines in something of positive value (money), so the Democratic party has brought about both long-term and continuing, recent declines in something of negative value (violence). And just as the first bank brought about corresponding increases in something of value, the Republican party brought about increases in something of negative value. So the decision the readers of this book now face is similar to the one the fictional investor in my analogy has to make: in which political party to invest their votes?

The relevance of this analogy can be brought home by another thought experiment. Suppose the Democrats had occupied the White House continuously from 1900 on, and had achieved the same reductions in violent death rates as they achieved during the 48 years in which they were in power (0.38 per year). Under those conditions, the violent death rate would have reached zero by 1941. Conversely, if the Republicans had been in power continuously from 1900 through 2007 and had achieved exactly the same increase in violent death rates (per 100,000 people per year) as those that occurred during the years they actually were in power (namely, an average increase of 0.34 per year), what would the death rate be by the end of 2007? It would be 52 (a net increase of 36.4, resulting from the yearly increase of 0.34 per year for 107 years, over the rate at which it already was, 15.6, or nearly three and a half times higher than the starting figure).

I am not suggesting that either of these counter-factual thought experiments represents what would necessarily have happened if either the Republicans or the Democrats had been in power continuously. Trees grow but they do not grow to the sky. And yearly rates of violent death rise and fall, but only in very exceptional cases do they fall to zero, or continue escalating indefinitely. Sometimes they do one or the other, of course, as in the complete extermination of a population group by genocide or a smallpox epidemic, or the complete reduction in violent deaths to zero that have occurred from time to time in one culture – or sub-culture – or another. (For example, the Hutterites, the highly religious, classless, pacifist Anabaptist sect that lives in small communal farms in the northern Midwest and southern Canada, whom I will discuss in more detail later in this book, are not known to have suffered a single homicide, or more than one suicide, during at least the first century following their immigration to North America in

1875.)[2] But both of those outcomes, which illustrate the fact that death rates from murder around the world and across the centuries vary from 100 percent to 0 percent, are exceptional. The purpose of the hypothetical scenarios that I just imagined was simply to illustrate how substantial the quantitative differences are between the effects on violent death rates that the two parties have had during the times they have actually been in office.

To put this difference into the language of public health and preventive medicine, the statistics reviewed in this chapter suggest that Republican administrations appear to be functioning as a "risk factor" for violent death and Democratic ones as a "protective factor," in the same sense that cigarette smoking is a risk factor for lung cancer and regular exercise is a protective factor against heart attacks. To continue that analogy further, we can remind ourselves that cigarette smoking is neither necessary nor sufficient to cause lung cancer; some people who have never smoked get lung cancer and some who do smoke never develop lung cancer. That is why even though there is a clear dose-response curve between the frequency of cigarette smoking and the frequency of lung cancer, it is still true that even if cigarette smoking dropped to zero, death rates from lung cancer would not also drop to zero.

---

[2] Joseph W. Eaton and Robert J. Weil, *Culture and Mental Disorders*, Glencoe, IL: The Free Press, 1955. Bert Kaplan and Thomas F. Plaut, *Personality in a Communal Society: An Analysis of the Mental Health of the Hutterites*, Lawrence, KS: University of Kansas Press, 1956; John A. Hostetler, *Hutterite Society*, Baltimore, MD: Johns Hopkins University Press, 1974; John A. Hostetler and Gertrude Enders Huntington, *The Hutterites in North America*, Fort Worth: Harcourt Brace, 1996; John A. Hostetler, *Hutterite Life*, Scottdale, PA: Herald Press, 1983.

By the same token, we can say that in order to begin or end an epidemic of lethal violence in the United States, it is necessary but not sufficient to have a Republican or a Democratic president, respectively. Just as the tubercle bacillus is necessary but not sufficient for the causation of tuberculosis, the data we have on violence suggest that you can never start an epidemic without a Republican, and you never end one without a Democrat. Among the 18 twentieth-century presidents, there was one Republican president who did not begin or continue an epidemic of lethal violence (Eisenhower), and one Democratic president who did not decrease violent death rates below the epidemic range he inherited from his Republican predecessors (Carter). Since we do not yet have the violence rates for 2008, all we can say about George W. Bush is that, although violent death rates increased during his presidency (in contrast to Eisenhower's), they had not reached epidemic levels as of 2007. He may turn out to be further proof that being Republican, although necessary, is not sufficient.

Why have these correlations not been noticed until now?

Before proceeding further with my investigation, I want to ask my readers: do you find yourself as puzzled as I am by one further mystery about all these murders and suicides – namely, why have these remarkable correlations between political party in power and violent death rates not been noticed up until now? One possible contributor to the overlooking of these correlations by almost everyone[3] who has studied them before may be that, despite the fact that suicide and homicide rates have cumulatively risen during Republican administrations and declined under Democratic ones, the *average* rates of suicide and homicide over the years each party was in power are almost *identical*. The reason for this is easy to understand. To simplify the math, suppose that in one ten-year period, the violence rate is going up 1 point per year, from 1 to 10, and in another ten-year period it is going down by 1 point per year, from 10 to 1. If you add up all the numbers and divide them by 10, you find that the average of the two different series is exactly the same, even though the net effect of the two series is exactly opposite. That is precisely what has happened, time after time, over the past century, with the rates cumulatively going up under Republicans and down under Democrats. So while the Republicans have accumulated massive net rate increases over the years, and the Democrats massive net rate decreases, the average rate in all the years taken together is about the same for both parties. The fact that these two pat-

---

[3] There are two exceptions to that generalization, though both are cross-sectional studies rather than longitudinal ones, and both were published in the mass media (a newspaper and a popular magazine), not a scientific journal. Michael Miller, a psychiatrist who is the editor of the *Harvard Mental Health Letter*, observed in an op-ed. piece in the *Boston Globe* that suicide was more frequent in the "Red States" that voted for Bush Jr. in 2000 than in the Democratically oriented "Blue States" ("A Suicide Map of the U.S.," August 22, 2004). And in a similar vein, *James Wolcott* reviewed a good deal of evidence that suicide as well as violent crime and many other symptoms of social pathology have been more common in the Red States than in the Blue in recent years ("Red State Babylon," *Vanity Fair*, Nov. 2006, p. 162).

terns of changes in death rates have an exactly opposite effect on the welfare of the American people may have been overlooked because of that.

The death rates I have summarized here have been part of the public record, and freely available to anyone who wanted to review them, since 1900. In that sense, they have been, so to speak, hiding in plain sight. An additional reason for our collective failure to notice these egregious facts may be directly related to what I just said: because the increases in lethal violence rates that occur under Republicans have regularly been compensated for by the almost exactly equal decreases that have occurred under Democrats, there has been, over time, essentially no net change in violent death rates for the country as a whole. For example, the homicide rate in 2000 (6.4 deaths per 100,000 population per year) was exactly what it had been in 1900, and the suicide rate in 2000 (9.6 per 100,000) was almost exactly what it had been in 1900 (9.2). That is true despite the fact, as we have already seen, that there were huge "swings" in both death rates when the presidency changed from one party to the other.

This absence of any net long-term increase or decrease in those rates could easily mislead people into thinking that there were no significant differences between the two parties with respect to the rate of violent deaths during their respective terms in office. That in turn would make it easy to forget that the only times the Republicans' violent death rates were *not* in an epidemic range were when they had inherited low rates from their Democratic predecessors. And the only times the Democrats' death rates were *in* an epidemic range were when they had inherited those high rates from Republicans.

In fact, there is only one reason that our homicide and suicide rates today are not at disastrously high epidemic levels, and that is because the Democrats have regularly undone the Republican rate increases with decreases of equal magnitude. Specifically, the Republicans increased the suicide and homicide rates by net cumulative totals of 14.5 and 5.4 per 100,000 respectively between 1900 and 2007, while the Democrats reduced those totals by almost exactly equal amounts (13.3 and 5.0, respectively). If the lethal violence rates in 2007 were determined only by the Republicans' influence on them during their 59 years in office, the suicide rate would have been 23.7 instead of 10.4 in 2007, and the homicide rate, 11.8 instead of 6.8. That would have resulted in a total violent death rate of 35.5 per 100,000, more than twice as many violent deaths as actually occurred – roughly 106,500, as opposed to the 52,000 that there actually were, if we apply those death rates to the current US population level of 300 million.

In this chapter I have summarized some of the data that create the murder mystery. In the chapters that follow, I will attempt to solve the mystery by seeing if there is any evidence that might explain why rates of suicide and homicide rise to epidemic levels only under Republican presidents, and fall to non-epidemic levels only during Democratic administrations. But statistics are one thing and feelings another, and statistics do not motivate people to commit suicide or homicide.

2

What Kind of a Man Are You?

In 1992, a gaunt, disheveled man in his mid-40s was admitted to the prison mental hospital in Massachusetts. He appeared half-dead: mute, motionless, unresponsive. Like a zombie, I thought. Since he was either unable or unwilling to talk – it was difficult to know which – I could only read the police report that accompanied him. It told me that on the day before, he had shot his wife and children to death with a hand gun. The man – I'll call him Paul Williams – was admitted to the hospital and placed on suicide precautions. I waited for him to tell me where he was mentally and who he was.

The next day, when he began to speak, it was like hearing someone talk to you from deep inside a cave. To speak and organize his thoughts appeared to require so much effort, it was as if he were trying to pick up the largest boulder imaginable and throw it, when he could hardly sustain the weight. He looked drained of all emotion, all feeling, and could only slowly and with great effort try to piece together for me the story of what happened. Over the duration of the next few days, here is what he managed to tell me.

He had been a hard worker all his life, and now, in his 40s, he had had a good job as a foreman at a factory in Boston. He was living with a woman who, like him, was African-American, and, although they had never married, each had a child from a previous partner, and they had a stable relationship. She was a school teacher, made a comfortable living just as he did, and he felt she was a good mother to her child and his.

Two months ago, Paul had been notified that he was going to be laid off at work – not fired, he insisted, "laid off." Not because he didn't do his job well enough. He was a good worker. The company just couldn't afford to pay him. Other men lost their jobs too, but that was their problem. (This was during the recession that occurred during the first President Bush's last two years in office.)

Paul did not know what to do next. He felt ashamed, so ashamed that he couldn't bear to tell his woman, as he called her, what had happened – that he had lost his job. Instead, he would get up every morning in a daze, dress for work, and leave the house as if he were going to work. He would stay out until his usual hour of return. At first, he spent this time looking for another job, but then he gave up – there were no jobs, it was too shameful to be rejected when he applied, he just gave up. He had lost his manhood. He couldn't even bring any money home, he explained.

Finally, his wife – as he also called her sometimes – noticed that there was no money coming in, and she confronted him. Cornered, Paul had to admit the unspeakable truth. She was shocked and flew into a rage when she realized what he had been doing for the past two months, pretending to go to work when there was no work, fooling her with his foolishness. And then she uttered the fatal words, "What kind of a man are you, anyway? What kind of a man would do such a thing?"

All this happened with the children looking on.

Paul went into the bedroom and took his gun out of the drawer. He came back. And to show her what kind of a man he was, he shot her to death. Then he shot the children to stop the sound of their screaming, but that did not work. He could still hear them screaming. He thought he would hear that for the rest of his life.

Paul does not know why he did not shoot himself too. When I asked him why he thought he hadn't, he said, "I was already dead. I felt dead. I thought I was dead. I think I'm dead now."

Listening to Paul tell his tale, I could not help but think how often "unemployment" is spoken of as if it were just a statistic, a "rate," a passing number that will eventually change, get larger or smaller, but not affect real people. But as tragic as Paul's story is, what is even more tragic is how far from unique it is. Paul was only one of many men who respond in this or similar ways, with slight variations, to the stress of losing a job or experiencing some equivalent loss of status that destroys their sense of who they are – in fact, their sense that they still exist, that they are real people. This pattern is hardly unique to the United States. A Japanese movie, *Tokyo Sonata*, tells an almost identical story of an unemployed man who spends his days away from home, also pretending he still has a job, until this strategy fails and he kills himself along with his family.

Now, of course, it is true that most people who are laid off from their jobs do not become this desperate and violent. But it is also true that there are always a certain number of people whose sense of self-esteem is so fragile and vulnerable that they are able to maintain only a tenuous degree of self-control even when they do have a steady source of income and the prestige and sense of being recognized by others that comes from holding down a job. Deprive them of this powerful source of support, and all hell can break loose, as it did in Paul's case. Increase the unemployment rate enough, and more such individuals will resort, as they regularly do under such circumstances, to homicide or suicide, or both.

After hearing such a harrowing tale, it may seem a bit absurd to go back into the world of numbers, but it will probably be less surprising to hear that, throughout the past century, when the unemployment rate has gone up or down, so have the rates of suicide and homicide. It was not the loss of a job per se that led Paul to kill his wife and their children. It was the feeling of being emasculated, the shame of being exposed as not a man in the eyes of his wife that led him to get his gun and shoot her as a response to her question: "What kind of a man are you?" And then to kill the children whose screams conveyed what they had witnessed.

In the largest database previously published on this subject in the United States, a study of the period from 1900 to 1970, Paul Holinger[1] found that age-adjusted

---

[1] Holinger, *Violent Deaths in the United States*, p. 186.

US suicide and homicide rates not only correlated with each other (p < .01), they both also correlated with the unemployment rate (p < .01). My own analysis of the much larger database on which this book draws finds the same thing,[2] as have many other studies based on much more limited population samples or time-periods.

In an influential study of the double epidemics of unemployment and violent crime in ghetto neighbor-hoods, William Julius Wilson[3] speaks of the "direct relationship between joblessness and violent crime." Quoting Delbert Elliott's research, he points out that

> The black–white differential in the proportion of males involved in serious violent crime, although almost even at age 11, increases to 3:2 over the remaining years of adolescence, and reaches a differential of nearly 4:1 during the late twenties. However, when Elliott compared only *employed* black and white males, he found no significant differences in violent behavior patterns among the two groups by age 21.... Accordingly, a major reason for the racial gap in violent behavior ... is joblessness.

It becomes easy, then, to understand why inner-city black youth facing limited prospects for employment would be drawn into drug trafficking and thus become involved in the violent behavior associated with it. The unemployment rate among blacks has always been at least twice as high as among whites, regardless of

---

[2] The probability values for the three correlations with the US unemploy-ment rate from 1900 through 2007 are: p < 0.05 for homicide, p < 0.01 for suicide, and p < 0.01 for total violent death rates.

[3] William Julius Wilson, *When Work Disappears: The World of the New Urban Poor*, New York: Vintage, 1996, p.22.

whether the overall rate of unemployment is high or low. The truth of the old adage, "Last to be hired, first to be fired," is thus more than confirmed by the statistics, which also helps to clarify why the homicide rate is so much higher in the black community than in the white.

Unemployment rates are not the only socio-economic variable that predicts changes in suicide and homicide rates. In a study of the relationship between income inequality and violent crime, Hsieh and Pugh[4] performed a meta-analysis of some 34 studies exploring this relationship and found that both (absolute) poverty and income inequality (relative poverty) are significantly correlated with homicide, not just in the United States but throughout the world. Richard Wilkinson[5] has for many years been documenting the relationship between inequality and violence (and many other threats to health) by showing a significant correlation between the incidence of violence and various measures and types of economic inequality and distress, both from his own research and from reviews of the literature produced by other investigators.

[4] Ching-Chi Hsieh and M. D. Pugh, "Poverty, Income Inequality, and Violent Crime: A Meta-Analysis of Recent Aggregate Data Studies," *Criminal Justice Review*, 18: 182–202, 1993; reprinted as ch. 26 in Ichiro Kawachi, Bruce P. Kennedy, and Richard G. Wilkinson, eds., *The Society and Population Health Reader*, Vol. I: *Income Inequality and Health*, New York: The New Press, 1999, pp. 278–96.

[5] Richard Wilkinson and Kate Pickett, *The Spirit Level: Why Greater Equality Makes Societies Stronger*, New York: Bloomsbury Press, 2009, especially ch. 10: "Violence: Gaining Respect," pp. 129–44; Richard Wilkinson, "Why is Violence More Common Where Inequality is Greater?" pp. 1–12 in *Youth Violence: Scientific Approaches to Prevention*, Vol. 1036, *Annals of the New York Academy of Sciences*, ed. John Devine, James Gilligan, Klaus A. Miczek, Rashid Shaikh, and Donald Pfaff, 2004.

Another review article observed that "the vast major-ity of studies of income inequality and homicide rates have employed cross-sectional designs." [6] The short-coming of that approach is that it leaves the question of what is causing what ambiguous: in a population with a high degree of income inequality, is the increased rate of homicides occurring only among those who are rela-tively poor, or among the rich, or among both? And if it is primarily caused by the poor, is that because their homicidal behavior is being caused by their poverty, or is their poverty itself caused by the same personality characteristics that make them more likely to commit murder, like being so angry, threatening, and unpleas-ant to be around that their bosses want to fire them and no one else wants to hire them?

That is why longitudinal studies, such as the ones presented in this book, are more useful for purposes of clarifying the causal mechanisms responsible for these correlations. A study by LaFree and Drass[7] shows the advantages of this approach. They did a time-series analysis of the US from 1957 to 1990 that found that increases in economic inequality were followed by increases in homicide rates (for both blacks and whites). In other words, the same population that had *not* been committing homicides in all the years *before* the state

---

[6] Steven F. Messner and Richard Rosenfeld, "Social Structure and Homicide," pp. 27–41 in M. Dwayne Smith and Margaret A. Zahn, eds., *Homicide: A Sourcebook of Social Research*, Thousand Oaks, CA, London, and New Delhi: SAGE Publications, 1999, p. 30.

[7] Gary LaFree and K. A. Drass, "The Effect of Changes in Intraracial Income Inequality and Educational Attainment on Changes in Arrest Rates for African Americans and Whites, 1957 to 1990," *American Sociological Review*, 61: 614–34, 1996.

of the economy changed suddenly began doing so only *after* there was a recession, millions of people were laid off from their jobs (regardless of their individual personality characteristics or the quality of the work they were doing), and so on.

In a study of inequality and violent crime (including homicide) sponsored by the World Bank, Fajnzylber, Lederman and Loayza[8] studied the relationship between homicide rates and two related economic variables, income inequality and changes in gross demographic product (GDP), in 39 countries around the world, and concluded that homicide rates are positively correlated with inequality rates and negatively correlated with GDP both within countries and between countries: that is, higher levels of inequality were associated with higher homicide rates, and increasing GDP levels with lower homicide rates. They also concluded that their data provided evidence that inequality was causing violent crimes, not the other way around, and that the combination of decreasing unemployment and rising GDP reduced both absolute and relative poverty, with both changes leading to lower homicide rates.

Land, McCall, and Cohen[9] studied the correlation between six economic variables and homicide rates in cities and states across the United States in 1960, 1970, and 1980, and found that the strongest and most consist-

---

[8] Pablo Fajnzylber, Daniel Lederman, and Norman Loayza, "Inequality and Violent Crime," *Journal of Law and Economics*, 45: 1–40, 2002.

[9] Kenneth C. Land, Patricia L. McCall, and Lawrence E. Cohen, "Structural Covariates of Homicide Rates: Are There Any Invariances across Time and Social Space?" *The American Journal of Sociology*, 95(4): 922–63, Jan., 1990, p. 951.

ent one was between poverty (both relative and absolute) and homicide: "cities, metropolitan areas, or states that are more deprived have higher homicide rates, and those that are more affluent have lower rates."

Inequality of wealth is even greater than income inequality in the United States, and may also predict rates of lethal violence. The two periods in the United States in which, according to Edward N. Wolff,[10] inequality of wealth – as measured by both household wealth (including home ownership) and financial wealth (including ownership of stocks, bonds, cash, and other fungible resources) – reached its maximum, were both periods in which the lethal violence rate was consistently at epidemic levels. These were the period just before the Great Depression (the degree of inequality of wealth peaked in 1929), and the 1980s, during the Reagan and first Bush administrations, during which time wealth inequality reached the highest level since 1929, and recessions became deeper and unemployment higher than at any time since the Great Depression. Conversely, the quarter of a century from 1942 to 1968 (from Roosevelt's third term in office until the "New Deal Consensus" was ended by the conservative backlash that brought Nixon to power in 1969) was a period of the greatest economic equality of the twentieth century, *and* it was also, as we have already seen, marked by the longest uninterrupted period of well-below-average, non-epidemic lethal violence rates in the twentieth century.

---

[10] Edward N. Wolff, *Top Heavy: The Increasing Inequality of Wealth in America and What Can Be Done about It* (An Expanded Edition of a Twentieth Century Fund Report), New York: The New Press, 1996.

Finally, my own analysis of economic contractions (recessions and depressions, periods of declining GDP) has found statistically significant relationships between those economic conditions and rising rates of suicide and homicide. As we have already seen, the highest suicide rates (17 per 100,000) and the highest total lethal violence rates (26.5) of the century were reached in 1932, during the bottom of the worst economic depression in our history. That was also when the highest homicide rates ever recorded up to that time occurred (9.5 per 100,000). But even higher murder rates, the highest of the twentieth century, 10.8 and 10.9 per 100,000, were reached three times during the longest period of Republican hegemony of the century, the 24 years from 1969 through 1992. That was a period marked by repeated recessions lasting a total of nearly five years, some of which were deeper than any seen since the 1930s; by unemployment rates that reached levels not seen since the 1930s; and by increases in inequalities in wealth and income that had also not been seen since 1929 (i.e., during the last previous period of extended Republican hegemony that extended from 1921 through 1932). This period of extended and repeated economic stress and distress that occurred during five Republican terms in office (with the most socially and economically conservative Democrat of the century, Carter, sandwiched in between them) was also, as we saw in chapter 1, a time during which there was an extended and uninterrupted "mountain range" of suicide and homicide rates that never once dropped below epidemic levels. So we have good reason to think of those three inter-related economic variables

– unemployment, recessions, and inequality – as being risk factors for lethal violence.

The association between suicide and unemployment has been confirmed repeatedly in dozens of studies, and I think it is fair to say that there is a general consensus now among social scientists as to the validity of this correlation. Many studies have found equally powerful correlations between homicide and unemployment, though these findings have been less consistent than those for suicide. This book is not the place for a full review of the extensive literature on this subject.[11] In line with the majority of the published evidence, my own analysis of the database on which this book is based – which covers the longest time-period and the largest population of any study of this subject – along with that of Dr. Bandy Lee, my research partner, who performed a time series analysis of the data, showed that the correlation between the political parties in power and the violent death rates could be mediated, or caused, by changes in the unemployment rate and in the per-capita GDP (one measure of economic contractions and expansions) that occurred under the two different parties. That leads me to turn to the next step in solving the mystery about murder and its association with the political party ruling the country: is there a relationship

---

[11] For those interested in pursuing this literature further, Chiricos reviewed 63 studies, and concluded that the studies with negative findings were far outweighed, both numerically and on methodological grounds, by those that found statistically significant positive correlations between unemployment rates and homicide rates. See Theodore G. Chiricos, "Rates of Crime and Unemployment: An Analysis of Aggregate Research Evidence," *Social Problems*, 34(2): 187–212, April 1987.

between political parties and the three economic variables I have focused on in this chapter: unemployment, inequality, and recessions?

3

Nothing Succeeds Like Failure

Long before the most vehement critic of capitalism, Karl Marx, was even born, the chief philosophic supporter of capitalism, Adam Smith, noticed that one flaw in this economic system is that the laws of supply and demand make it to the advantage of employers to operate in an economic system that can create a large unemployment rate, because that lowers the "cost of labor," i.e., the wage the employer will need to pay people in order to induce them to work for him. The worst effect of this system is that it turns the laborer – who is, after all, a person with needs and feelings of his or her own – into a commodity, a carrier of labor power that can be bought and sold, and which can be more or less expensive to the employer. Consequently, the political party that is more supportive of and supported by employers (capital) than employees (labor) will have a vested interest in pursuing policies that have the effect of increasing the unemployment rate. This is one of the ways they serve their constituency, whose identity was "outed" by President George W. Bush

51

when he addressed them as "the haves and the have mores."[1]

Inequality, unemployment, and recessions

In comparing the economic performance of Republican and Democratic administrations over the past century, we see a polarization at least as great as that with respect to their effects on rates of lethal violence. Despite presenting itself as the party of prosperity, the Republican party throughout this time has had the effect, as I will show in this chapter, of increasing both the rate and the duration of unemployment, the frequency, depth, and duration of economic contractions (recessions and depressions), and inequalities of income and wealth, meaning increases in the size of the gap between the rich and the poor. They have also, relative to the Democratic party, been far more likely to achieve decreases rather than increases in the median wage, the minimum wage, overall prosperity (the per-capita GDP), and the "Commodification Index" (a measure of the package of benefits provided by the government, including unemployment insurance). As one would suspect, there is a great deal of overlap among these various measures in that they all tend to reinforce each other. For example, recessions increase the unemployment rate, and, as James

---

[1] "This is an impressive crowd – the haves and the have-mores. Some people call you the elites; I call you my base": CBS News, "Bush and Gore do New York," Oct. 18, 2002. Downloaded from www.cbsnews.com/stories/2000/10/18/politics/main24220.shtml.

Galbraith[2] observed, "when unemployment is high, inequality rises. And when unemployment is low, inequality tends to fall." Indeed, he shows mathematically that,

> movements of unemployment alone account for 79 percent of all variation in wage inequality. . . . Other forces are to be reckoned with . . . but changes in unemployment are overwhelmingly the main thing. . . . Nothing else in our history has had a comparable effect. . . . For those who are concerned with inequality, it should be an article of policy that unemployment be kept below the value at which it begins to lead to increased inequality.[3]

Galbraith then goes on to show how both unemployment and its close relative, inequality, dramatically increased during certain periods between 1920 and 1998 and diminished in others. He does not make the connection, but the years during which unemployment and inequality increased so markedly were those when Republican presidents occupied the White House, and the periods of diminishing unemployment and inequality occurred during Democratic administrations. A clear implication of Galbraith's argument, however, is that the unemployment rate can almost be used as a proxy for inequality, or, more simply, as a way of measuring it.

On a personal level, the moment one loses one's job, one experiences an increase in economic inequality between oneself and those who still have jobs. In this sense, the rate and duration of unemployment can be seen as another measure of economic inequality or

---

[2] James K. Galbraith, *Created Unequal: The Crisis in American Pay*, New York: The Free Press, 1998, p. 148.
[3] Ibid., pp. 147–9.

relative poverty, except to the extent – minimal in the US compared with all other economically developed nations – that the wages lost by unemployment are compensated for by unemployment benefits.

Unemployment rates and recessions, respectively, have been measured throughout the twentieth century by the Bureau of Labor Statistics and the National Bureau of Economic Research, and tracking these rates and recessions over time reveals that both of these forms of economic loss and distress have increased in frequency, depth, and duration during Republican administrations and decreased under Democratic ones.

I will deal with unemployment first. One of the most remarkable features of the unemployment figures is that both the rate and the duration of unemployment have increased during every Republican administration and decreased under every Democratic one, without a single exception. In other words, when Republicans have left the White House, the unemployment rate has been higher than it was when they entered it, and when Democrats have left, it has been lower than it was when they entered. If we count up the net sum of all the increases that occurred during all the Republican administrations from 1900 through 2008 (the last year of Bush Jr.), we find that the Republicans brought about a cumulative increase of 27.3 percent in the unemployment rate, and the Democrats an almost exactly equal decrease of 26.5 percent. Thus the net cumulative difference between the effect the two parties had on the unemployment rate during that entire period was 53.8 percent.[4]

---

[4] See table 1 in appendix B.

The Princeton political economist Larry Bartels[5] has found that in the post-war US, from 1948 to 2005, unemployment rates under Republican presidents averaged 30 percent higher than under Democratic presidents (6.26 percent vs. 4.84 percent respectively).

The duration of unemployment has only been measured since 1948, but it has shown the same partisan difference since that time. Without exception, the duration of unemployment has been longer by the time Republicans left the White House than it was when they entered, and shorter when Democrats left than when they entered. Over the period from 1948 through 2003, the Republicans brought about a net cumulative increase of 24.6 weeks of unemployment among those who were unemployed, and the Democrats, a net decrease of 13.6 weeks, for a net difference between the two parties of 38.2 weeks – nearly 9 months.[6]

The increase in the duration of unemployment not only increases the stress of unemployment and the sense of despair, failure, humiliation, rejection, and worthlessness it brings with it, for obvious reasons; it also has another important implication. Because of an important shortcoming in the data collection process by which the Bureau of Labor Statistics measures unemployment rates, people are simply not counted as unemployed once they have remained unemployed for a long time, on the grounds that, since their continuing inability to find a job has left them too discouraged to keep looking

---

[5] Larry M. Bartels, *Unequal Democracy: The Political Economy of the New Gilded Age*, New York: Russell Sage Foundation, 2007, p. 48, table 2.4.

[6] See table 2 in appendix B.

for work, they are not really unemployed. What that means is that the longer the duration of unemployment, the more extreme is the undercount of the true unemployment rate. And what that in turn means is that as high as the measured and reported unemployment rates were during Republican administrations, they were almost certainly much higher even than those reported rates. Thus the difference between the Republican and Democratic records with regard to unemployment is probably even greater than it appears to be. That conclusion is not an "opinion," as opposed to a "fact." It is a critique of the process by which something is reported to be a fact, namely, the recording of unemployment rates that are almost certainly, according to virtually every labor economist who has studied this matter, serious underestimates of the true rate of unemployment.

How about recessions? Before I began the research for this book, I had heard so many claims from Republican partisans that they were the party of economic growth, as opposed to their rivals, the Democrats, whom they claimed stifled economic growth with high income, capital gains, corporate and "death" (inheritance) taxes, as well as excessive regulations, that I simply assumed that that was true, and that, as with respect to other matters of public interest, you could vote for Democrats only if you thought the other advantages they could bring to the country outweighed the fact that they were bad for the economy and the Republicans were good for it. Therefore I was genuinely surprised – I would even say shocked – to discover that that reputation of the Republican party appears to be the diametrical opposite of what the numbers show. I am referring to the numbers gathered and published by the National Bureau of Economic Research, which is hardly a liberal or left-wing think tank. Its president for many recent years was Martin Feldstein, who has been an economic advisor to a number of conservative Republican presidents. Yet this group has the reputation of being as objective, non-partisan, and economically expert as any single monitor of the US national economy. One of their most important and influential functions is to determine when the country has gone into a period of economic contraction (a recession or depression) or of expansion. I have reviewed their tabulations of contractions and expansions from 1900 through October 2010, as a way of differentiating between opinion and fact. The conventional opinion is that Republicans are the ones to vote for if you want economic growth, whereas Democrats stifle growth. What do the facts show?

What they show is that, from 1900 through October 2010, the country suffered approximately three times as many months of recessions during the times Republicans were governing the country as during the times Democrats were: 246 months (more than 20 years) compared with 86 – a discrepancy that could not have happened by chance more than 1 time out of 10,000. If we qualify that by examining how many months of contractions they had per year in office (since they occupied the White House for 61 years, as opposed to the Democrats' almost 50 years [through Oct. 2010]), we still find a large discrepancy. The Republicans brought us 2.3 times as many months of recessions per year they were in power as the Democrats did. Furthermore, Republican recessions, when they did occur, lasted more than 4 months longer than those that occurred during Democratic administrations: 14.2 months, as opposed to 9.8. So recessions were more than twice as frequent, and lasted 45 percent longer, under Republicans than under Democrats.

Another difference: recessions began during Republican presidencies 17 times, almost 3 times as often as they did during Democratic ones, when they began only 6 times. In addition, Democrats inherited recessions from outgoing Republican administrations 4 times (in 1913, 1933, 1961, and 2009). By contrast, Republicans inherited recessions from Democrats only once throughout the past 111 years, in 1921, after the ending of which they soon initiated 3 recessions of their own, in 1923 (for 14 months), in 1926 (for 13 months), and then the big one, the Great Depression, which they showed themselves incapable of reversing throughout the entire 43 months in which they remained in office, from August 1929 to March 1933. Franklin Roosevelt then immediately reversed it and began a period of economic expansion that lasted uninterruptedly for the next 50 months. It was then interrupted once, for 1 year (May 1937 – June 1938), by Roosevelt's decision to go back to the kinds of economic policies the Republicans had used and continued to advocate, following which he returned to his original strategies and once again succeeded in bringing about an uninterrupted period of expansion that, contrary to much of the conventional misinformation about the ending of the Depression, continued for 42 months (June 1938 – December 1941) even *before* the US entered the Second World War.

To sum up:

1) Recessions began 3 times as frequently during Republican administrations as during Democratic ones (17 vs. 6). These recessions lasted 45 percent longer per recession, and led to 4 times as many years of recession as occurred during those that began under Democrats (more than 20 years vs. fewer than 5 years).

2) Republicans were 4 times as likely as Democrats to "bequeath" a recession that had begun during their own administration to their successors. They did this 4 times, to Wilson, Roosevelt, Kennedy, and Obama, whereas the Democrats did this to their Republican successors only once (in March 1921, a recession that had begun during Wilson's administration).

3) Nearly a third of the total months of recession that occurred during Democratic administrations were the result of recessions they had inherited from their Republican predecessors (27 out of 86), whereas fewer than 2 percent of the total months of recessions that occurred during Republican administrations were the continuation of the 1 recession they inherited from 1 Democrat (4 months out of a total of 242).

4) This implies that the recessions Republicans handed on to their Democratic successors were deeper, more malignant, and harder to "cure" than the relatively milder and shorter-lived single recession that 1 Democrat left his Republican successors. As a result, the 1 recession Republicans inherited from a Democrat, which occurred in 1921, lasted only

4 further months, whereas the 4 recessions that Democrats inherited from 4 different Republican presidents took a combined total of 27 months to end.

5) This implies further that all 17 of the recessions that began during Republican administrations were largely self-caused, as were all 6 of the recessions that began during Democratic administrations; but that the remaining 4 recessions that existed during Democratic presidencies, which led to almost one-third of the total months of recession that occurred during their administrations, were largely caused by the economic policies of their Republican predecessors. For example, virtually no one believes that Roosevelt caused the Great Depression that he inherited in 1933, which began under Republicans in 1929–30, years before he took office. And no one could reasonably believe that Obama caused the Great Recession that he inherited in 2009, which began under a Republican during 2007. The same applies to the Republican-caused recessions that were inherited by Wilson and Kennedy.

6) The alternative hypothesis, that Republicans were simply more skillful in ending the 1 recession they inherited than the Democrats were in ending the 4 they inherited, does not seem to be supported by the following facts:

7) a) A Democratic president, Roosevelt, in fact succeeded in ending the most serious economic contraction in the history of capitalism, the Great Depression of the 1930s – from the time he first entered office he began taking radical emergency

action that had the effect of reversing the contraction into an expansion, a feat that was never
matched by, nor ever needed to be matched by,
any Republican president (or, for that matter,
any other Democrat).

b) Given that the Republicans showed themselves
on 17 different occasions to be incapable of
preventing even *non-inherited* recessions during
their administrations (as opposed to only 6 comparable failures by Democratic presidents), and
less capable of ending those recessions, once they
had begun (as was most powerfully shown by
their inability to reverse the economic contraction
called the Great Depression that started in 1929),
as speedily as the Democrats did with their own
self-caused recessions, it would be difficult to
support the proposition that they were capable
of ending *inherited* recessions more rapidly than
the Democrats were. It seems more likely that the
single recession that a Democrat, Wilson, handed
on to his Republican successors in 1921 was less
severe than the ones that 4 different Republican
presidents left to their Democratic successors.

If we look at the opposite effect, and compare the
ability of the two parties to bring about economic
growth and expansion, we find that during Democratic
administrations the economy was expanding 86 percent of the time, as compared to only 66 percent under
Republican presidents.

Another way of measuring the differences between
the two parties' ability to increase overall US prosperity

by bringing about economic growth is to compare the rate at which the per-capita Gross National Product (GNP) showed a net increase during the years each party was in power. As Bartels[7] has shown, between 1948 (the year in which this concept was first measured and reported) and 2005, the real (inflation-adjusted) per-capita GNP growth rate was 1.64 percent during the years Republicans were in power. What was the growth rate under the Democrats when they were in power? The answer is quite startling: 2.78 percent, which is a full percentage point higher (or, to be more exact, 70 percent higher) than the Republicans' rate, over that 58-year period.

Why has unemployment increased and then lasted longer, and why have recessions occurred so much more frequently and then lasted longer, during Republican administrations than during Democratic ones? And why have declines in unemployment and growth of the economy been so much greater when there was a Democratic president rather than a Republican in the White House? Is this simply a matter of bad luck for the Republicans and good luck for the Democrats? Is it a function of the "business cycle" that operates independently of human political choices, like a force of nature or an act of God that just happens to coincide with times when Republicans are presidents? A misfortune, to be sure, but not their fault?

As opposed to that supposition, many experts on the relationship between the political parties and the

---

[7] Bartels, *Unequal Democracy*, pp. 48–9 (including table 2.4 and figure 2.3).

functioning of the economy have concluded that the latter is very much a function of the difference between the economic policies of the two parties. This has been shown, for example, with respect to why economic inequality increases under Republicans and decreases under Democrats. Writing in 2007, the Princeton political economist Larry Bartels[8] concluded that:

> The most important single influence on the changing US income distribution over the past half-century [has been] the contrasting policy choices of Democratic and Republican presidents. Under Republican administrations, real income growth for the lower- and middle-income classes has consistently lagged well behind the income growth rate for the rich – and well behind the income growth rate for the lower and middle classes themselves under Democratic administrations.

Furthermore, Bartels observes that "these substantial partisan disparities in income growth . . . are quite unlikely to have occurred by chance. . . . Rather, they reflect consistent differences in policies and priorities between Democratic and Republican administrations."

Bartels also points out that one measure of inequality, "the 80/20 income ratio, increased under each of the six Republican presidents in this [post-World War II] period. . . . In contrast, four of five Democratic presidents – all except Jimmy Carter – presided over declines in income inequality. If this is a coincidence, it is a very powerful one."[9] He then goes on to show reasons why it "seems hard to attribute this to a mere coincidence in

8 Ibid., p. 30.
9 Ibid., p. 36.

the timing of Democratic and Republican administrations."

To extend the argument, the political economist Douglas Hibbs[10] points out that "Democratic administrations are more likely than Republican ones to run the risk of higher inflation rates in order to pursue expansive policies designed to yield lower unemployment and extra growth." Hibbs notes that "six of the seven recessions experienced since [1951] . . . occurred during Republican administrations. Every one of these contractions was either intentionally created or passively accepted . . . in order to fight inflation." The cruelest irony of all, in this regard, is that from 1948 through 2005 the inflation rate during Republican administrations has been virtually indistinguishable from that achieved under Democratic ones (3.76 percent vs. 3.97 percent), while the degree of overall prosperity (real per capita GNP growth per year) has been 70 percent higher under Democrats than under Republicans (2.78 percent vs. 1.64 percent), as Bartels[11] has documented. So, while the Republicans have pursued economic policies that have increased unemployment, recessions, and inequality, all ostensibly in order to prevent inflation, they have not in fact succeeded in preventing inflation noticeably better than the Democrats have.

In an analysis of the relationship between recessions and unemployment, Theodore Chiricos has pointed out that, beginning in the 1970s,

---

[10] Douglas Hibbs, *The American Political Economy: Macroeconomics and Electoral Politics*, Cambridge, MA: Harvard University Press, 1987, p. 218.

[11] Bartels, *Unequal Democracy*, pp. 48–9.

unemployment rose more sharply and to higher levels than at any time since the 1930s. In 1969, civilian unemployment reached a fifteen year low of 3.5 percent. Then, three consecutive recessions pushed unemployment to progressively higher levels in 1971 (5.9 percent), 1975 (8.5 percent) and 1982 (9.7 percent). By the spring of 1982, unemployment topped 11 percent in six states. Hardest hit were teenagers, young adults, minorities, and blue-collar workers. For example, unemployment during 1982 reached 14 percent for 20–24-year-old adults, 18 percent for construction workers, 28 percent for auto workers, and 42 percent for black teenagers. By the spring of 1982, fears of economic depression were openly discussed in the national media.[12]

What he did not point out was that these years of increasing unemployment were all years in which Republicans occupied the White House. For example, 1969 was precisely the first year of the new Republican hegemony that replaced the New Deal Consensus that had ruled Washington for the previous 36 years. As a result, "unemployment climbed to levels unmatched in 40 years," i.e., since the last period of Republican hegemony that ended in the Great Depression. Again without mentioning the political parties involved, or the partisan ideological identification of the economists and commentators to whom he refers (such as Martin Feldstein, Milton Friedman, William Safire, James Q. Wilson, and Richard Herrnstein), he points out that, even as this economic disaster was unfolding,

---

[12] Theodore G. Chiricos, "Rates of Crime and Unemployment," p. 187.

the significance of this trend was being discounted in a variety of ways. For example, government economists periodically redefined the concept of "full employment" to include progressively higher levels of unemployment. Some argued that the "new unemployment" was less harmful because it increasingly involved women, teenagers, and voluntary job leavers. Others argued that high unemployment was unavoidable and necessary to combat inflation, or would soon be diminished by the growth of jobs in service industries. Still others claimed that rising unemployment had little or no impact on rates of crime.[13]

And yet, of course, as we have already seen, these were precisely the years when the US entered into the most prolonged epidemic of homicide and suicide of the twentieth century.

Referring to a more recent period, Daniel Hojman and Felipe Kast[14] have shown that during the 1990s (the decade when Clinton was president), significantly fewer people entered poverty and more escaped it than during the 1980s, the Reagan–Bush years.

As I mentioned in the last chapter, the unemployment rate by itself (independent of which party was in power) from 1900 through 2007 correlated positively with changes in all three of the violent death rates that have been measured during that time, to a statistically significant degree ($p < 0.05$ for homicide, $p < 0.01$ for suicide, and $p < 0.01$ for total violent death rates). A time series

---

[13] Ibid.

[14] Daniel Hojman and Felipe Kast, "On the Measurement of Income Dynamics," Harvard University, Kennedy School Working Paper, Oct. 2009.

analysis performed by Dr. Bandy Lee showed that the effect of the political party in power on violent deaths could be largely explained by the unemployment rate change. Since the parties themselves determine the unemployment rate, however, it is clear that what we have here is a causal circle or an interaction between causal mechanisms, not a reduction to one "true" cause and the elimination of bogus ones. If Republican politicians cause the unemployment rate to rise and the rise in the unemployment rate causes the violent death rates to rise, then it is clear that the Republican party is as responsible as, say, the man who pulls the trigger of the gun, even though it is the bullet not the man that kills the victim.

But a further refinement can be made, indicating that it is not the party label per se that is important but rather the policies of the politician who becomes a Republican president. And here the example of Eisenhower is invaluable. Eisenhower was nominally a Republican president, but he endorsed and supported many of the policies and values that are identified with the Democrats, such as the largest expansion of social security and unemployment benefits since those programs were begun, continuation of the highest marginal income tax rates in our history (91 percent), enforcement of the Supreme Court's desegregation decision, and the promotion of the Department of Health, Education, and Welfare to cabinet status. As a result, many conservative politicians felt that Eisenhower was not one of them (just as Eisenhower himself often felt alienated from the Republican party, on more than one occasion talked of changing parties, and explicitly declared his determination to continue the social and economic policies of

Roosevelt's New Deal). For example, the late William Buckley, whom many people credit with the success of the modern conservative movement that was responsible for the huge Republican gains made throughout the country (from state houses to the Congress) from 1966 to the present, refused to support Eisenhower. And the late Barry Goldwater based much of his campaign to turn the Republican party to the far right on what he claimed was the necessity to move it away from what it had become under Eisenhower.

Just as Eisenhower was the one Republican who did not increase the low rates of lethal violence that he had inherited from his Democratic predecessor, Truman, Jimmy Carter was the one Democrat who did not end the epidemic of violent death that he had inherited from his Republican predecessors, Nixon and Ford. In a recent analysis of the Carter presidency, Hacker and Pierson[15] have pointed out that in many ways Carter's economic policies were more conservative even than Nixon's had been. And just as Eisenhower fantasized about switching to the Democratic party, Carter talked about feeling more comfortable with the Republicans than with his fellow Democrats. And just as many of Eisenhower's fellow Republicans regarded him as not "one of them," so many of Carter's fellow Democrats felt the same way about him. Arthur Schlesinger Jr., for example, as well as many labor leaders, called Carter a Republican and refused to support him. Ultimately, it is policies,

---

[15] Jacob Hacker and Paul Pierson, "The Unseen Revolution of the 1970s," pp. 95–115 in *Winner-Take-All Politics: How Washington Made the Rich Richer – And Turned Its Back on the Middle Class*, New York: Simon and Schuster, 2010.

not party, that determine both economic and behavioral outcomes. The reason the latter are almost always associated with one party or the other would appear to be because the policies of each of the two parties have almost always differed in the same ways from those of the other party. And when that is not true – and only when that is not true – the parties achieve results (or failures) that are otherwise associated with the other party.

Our mystery deepens, although not about murder for the moment. According to the most objective and reliable data that we have concerning prosperity and public safety, the Republican party is the party of poverty and violent death. And yet Republicans regularly come to power by claiming that they are the party of prosperity and public safety. Their failure to succeed in achieving prosperity and decreasing the rates of lethal violence, however, benefits the very constituency to which they appeal, for reasons I will discuss below.

Why the President? Why not the Congress?

But first, I can imagine your asking me why I am concentrating only on the party of the president, not the partisan make-up of the Congress. Why the presidency? There is no question that Congress plays or can play a role with respect to matters of prosperity and public safety. For example, during Johnson's last two years in office (1967–8), the Republican Congressional opposition was sufficiently powerful to block all further progressive civil rights legislation. But it is also true that, to everyone's surprise, the 1994 Republican majority in

Congress was outfoxed by Clinton's brilliant political skills and was unable to stop the passage of many progressive laws and policies.

As the Clinton example illustrates, for the most part the data do not support the notion that Congress influences violent death rates in this country with anything approaching the magnitude, consistency, and statistical significance that the president does. The evidence for the most part supports the position that the president usually wields far more power than the Congress with respect to the matters I am considering here. In any event, the statistical regularities I have uncovered – the correlations between Republican administrations and increases in violent death rates and between Democratic administrations and decreases in violent death rates – are associated with presidential party affiliation (with only two exceptions), not with the partisan majority in Congress.

This same conclusion was reached by Larry Bartels[16] in his studies of the relationship between the political parties in power and rates of unemployment and other forms of economic distress and inequality: he found that the president is far more important in influencing these variables than the Congress is. When Congress does have an effect, it is more likely to consist of stopping the president from doing what he wants to do than of forcing him to do something he does not want to do (which he can usually prevent in any case by means of his veto power).

In short, whether we can explain it comprehensively or not (and I do not pretend to have done so in this short

[16] Bartels, *Unequal Democracy*, pp. 34–6.

discussion), it appears, on the basis of the empirical evidence, that the political affiliation of the president is a more powerful determinant of the violent death rates in the US than is the partisan identity of the Congress. How can we understand this, if the "separation of powers" in our national polity is truly between separate but equal branches of government?

This paradox might be explained by Schlesinger's observation that the president of the US has become more powerful than the Congress, especially and increasingly since the beginning of the twentieth century. As Schlesinger[17] put it, "the imperial presidency began with the first Roosevelt and was nourished by the second Roosevelt. It burst into full splendor in the days after the second World War." And he quotes Woodrow Wilson's assessment that the president remains "the only national voice," and the presidency "the vital place of action in the system."

Nor are Schlesinger and Wilson the only ones to reach that conclusion, as is shown by Richard E. Neustadt's study, *Presidential Power and the Modern Presidents*.[18] Neustadt quotes with approval, as does Schlesinger in his book, this passage from an analysis called *The Rise and Growth of American Politics*, published in 1898 by another political scientist, Henry Jones Ford:[19]

---

[17] Arthur Schlesinger Jr., *The Imperial Presidency*, Boston: Houghton Mifflin, 1989.

[18] Richard E. Neustadt, *Presidential Power and the Modern Presidents: The Politics of Leadership from Roosevelt to Reagan*, New York: The Free Press, 1990.

[19] Henry Jones Ford, *The Rise and Growth of American Politics*, New York: Macmillan, 1898, ch. 22, p. 185.

The agency of the presidential office has been such a master force in shaping public policy that to give a detailed account of it would be equivalent to writing the political history of the United States. The evidence . . . history affords seems conclusive of the fact that the only power which . . . defines issues in such a way that public opinion can pass upon them is that which emanates from presidential authority. The rise of presidential authority cannot be accounted for by the intention of presidents; it is the produce of political conditions which dominate all the departments of government, so that Congress itself shows an unconscious disposition to aggrandize the presidential office.

Why do Republicans win elections?

This still leaves a major mystery unsolved: why would the American people continue to vote into power a political party whose presidents expose them to increased rates of inequality (relative poverty) and violence? And secondly, why would that political party and its presidents continue to pursue policies that lead to those outcomes? It may surprise the reader, as it surprised me, to discover that there is a single answer to both questions. But to discover that answer, we must begin by asking a third question: namely, given that we live in a democracy, why is it that 99 percent of the voters in the United States give 1 percent of the population possession of more than 40 percent of the net wealth of the entire country?

The greatest increases in the concentration of wealth in the twentieth century occurred during the Republican administrations of the 1920s, which led to the Great Depression, and during those from the late 1960s into the 1990s (especially during the 1980s, the Reagan years). The polarization of wealth attained by the Republicans during the "Roaring Twenties" was reversed by the New Deal Consensus from 1933 to the late 1960s. This was accomplished by introducing income supplements for the needy (social security, unemployment benefits, etc.) that had not existed before, reducing unemployment, and creating not only a "minimum wage" but also what was in principle a "maximum wage," by raising the highest marginal income tax rates above 90 percent. The result of these and other policies was what some economic historians have called the "Great Compression" in incomes and wealth that occurred during the most prosperous – and also the most economically equal, and the most non-violent – period in American history (at least with respect to domestic or intranational violence), from roughly 1940 to 1970. Once the Republicans returned to power in 1969, however, that period ended, and inequalities in wealth and income once again reached the same – or nearly the same – levels under Reagan as they had in the 1920s (as did the rates of lethal violence). The rate at which inequality was growing slowed down during the Clinton administration in the 1990s to only about a third of the rate at which it had been growing under his Republican predecessors. This may have been because he succeeded in reducing both the rate and the duration of unemployment, and increasing the highest marginal income tax rates, the Earned Income Tax Credit (the negative income tax which gives money to those who are poor despite having a job), the median and minimum wages, and applying other policies whose effect was to redistribute at least a bit of the national collective income and wealth from the rich to the poor. However, the momentum of the forces producing inequity was still so strong that by 1998 the wealthiest 1 percent of US citizens still owned 38 percent of the total household wealth of the country and 47 percent of the total financial wealth. In other words, the richest 1 percent owned nearly 40 percent of the country's real estate and almost half of its money and other liquid assets (stocks, bonds, etc.).[20]

Although we do not have comparable data yet for rates of lethal violence during the last year of the second Bush administration or the first two years of Obama's presidency, we do know something about their economic policies, and their results. First of all, the current "Great Recession" – as it has been called, in acknowledgment of the fact that it is the worst economic failure the US (and perhaps the world) has suffered since the "Great Depression" of the 1930s (a description that would also describe recessions that occurred during the prior Republican administrations of Nixon, Ford, Reagan, and Bush Sr., although this one is even worse) – occurred right on schedule – after one of the most conservative Republican presidents in US history had been in office for seven years. We also know that when Obama cut a deal with Congressional Republicans to extend unemployment benefits for the long-term unemployed, and to renew tax cuts for middle-class and poor

---

[20] Wolff, *Top Heavy*.

families, he spoke of those groups as being taken hostage by the Republicans, who would not agree to help the unemployed and the two lower classes unless the Democrats would agree to continue the comparatively enormous income tax cuts that the Bush administration had given to the extremely rich, and to give even larger cuts in inheritance taxes that would primarily be of benefit only to the wealthiest 1 to 1/10 of 1 percent of the American population.

So the mystery is this: how can the wealthiest 1 percent of the population persuade the other 99 percent to agree to a system that is so clearly biased against their economic interests? The Republican party's solution to the problem of how to persuade a majority of the voters to support the party that increases their relative poverty has been to pit the members of the lower middle class against the very poorest lower class, thus distracting the attention of both classes from the fact that it is the upper class (and the party that represents its interests) that is picking their pockets, not each other. As long as the near-poor are fighting with the very poor, neither will fight against the rich – or, to be more exact, against the whole social and economic system that divides the population into a tiny number of very rich people and a huge number of poor and near-poor.

How do they do this? By perfecting the oldest strategy in politics by which a minority can dominate a majority: as the Roman emperors put it, "divide and conquer." But how do they do that?

One means was what Lyndon Johnson called the "Bourbon strategy" in Southern society and politics. He was referring not to the whiskey but to the wealthy white ruling class in the South, the "Bourbons." He said that it was to the political and economic advantage of the Bourbons that racial discrimination continue in the South, because, as long as it did, the poor whites would have an even poorer group of blacks whom they could look down upon and to whom they could feel superior, thus distracting them from feeling envy and resentment toward the rich whites because of their much greater wealth – a clear example of the "divide and conquer" strategy by which a wealthy minority can dominate and exploit a much larger and poorer majority, even in a governmental system that calls itself a democracy. So, of course, the conservative Republicans' "Southern strategy" (which now means the main-stream Republicans' strategy), which many observers have claimed is more responsible than any other single historical development for bringing them back into power in 1969 after 36 years in the political wilderness, has been based on fighting against racial equality by virtually every means at its disposal, including (but not limited to) the following:

1) The policy of mass incarceration, by which I mean the historically unprecedented seven-fold increase in the US imprisonment rate since the mid-1970s, in response to President Nixon's declaration of a "war on crime," which has imprisoned African-Americans to a disproportionate degree, especially for non-violent violations of drug laws which many studies have shown they break no more frequently than whites do, but for which they are imprisoned much more frequently than whites are. The fact that mass incarceration serves no rational interest in increasing

public safety is demonstrated by the evidence that it is both unnecessary and ineffective as a means for preventing violence, as I discuss elsewhere in this book. The irrational interest this policy serves, however, is very clear: it is a means of re-instituting "white supremacy," after the partial successes of the civil rights movement from 1954 to 1965 threatened to reduce racial inequality by legally prohibiting older methods of enforcing it, such as lynching and racial segregation.[21]

2) The disenfranchisement of millions of African-Americans, most of whom would vote for Democrats if they could vote, by defining them as felons (as just described), and then barring them from voting, often for the rest of their lives. This too is a way of finding a substitute for older ways of maintaining white supremacy that are now legally prohibited, such as disenfranchisement of blacks through "poll taxes" and "literacy tests."

3) Supporting litigation whose purpose is to re-institute racial segregation.

4) Opposing laws whose effect would be to increase racial equality.

But there is another historical development that has also had the effect of dividing and conquering the middle and lower classes – indeed, the poorest 99 percent of the population – to the benefit of the Republican party. That is by pursuing policies whose effect is to raise the level

---

[21] See Michelle Alexander, *The New Jim Crow: Mass Incarceration in the Age of Colorblindness*, New York and London: The New Press, 2010.

of criminal violence. I am not suggesting that increasing the rates of violent and other crimes is necessarily, usually, or ever the conscious intent behind those policies, nor do I regard the intent as particularly relevant here. I am talking about the *effect* these policies have, which is to benefit the Republican party whether they are consciously aware that that is what they are doing or not.

How would increases in the homicide rate divide the poorest 99 percent of the population, to the benefit of the wealthiest 1 percent? The answer is simple: most of the violence that our laws define as criminal is committed by poor people, so when criminal violence increases, members of both the upper and the lower middle classes tend to become frightened of and angry at the lower class, which distracts them from noticing that it is the upper class that is actually expropriating the majority of the country's collective wealth and income.

And while most of the violence that our legal system defines as criminal is committed by poor people, most poor people do not commit violent crimes (or any other kind). But most of the victims of violence are poor people. Therefore, a high violent crime rate also tends to divide the poor from each other – that is, to divide the non-violent and non-criminal majority of the poor from that minority among them that is violent and is immediately threatening to them (such as youth gangs, drug dealers, etc.). The effect this has on the inhabitants of crime-ridden inner-city urban ghettos is to distract them from noticing or caring that tax and other laws are written so as to increase the wealth of those who are already rich, and to do so at the expense of the poor. They are too preoccupied with the need to protect themselves from their violent neighbors.

In presenting this analysis, I am not offering a conspiracy theory. I am not suggesting that there is a committee of the Republican party or of the "ruling class" that meets every Monday morning to decide how they can increase the rate of violent crime that week. I am simply describing the way the economic system works of its own volition, so to speak, when the tax laws and other regulations are written so as to benefit the Republican party's main constituency, the super-rich.

What I am describing here is not a conspiracy, it is a conflict of interest. In fact, there are two conflicts of interest, an economic one and a political one. Between whom and whom? First of all, between the *economic* interests of the richest 1 percent of the American population (and the political party that represents their interests), and the interests of the other 99 percent. We know that increases in economic inequality lead to increases in homicide and suicide. But we also know that increases in economic inequality are in the interest of the very rich by definition, because that is what inequality means. When the gap in wealth and income between the rich and the poor increases, what that means is that the rich are getting a larger share of the country's collective income and wealth, and the poor, a smaller share. Thus there is an objective conflict of interest between the *economic* interest the richest 1 percent of the country has in becoming even richer, and the interest the other 99 percent have in living in a less violent society, as well as the interest they have in gaining access to a larger share of the country's collective wealth and income.

As I said, the main victims of violent crime are the poor, and an increase in the rate of criminal violence offers minimal threat, if any, to the rich, who live in gated communities or are otherwise protected by expensive security arrangements. One of the more astonishing facts about the United States today is that more money is spent on private security forces for the rich than on police forces and other security arrangements for the rest of the population.

But there is also another conflict of interest here: a *political* one. It is in the political interest of the very rich for the country to have high rates of violent crime, since the higher the crime rate, the more the voting population is able to be divided and conquered, as the high crime rate alienates the middle class from the poor, and the poor from each other – the non-violent majority from the violent minority by whom they feel most directly and immediately endangered. When that happens, the middle classes are less likely to vote for the party that identifies itself with the interests of the poor (who are seen as violent and dangerous); and the poor are less likely to vote for the party that is less punitive toward the criminals (since they have been misled into believing that increasing the amount of punishment will reduce the rate of violence, rather than increase it). Since both poverty and violence are concentrated among easily identifiable racial and ethnic groups, the Republican party has been able to play on the fears of poor and lower-middle-class voters from majority racial and ethnic groups who feel threatened by those who belong to minority groups.

The higher the rates of crime and violence, then, the

more that members of the middle and lower classes become manipulated into fighting against each other, and distracted from noticing that the people by whom they are most in danger of being robbed are not the relatively small number of armed robbers among them, but the even smaller number of very wealthy people and their agents, the Republican politicians who write the laws that divert money into their hands and out of the hands of the lower and middle classes. As the old saying goes, the poor man robs you with a gun, the rich man with a pen.

In advocating policies that increase the level of social and economic stress and distress to unbearable levels, and thus increase the rates of suicide and homicide, the Republican party succeeds in winning elections precisely by failing to achieve its stated goals of prosperity and public safety. Thus "nothing succeeds like failure."

In this analysis, I am not assuming that many individual members of any of these classes – the upper, middle, or lower – are actually consciously aware of the role they are playing in this conflict. Some in each class are aware of it, and, of those who are, some work consciously to support this system and some work consciously to oppose it. But the beauty of the system, from the standpoint of the interests of the rich, is that the vast majority of people whose lives are affected by it, whether for good or for ill, do not have to understand the system or consciously support it in order for it to work. The socio-economic and criminal justice systems themselves do that job for them, so that individuals do not have to do anything different from what they have always done for the system I have just described to work and perpetuate and reproduce itself. Simply maintaining the status quo, individual by individual, maintains the status quo for the social system as a whole.

Representative strategists in both major American political parties are aware of these facts, and use them consciously in devising their political strategies. For example, Barry Goldwater's campaign manager in 1964 said that crime in America was a free, multi-million-dollar gift to the Republican party, and, as the senior President Bush's campaign strategist Lee Atwater put it, "Crime was a 'wedge issue' to be driven into the Democratic party in order to fragment it."[22] In other words, Divide and Conquer!

And Democratic strategists are fully aware not only that this is the strategy of the very wealthy, but that it has been a very powerful and largely successful strategy. As the Democratic representative Barney Frank said, "There is an important political imperative: for the Republicans not to be able to accuse the Democrats of being soft on crime. Period. We have a dilemma – division within the party."[23] Again, divide and conquer. And as Senator Charles Schumer put it, referring to the Republican party strategists, "they want a lot of criminals. The Republican party only succeeds when the race issue is the divide . . . When they try to win on non-race – abortion, gays – they lose. That's why they're going to crime . . . That's when they win. They know it."[24]

Perceptive social scientists have long known this. As Christopher Jencks[25] put it:

[22] Sidney Blumenthal, "Crime Pays," *The New Yorker*, May 9, 1994, p. 44.
[23] Ibid.
[24] Ibid.
[25] Ibid., p. 33

Like rain on election day, crime is good for the Republicans. Whenever crime seems to be increasing, significant numbers of Americans tend to blame liberal permissiveness and turn to conservative political candidates, partly because they endorse a sterner approach to raising children, policing the streets, and punishing criminals, and partly because they oppose government "give aways" to the poor – blacks and other groups that commit a lot of crimes. While orthodox liberals answer that "getting tough" won't really help and that the way to reduce crime is to make society more just and opportunity more equal, this response to crime has seldom moved the electorate. When crime rates rise, liberals almost always find themselves on the defensive.

And, as Edgar Z. Friedenberg[26] wrote, it is important

> to demonstrate the ways in which crime *does* pay – not for criminals but for certain elements in the community at large . . . For dominant social groups, it is an epiphenomenon that is costly mostly to lesser people whose lives are not so well guarded, a side effect of the operation of the kinds of values that have made our capitalism effective. Eliminate violent crime? We couldn't leave home without it!

The true brilliance of the Republican party's strategy is that the real interests which that strategy is serving, and the means by which it serves them, are concealed by a rhetoric that states the strategy is serving exactly the opposite interests and pursuing exactly opposite goals from those that it is actually serving and pursuing. And despite the fact that Orwell anatomized this rhetoric

[26] Ibid.

with the utmost clarity in his concept of "double speak," it still deceives millions of voters. Thus, instead of openly acknowledging that it is in the interest of the rich to have a high crime rate, the political rhetoric of the Republican party claims to want to decrease the rate of violence.

But the brilliance of this strategy does not end there. For it also includes a corresponding form of double speak – namely, labeling those policies that would actually decrease the rates of violence as being "soft on crime." That is how "the Republicans have used the law and order issue for a generation to kneecap Democrats at will," as Sidney Blumenthal put it; "From the election of Richard Nixon through the election of George Bush, the Republicans held a strategic advantage on crime which was the domestic political equivalent of their advantage in foreign policy."[27] Without a high crime rate, in other words, the Republican party would lose one of its major political advantages, one of its strongest vote-capturing issues – "the war on crime," "law and order," "getting tough on crime," and so on.

It would take another George Orwell to do justice to the irony in the fact that it is precisely the failure of the Republican party to diminish criminal violence that is responsible for its success in dividing and conquering the electorate; and it is precisely the failure to create prosperity and diminish poverty that is responsible for the elevated crime rate which is responsible for Republicans' electoral victories. In other words, the motto of the Republican party is, in effect, "nothing succeeds like failure." The more they fail at

[27] Ibid.

providing prosperity and public safety, the more they succeed.

Thus, we are able to answer the question: if Republican administrations do in fact elevate violent death rates, and if practically none of those who vote for a Republican president in any particular election has the slightest desire to bring about that outcome (an assumption that I will simply take for granted), then why do people vote for Republicans? When investigating crime and corruption, the Roman lawyer Cicero asked: *Cui bono* – Who benefits? If Republicans regularly bring about epidemics of lethal violence once they come into power, we similarly can ask: who benefits? For it is hard to imagine that a political party would continue to repeat the same manifestly destructive policies unless it, and the interest groups it was serving and being supported by, were in some way benefiting from them. I have suggested that this question can be answered not by assuming some complicated conspiracy theory, but rather by noticing the simple and obvious conflicts of interest that exist between the Republican party's main constituency (the richest 1 percent of the population), and the interests of the other 99 percent of the population.

We all know what conflicts of interest are, and why we have laws against them. It is not that people always sacrifice the public interest in favor of their private interest when they are faced with such a conflict. Indeed, some of the very rich fight against the inequities in our political and economic system more vigorously than do most of us who are less well-off. I am thinking here of people like Franklin Delano Roosevelt, who was called a "traitor to his class," though it would be more accurate to say that he was a traitor to a class system that deserved no loyalty – indeed, that was a central part of his greatness. In the contemporary world, George Soros has generously lavished his considerable fortune on groups that fight to increase political and social democracy both in the United States and around the world. But we also know that, human nature being what it is, most people are not Franklin Roosevelt or George Soros, and, when faced with a conflict of interest, will often sacrifice the public interest to their own private interest, which is why we outlaw such conflicts (when we do).

How (and why) to increase the level of violence

The main obstacle to preventing violence is not lack of knowledge as to how to do it; rather, it is lack of the political will to make the changes in our society that would prevent violence, or, in other words, lack of the political will to discontinue the policies that cause violence. This simple fact has been largely obscured by a great deal of political propaganda whose effect is to persuade people that policies that stimulate violence actually prevent it, and that policies that prevent it actually stimulate it. Another way to say this would be to point to a paradox: although most voters and most politicians claim to want to diminish the level of violence in the world, they repeatedly pursue policies whose effect is to increase the frequency and intensity of violence. How can we understand this paradox? For unless we can learn how to understand it and to discontinue this self-defeating behavior, we will never be able to implement the policies that we now know are both necessary and sufficient for the prevention of violence.

What do I mean by self-defeating behavior that stimulates violence rather than preventing it? For the sake of brevity, I will mention only a few particularly egregious examples, though one could easily come up with a list of dozens.

1) Among the only drugs we know of that actually inhibit, and thus can be said to prevent, violence, two of them, marijuana and heroin, have been declared illegal and their use has been made punishable by increasingly severe prison sentences ever since our first modern Republican president, Richard Nixon, declared his "war on drugs" during his election campaign in 1968. When I say that they prevent violence, I mean exactly that: people who are under their pharmacological influence are less violent than when they are not exposed to the effects of these drugs.[28] The only drug that we know of that causes violence (alcohol) is legal, as is the most addictive and deadly of all the drugs of abuse (tobacco). And the main cause of the association between illegal drugs and violence is not the drugs (not even cocaine). It is the

---

[28] Klaus A. Miczek et al., "Alcohol, Drugs of Abuse, Aggression, and Violence," pp. 377–570 in Albert J. Reiss and Jeffrey A. Roth, eds. (Panel on the Understanding and Control of Violent Behavior, National Research Council, National Academy of Sciences), *Understanding and Preventing Violence*, Vol. III, Washington, DC: National Academy Press, 1994. See also, among many excellent studies documenting how counter-productive the "war on drugs" is, Steven B. Duke and Albert C. Gross, *America's Longest War: Rethinking Our Tragic Crusade against Drugs*, New York: G. P. Putnam's Sons, 1993.

criminal justice system itself, i.e., the laws declaring the drugs illegal, which have the effect of providing a multi-billion-dollar, tax-payer-financed subsidy of the various drug cartels throughout the world and the inner-city drug dealers in our own country who engage in violence to increase their share of an illegal drug market which would not exist in the first place if conservative lawmakers had not created it by criminalizing the drugs.

Much careful epidemiological research has shown that the main source of the violence associated with illegal drugs is the war between the different drug dealers and gangs, not violence committed by those currently intoxicated (most of whom become less violent, not more so, as long as they have their drug of choice). And yet this exorbitantly expensive method of stimulating violence is done in the name of preventing violence. The criminalization of these drugs is one of the main causes of violence throughout the world. If they were decriminalized, the drug cartels would go out of business tomorrow, just as the bootleggers did when the prohibition of alcohol in the US was repealed right after Franklin Roosevelt was elected in 1933. Until our legislators do this, the criminalization of drugs will continue to provide the main source of funding for: (a) the Taliban, Al Qaeda, and other groups, in the fight against whom we have spent an estimated trillion dollars and sacrificed thousands of military and civilian lives; (b) the Mexican drug cartels who have so much money they have been able to corrupt most of the government and purchase weapons more powerful than even the Mexican army can use against them, and thus threaten to turn that country into a failed state unable to defend its own citizens; (c) other drug cartels throughout the world who are so affluent they are able to destabilize whole national governments, for many of whom their GDP is less than the wealth and income of the cartel owners.

While the drugs we have criminalized do not, in and of themselves, cause violent behavior, they can cause medical problems. That is why it would be appropriate to treat their use as a problem in public health, not as a crime. Substance abuse treatment has been shown to be much more therapeutically effective than imprisonment in enabling drug addicts to overcome their addiction, and is vastly less expensive than imprisonment. And yet, because of the Republican-initiated "wars" on "crime" and "drugs," we continue to waste billions of dollars of taxpayers' money, and to turn our country into a virtual police state, with the highest imprisonment rate of any country in the world (including those that actually are police states), by building more and more prisons and overcrowding them with non-violent drug addicts (whom we confine in prisons where they are all too often forced into becoming either victims or perpetrators of violence), rather than offering them the treatment that could actually cure their addiction, by means that would be: (a) less expensive than imprisonment, (b) less cruel than imprisonment, and (c) more therapeutically effective than imprisonment.

2) Earlier in my career, in the 1970s and 1980s, I

headed the Institute for Law and Psychiatry at the Harvard Medical School. In that capacity, I served as Medical Director of the prison mental hospital, as well as of mental health services for all of the state prisons in the Massachusetts Department of Correction. A major responsibility I had was to end an epidemic of violence – i.e., suicides and homicides – in the prison system, since the federal courts that ordered the state to let us provide psychiatric treatment to the prisoners had determined that much of this violence was associated with undiagnosed, untreated, and overwhelming mental and emotional stress and distress.

One year, my colleagues and I investigated which of the various rehabilitative and therapeutic programs available to the prisoners had been most effective in preventing recidivism, or reoffending, among those who left the prison and returned to the community. What we found was that there was one program, and only one, that had been 100 percent effective in preventing recidivism, and that was gaining a college degree while in prison. For 25 years, Boston University professors had been volunteering their time to teach college-credit courses in Massachusetts prisons. Between 200 and 300 prisoners had gained at least a bachelor's degree over a 25-year period, and we found that not one of them had been returned to any prison for a new crime. At first I thought that perhaps we had made a mistake, that perhaps we had missed some, but then we discovered that several other prisons or prison systems had had the same result – zero recidivism in the

Indiana state prison system, 0 percent at the Folsom State prison in California, and so on among those who had gained at least a baccalaureate in prison. Not every prison had such perfect results, of course, and neither did we when we extended the study to 30 years and discovered 2 recidivists over a 30-year period – less than a 1 percent recidivism rate over 30 years, compared to the US rate of 65 percent after only 3 years. Similarly, state prison systems throughout the United States have repeatedly found college education to be not only effective, but the most effective single program capable of reducing recidivism rates.

Now, of course, this was an atypical group of prisoners, clearly more motivated and already more educated than most prisoners. On the other hand, they had committed crimes just as serious as anyone else – murder, rape, etc. And given the prison system's usual scandalously high recidivism rate, it seemed to me that any government official interested in reducing the incidence of violent crime in our communities would immediately do everything possible to increase the availability of college education to every prisoner who had the slightest degree of interest or ability.

Little did I know. When I reported the results of my research on this issue in a lecture series I gave at Harvard, a friend who attended gave a copy of my lectures to our new governor, a Republican Harvard graduate and former prosecutor who had been elected to office on the campaign promise to "reintroduce prisoners to the joys of busting rocks."

He had not realized until then that there was a program of free higher education in the prison system. Within days, he gave a press conference in which he stated that we should abolish this program, or otherwise people who could not afford to go to college would start committing crimes so they could go to prison and get a free college education. And he in fact did succeed in effectively vitiating the program. Nor is this simply the behavior of one politician in one state: three years later, the Republican majority that was elected to the US Congress under Newt Gingrich's leadership in 1994 repealed the federal grant that provided the relatively small amount of funds necessary to pay for college textbooks and tuition for inmates in prisons throughout the country. So, in the name of fighting crime and being tough on criminals, Republican politicians systematically and deliberately dismantled the single most effective program we have yet discovered for enabling people to leave a life of crime and violence. And the "war on crime," as this irrational and self-defeating behavior is called, is just as Orwellian a reversal of the plain meaning of the words of the English language as is the "war on drugs." Indeed, all these slogans have their model in Orwell's *1984*: "War is peace," "slavery is freedom," etc.

3) Studies have repeatedly found that when juveniles (children under the age of 18) are sent to adult prisons, not only are they more likely to be raped and to commit suicide, but also those who survive long enough to be released from these prisons reoffend at higher rates and commit more violent offenses

than when they are sent to juvenile detention centers and housed with other children. Yet many state
legislatures have passed laws mandating the transfer
of juveniles to adult prisons. They do not say that
their purpose is to raise the rates of violence and
recidivism to the highest possible level, but that is the
effect of the laws they have been passing.

4) Studies consistently show that the more severely
children are punished, the more violent they become.
Yet our courts and legislatures have continued to
authorize the corporal punishment of children,
a practice that is most strongly approved of by
Republican voters and legislators, and residents of
the Republican-dominated "Red States" (as I will
discuss in chapter 6).

5) Between 1984 and 1994, the rates of both committing homicide and being a victim of homicide tripled
among 14- to 17-year-old American boys. This explo-
sive increase in the murder rate was caused by one
weapon and one weapon only – hand guns. Yet the US
Congress and virtually every state legislature refuses
to outlaw the private possession and use of these
weapons, despite the fact that people are far more
likely to be killed by whatever guns they have in their
own homes (where they cause fatalities in family quar-
rels, suicides, and so-called accidents) than they are by
the guns of criminals invading their homes (a phenom-
enon so rare it can be considered more of a paranoid
fantasy – or delusion – than a reasonably probable
reality). The Republican party both supports and is
supported by the National Rifle Association, the main
lobbying group opposing the banning of hand guns.

I could go on and on, but I think I have made my point: there is a disconnect between what the Republican party says it is doing (preventing violence) and what it is actually doing (stimulating violence).

There are undoubtedly several additional factors that explain the Republican party's surprising degree of electoral success, including the facts that the wealthiest 1 percent of the population owns the mass media which tell people what to think, what to believe, whom to vote for, and so on (as someone said, the press is free – for anyone who owns one), and that the wealthiest individuals and corporations donate a disproportionate percentage of the campaign funds that are the prerequisite for running for office in the United States, so that most politicians – Democrats as well as Republicans – are under tremendous pressure to serve the economic and political interests of the very wealthy.

The politics of suicide

One mystery remains here: how has the public been led to overlook the relationship between suicide and politics? At least a partial answer to this might be that there is another divide and conquer strategy going on here, even if it is completely unconscious – namely, the division between suicide and homicide. Clearly, it is in the interest of conservative political parties to deny, as far as possible – as Margaret Thatcher did – that there is any such thing as society, because society is the arena in which politics exerts its effects. Therefore, if you want to make a political party immune to being accountable for what happens in society as a whole – such as increases in unemployment, recessions, and poverty, or in the rates of either suicide or homicide that those economic stresses increase – you will want to isolate those disasters from the range of events for which the political parties can be held responsible. That is, you will want to claim that the economic system functions according to natural laws that can no more be changed than we can change the laws of gravity, rather than that it is a game that functions according to the laws and rules we write regarding how to play the game. And it is also to the political advantage of the conservative parties whose impact on the suicide rate is only to elevate it (as has been documented, in the United States, the United Kingdom, and Australia, at least), to deny that there is any relationship between what happens in and to "society" – or, in other words, their policies and practices – and the suicide rate. One way to do that is to insist that suicide is a completely personal, individual act which is caused exclusively by an individual's private mental illness or despair, not by public policies or societal trends. The conservative party in the United States, the Republican party, has been all too successful in achieving this goal.

What I find more surprising is the degree to which the social sciences and the mental health professions have sometimes unwittingly colluded in this. To see suicide as an act of violence seems self-evident. From the standpoint of public health and preventive psychiatry, the discovery of the social and environmental causes or risk factors that can lead to epidemics of this form of premature, unnecessary, and often preventable death is of the utmost importance. Tens of thousands of deaths a year in the US alone, and hundreds of thousands around the world, are at stake.

But the moment we take that approach, we threaten those who have a stake in blinding themselves to the impact of social, economic, and political forces on the suicide rate. To see suicide simply as an individual mental illness and homicide as a similarly individual moral failing is to ignore the degree to which both are caused, in part, by social, economic, and political forces. There are many individual factors that can increase or decrease a person's tendency to both suicide and homicide, including heredity, life experience, individual personality structure and the like, but the *epidemics* of both of these forms of lethal violence are clearly caused by changes in the social environment, including economic and political events, rather than by some sudden change in the genome or the personality structure of the tens of thousands of additional people who just happen to decide to commit murder or suicide only after a Republican becomes president.

4

The Shame of It All

None of this can be understood, however, without understanding the individual psychology involved. We cannot understand or explain epidemics of lethal violence without understanding what leads individuals to become violent, since it is individuals, after all, who are the perpetrators of violence, whether their victims are themselves or other people. Whether one reads the story of Cain and Abel or the *Iliad* or the plays of Shakespeare or the daily newspaper, or talks with people who have committed murder, or listens to people who are suicidal, when it comes to violence, all roads lead to shame. In previous publications,[1] I have identified shame as the proximal cause of violent behavior, the necessary – though not sufficient – pathogen, in the same sense that the tubercle bacillus is necessary but not sufficient

---

[1] Gilligan, *Violence*; Gilligan, "Shame, Guilt and Violence"; James Gilligan, "Exploring Shame in Special Settings: A Psychotherapeutic Study," pp. 475–90 in Christopher Cordess and Murray Cox, eds., *Forensic Psychotherapy: Crime, Psychodynamics and the Offender Patient*, Vol. II, London: Jessica Kingsley, 1995.

for the development of tuberculosis. Everybody experiences feelings of shame at one time or another, yet most people never commit an act of serious violence (just as most people exposed to the organism that "causes" tuberculosis do not come down with the disease). Therefore, it is clear that there are other determinants of violent behavior, such as biology, culture, social class, age, sex, and many others. But when violence does occur, experiences of shame and humiliation or the fear of undergoing these experiences, is an ever-present prerequisite.

There is a paradox at the heart of shame. Although we usually think of shame as an emotion, and an extremely painful one at that, the paradox is that shame is actually the absence of an emotion, namely, the emotion of self-love (or, as it is also called, pride, self-respect, self-esteem, or the feeling of self-worth). The power of shame is often overlooked because of the fact that the most painfully shameful experiences are frequently those in which the provocation of shame seems most trivial, objectively. The greatest psychologists are often novelists, and William Faulkner illustrates this point powerfully in his tragic novel about the antebellum South, *Absalom, Absalom*, in which he shows how his protagonist's entire life becomes consumed and ultimately destroyed by his attempt to heal the shame caused by an incident in which, when he was young and penniless, a black slave who was serving as butler to a rich white plantation-owner imperiously and contemptuously orders him to enter by the back door of the mansion, not the front.

Shame is often overlooked because people who feel

ashamed are often ashamed to reveal that they feel ashamed and how ashamed they feel, because it is shameful to feel ashamed, since that implies that one is so weak, incompetent, inadequate or, inferior that one can be shamed – which is more true, the more objectively "trivial" the incident was by which one was shamed. Therefore, the more deeply shamed people feel, the more likely they are to conceal their shame behind a mask of bravado or *braggadocio* – or violence.

People don't have to have had the kind of specialized experiences I have had with both homicidal and suicidal individuals in order to recognize how central shame is to the genesis of violence. For example, every reader of newspapers in the United States read recently the tragic story of a college student who jumped off the George Washington Bridge after some of his classmates secretly filmed him having sex with one of his male classmates, and then posted the video on the internet where everybody could see it.

When I have asked murderers in prisons why they assaulted, or even killed, someone, the answers I have received have been astonishingly similar: "because he (or she) disrespected me." They used the word "disrespect" so often that they abbreviated it into the slang term "he dis'ed me." When people use a word so often that they abbreviate it, that may tell you how central the word is in their moral and emotional vocabulary. But you do not need to go into prisons and talk with murderers in order to know this for yourself. In the book of Genesis, the relation between disrespect and violence is described with utmost clarity in the story of the first recorded murder in Western history, the story of Cain's murder of his brother Abel. The Bible says very clearly why Cain killed Abel; it was because "God had respect unto Abel and unto his offering and unto Cain and his offering God had not respect." In short, God "dis'ed" Cain; or Cain was "dis'ed" because of Abel, and he acted out his anger at being disrespected in exactly the same way as the murderers I saw had done.

People commit homicide and other acts of violence on others in order to undo feelings of shame that are intolerably painful (or to avoid feelings of shame that would have that effect), by transferring their shame from themselves to their victim. By assaulting the other person, they prove that the victim is weaker than they are and therefore more shameful. Our language alone tells us this. Two of the words that we use with which to describe acts of violence are "assault" and "injury." "Assault" comes from the same Latin roots as the word "insult," and, even in English, the word "insult" also has the meaning of a physical assault or injury, as when surgeons refer to an incision as the surgical insult. And "injury" is the English descendant of the Latin word *iniuria*, which means "insult" (it also means "injury," as well as "injustice," and also is used to refer to rape). One does not have to add insult to injury; it is already there, in the word, the feeling, and the act itself. To assault or injure someone is to insult or, in other words, shame them.

But what about suicide, which in many ways is the opposite of homicide? People can also commit suicide as the only means they have available by which to escape from intolerable intensities of shame, even though they might prefer to commit homicide instead if they had the power to do so. Examples would include defeated Japanese Samurai, who would commit the ritual form of suicide called *seppuku* or *hara kiri* as a means of proving their courage and to avoid being executed in a shameful manner, even though their first choice, if they had not been defeated and disarmed, would have been to continue killing the enemy. Likewise, and for much the same reason, Antony and Cleopatra killed themselves (as Cleopatra made clear in her suicide note) in order to avoid the shame of being led through Rome in chains so that Octavian could celebrate his victory over them. While the suicides of many of the violent criminals in prisons today may have analogous motives, the motives of most suicides and suicidal people in the community are, in my experience, not that simple.

To understand suicide more fully, we must also consider another emotion, the feeling of guilt. Guilt is the emotion that motivates self-punishment. The paradox about suicide and guilt is that, while guilt is in some respects the opposite of shame – that is, its causes tend to be the opposite of those that cause shame and the behaviors it motivates tend to be the opposite of those motivated by shame – it nevertheless is inextricably related to shame. Shame motivates active, aggressive behavior toward other people, which can escalate to homicide under certain exceptional circumstances. The psychological function of guilt feelings is to inhibit (i.e., prohibit) the hostility toward others that shame has stimulated, which people can sometimes manage to do only by redirecting their hostile and violent impulses toward themselves instead. Thus, shame can motivate homicide as well as suicide, depending on whether the person believes he can succeed in wiping out his shame by means of violence toward others, or can only put an end to this intolerably painful feeling by killing himself.

However, for people who have developed an internalized conscience and the capacity to feel guilty and remorseful over impulses and wishes to harm others, the motivation for suicide is more likely to involve both shame and guilt. The emotion of guilt consists of anger and aggression that are directed against the self. But the aggression that is the essence of guilt has actually been stimulated by the experience of feeling shamed. Most people, except for psychopaths, have developed at least some capacity to feel guilt and remorse, and have developed an internalized conscience that forbids them from harming other people. When they experience a major shame-provoking event such as being ruined financially, or being fired from their job, or being rejected by a lover or betrayed by a spouse, or losing their home in a foreclosure, they can be expected to experience a steep intensification of anger, which shame always stimulates, but which, because of the power of their conscience and their guilt feelings, they internalize and direct against themselves, sometimes leading to suicide.

This is one way of understanding how the same social and economic stresses, such as unemployment or bankruptcy or homelessness, can lead to increases in the rates of both homicide and suicide, even though the people who respond to these stresses with homicide may have very different personalities and very different motivations from the people who respond to them with suicide. And, not infrequently, as everyone knows who reads the newspapers, those who kill others may go on to kill themselves as well.

We do need to recognize, however, that suicide and homicide are simply the most extreme and least common of all the responses to socio-economic stress. They are the tip of the iceberg, so to speak, underneath which are many times more people who suffer grievously from these stresses but do not respond to them by killing others or themselves. The fact that suicide and homicide rates do increase with a magnitude so great that they look like mountain peaks on a graph becomes an indicator of the degree to which many more people are affected by changes in the political party of the occupant of the White House and the social and economic consequences of these shifts in political party.

Psychodynamically, shame functions as a motive for stifling wishes that are experienced as shameful, such as wishes to be loved and taken care of by others, which may be seen as rendering one passive, dependent, childish, or (for men) "feminine" in nature, as opposed to being an active, self-sufficient, autonomous, and independent adult who takes pride in being able to "take care of himself." The capacity to feel shame can play an adaptive role in human life to the extent that it motivates ambition, maturation, development, achievement, the acquisition of skills and knowledge, and the other prerequisites of autonomy, self-respect, and the capacity to win respect from others. The problem with this, however, is that none of us is ever completely dependent or independent; we are all, always, interdependent. To the extent that people misidentify their own need for help and support from others as a shameful sign of personal failure or weakness rather than a feature of the human condition (as I have sometimes said to my patients, "we all need all the help we can get"), they are likely to project their own need for support onto so-called "welfare queens" whom they can then shame, reject, and punish. That is one way in which shame can stimulate right-wing political and economic attitudes and values. To the shame-driven person, "dependency," such as being dependent on "welfare," is not something to be sympathized with, it is one of the worst evils, something to be shamed, condemned, ostracized, and punished.

But an even more destructive by-product of shame will occur when a person defends against his wish to be "passive and dependent" (i.e., loved and taken care of by others) by going to the opposite extreme, and becomes active and aggressive toward others, even to the point of violence. For example, the health care reforms that were proposed by the current Democratic president, Obama, and passed by the Democrats in Congress over the almost unanimous opposition of Republicans, were responded to in many different parts of the country with death threats against those who had supported this attempt to ensure that the sick would be taken care of. What one sees here is the depth and intensity of a psychology of shame.

Shame ethics vs. guilt ethics

Shame and guilt are the emotions of morality, and therefore also the emotions of politics. To be more exact, they are the emotions of the two antagonistic moral and political value systems that exist in the world – in political terms, "right-wing" vs. "left-wing" ideologies. To understand moral conflict and therefore political conflict, it is absolutely essential to realize that there is not just one morality but two, and not just one politics but two. Despite the fact that morality is often spoken of as though there were only one moral value system, to which people adhere or else they are immoral, the fact is that there have always been two opposite moralities and they have been recognized by moral thinkers from the very beginning of moral and political discourse, which, in the West, at least, means from the time of ancient Greece and Israel.

Shame ethics is a moral value system in which the greatest evil is shame and humiliation, i.e., dishonor and disrespect, and the highest good is the opposite of shame, namely, pride and honor (respect). Guilt ethics is a moral value system in which the greatest evil is guilt (also called sin), and the highest good is the opposite of guilt, namely, innocence. But these two value systems are opposites. For example, in the guilt ethic of Christianity, the worst evil, the deadliest of the seven deadly sins, is pride, which is the highest good in a shame ethic. Thus guilt ethics supports egalitarianism, so that nobody can experience the pride of being superior to others (and no one will be shamed or humiliated by being considered inferior to others), just as shame ethics valorizes a hierarchical social system in which some people are superior and therefore experience pride and honor, meaning that others are inferior and subjected to feelings of inferiority or shame. The guilt-ridden person recognizes that we are all sinners, and that we all stand in need of forgiveness from others for the harms we have done to them, so that it would be utter hypocrisy not to forgive others for the harm they do to us. On the day of Atonement, in the guilt-ethic of Judaism, Jews are called upon to ask forgiveness from those they have offended or sinned against, and a person's failure to forgive after the third request makes him or her guilty of the sin they refused to forgive. The shame-driven person, by contrast, sees revenge as not only permitted but even required, for the failure to revenge yourself on someone who has harmed you (or a member of your family or cultural group) deprives you of "honor."

The opposite of pride is humility, which is a prerequisite for innocence, so that humility is valued as one of the highest goods in a guilt ethic; whereas for a shame ethic, humility is tantamount to self-humiliation, which is the worst evil. One consequence of these value differences is that people who live by a guilt ethic will identify with those of low social status as a way of renouncing pride and embracing humility, whereas people who live by a shame ethic will identify with those of superior social and economic status as a way of enhancing their pride and assuaging their own feelings of shame and inferiority. To put it in everyday English, those who live by a guilt ethic are likely to identify with the underdog, and those who are ruled by a shame ethic have an incentive to identify with the overdog (or the *Ubermensch*, the "superman," in the shame-ethic of Nietzsche – who emphasized that his "master-morality" is the opposite of Jesus' "slave-morality" by identifying himself, in one of his last writings, as "The Anti-Christ").

Political examples of these two different attitudes can

106

be seen in the contrast between the goals enunciated by Franklin Roosevelt and Ronald Reagan. As Roosevelt put it, "The test of our progress is not whether we add more to the abundance of those who have much; it is whether we provide enough for those who have too little."[2] Reagan, by contrast, said (speaking of the Republican party) that "We're the party that wants to see an America in which people can still get rich."[3] Roosevelt was identifying with the underdog, the person who has too little, and advocating the reduction of inequality, which he in fact achieved through his economic policies and his political activities; Reagan, with the overdog, the person who could still get rich (which is a meaningless concept unless there are others who, by comparison, are relatively poor), so he can be seen as advocating an increase in inequality (which is exactly what he achieved through his economic policies and political activities, such as decreasing taxes on the rich, welfare payments to the poor, the regulation of corporations, and the power of labor unions).

A further contrast between shame ethics and guilt ethics that is relevant to this book is that a central moral commandment of a guilt ethic is "Thou Shalt Not Kill," even when failing to kill makes you vulnerable to being called dishonorable, a coward, a deserter, "soft on crime," etc. A central commandment of a shame ethic is "Thou Shalt Kill," meaning not just that you

---

[2] Franklin D. Roosevelt, "Second Inaugural Address," January 20, 1937 (quoted in Justin Kaplan, gen. ed., *Bartlett's Familiar Quotations*, Boston: Little, Brown, 1992).

[3] Remark at Republican Congressional dinner, Washington, DC, May 4, 1982 (quoted in Kaplan, gen. ed., *Bartlett's Familiar Quotations*, p. 730).

are permitted to kill, but that you are even obligated to, when honor is at stake – which it usually is, for the shame-driven personality. For example, shame ethics supports capital punishment, war, violent self-defense and retaliation, feuds, duels, lynching, torture, and other forms of violence, including "honor killings" – and it defends all of them on moral grounds. In other words, shame ethics and guilt ethics are the same value system except with the value signs reversed, so that what is positively valued by the one is valued negatively by the other.

Among the many thinkers in the past, from the time of the very beginnings of ethical reflection in Western history, who have noticed that there is not just one morality but two and they are opposites, we can include Plato, Aristotle, St. Augustine, and in more recent times, Nietzsche, Thorstein Veblen, and Jean Piaget. Perhaps the most famous such dichotomization of moral value systems is Nietzsche's distinction between "master morality" and "slave morality,"[4] which corresponds very closely to the distinction I am making here between shame ethics and guilt ethics. "Master morality" is the moral value system that justifies being a "master," i.e., a slave-owner (as in the Old South, in the US), and violence in general (e.g., warfare, revenge, sadism). "Slave morality," which Nietzsche identified with Christian ethics as proclaimed by Jesus in his Sermon on the Mount, is the ethic that Nietzsche said would subject

---

[4] See Friedrich Nietzsche, "Beyond Good and Evil" and "The Genealogy of Morals," from *Basic Writings of Nietzsche*, translated, edited, and with an Introduction and notes by Walter Kaufmann, New York: Random House, 2000.

people to becoming or remaining slaves, since it forbids violence even for purposes of self-defense, and recommends that people "turn the other cheek," "resist not evil," forgive those who have hurt them, and love their enemies.

Silvan Tomkins,[5] one of the greatest psychologists of shame in the twentieth century, declared that shame was the dominant motive or dominant emotion motivating right-wing political values and ideologies, and that guilt was the primary motivating force behind left-wing politics. In the contemporary American political climate, left-wing policies, with their emphasis on social and economic equality and providing universal health care, are perceived by many of those who identify with right-wing politics, i.e., the Republican party, as "socialism," if not communism and totalitarianism, whereas the social policies of the right wing are perceived by members of the left wing, the Democrats, as heartless and cruel, even fascism. It is not surprising that those on the left are sometimes called, by their right-wing opponents, not just liberals but "bleeding heart" liberals – for "bleeding heart" is an ancient iconographic symbol for Jesus, whose ethical principles correspond, as Nietzsche saw, to slave-morality or what I am calling guilt-ethics.

Plato and Aristotle distinguish between democracy, an egalitarian political system based on the principle of

5 See Silvan S. Tomkins, "The Right and the Left: A Basic Dimension of Ideology and Personality," pp. 389–411 in R. W. White, ed., *The Study of Lives*, New York: Atherton Press, 1963; and "Ideology and Affect," pp. 109–67 in E. Virginia Demos, ed., *Exploring Affect: The Selected Writings of Silvan S. Tomkins*, Studies in Emotion and Social Interaction, Cambridge: Cambridge University Press, 1995.

rule by the people, and timocracy, whose literal meaning is rule by the honorable (*time*, honor, and *kratia*, rule). The actual, practical meaning of this term, for Plato, was a state governed on principles of honor and military glory (two principles that in historical practice have often been virtually synonymous or indistinguishable, as seen in the fact that throughout history and in cultures around the world aristocrats have most often constituted the military class). To Aristotle it meant a state in which civic honor, i.e., political power, was proportional to one's ownership of property, i.e., one's wealth; i.e., it was rule by the rich, and corresponds to what in today's English adaptations of Greek roots we more commonly call "plutocracy." The latter is a reasonable description of the political system favored by the current conservative Republican majority in the US Supreme Court, with its renunciation of limits on political campaign contributions by the wealthiest individuals and corporations.

Time or honor is the highest value in a shame ethic and in a shame-dominated political culture, and it is often closely associated, and more or less synonymous, with wealth and power. The current US debates over tax policy and many other social and economic debates reflect these distinctions. But they go back to the very beginnings of American democracy, in which the right to vote was originally restricted to those who owned property, or, in other words, capital (i.e., capitalists), as well as to the very beginnings of political thought and practice in Western civilization.

Shame and honor cultures vs. guilt cultures

Anthropologists have made a distinction between shame cultures and guilt cultures, although, in more recent times, the former have more frequently been referred to as honor cultures, or honor and shame cultures. Not all shame cultures are the same, however. Some, recognizing how much destruction and violence can be provoked by shaming people, have institutionalized elaborate rules of courtesy – deep bowing, etc. – which involve humbling oneself so as to avoid shaming anyone else (as in Japan, which, since the end of the Second World War, has come to have both the least economic inequality and the lowest homicide rates in the world). Other, more violent shame cultures specialize in shaming some people in the population as a way of enabling those at the top of the social hierarchy to feel pride and superiority. These are cultures associated with high levels of violence, as I will go into in more detail in the next chapter.

While many different cultures throughout the world have been identified as shame cultures, guilt cultures appear to be extremely rare. Certainly the United States cannot be so described (though it might be called a mixed shame- and guilt-culture, like many others around the world). The clearest example of a relatively pure and extreme guilt culture that I'm aware of is the Hutterites, a very religious, pacifist Anabaptist sect that believes in living according to the precepts of the New Testament. They "consider themselves to ... live the only true form of Christianity, one which entails communal sharing of property and cooperative production and distribution of goods," as Kaplan and Plaut[6] described them. That is, they conform to the pattern of the earliest Christian communities, as described in the Acts of the Apostles (2:44–5): "all that believed were together, and had all things in common; And sold their possessions and goods, and parted them to all men, as every man had need." In other words, they live according to the principle "from each according to his ability, to each according to his need." As a result, the Hutterites experienced "virtually no differentiation of class, income, or standard of living.... This society comes as close to being classless as any we know."[7] This has been called "primitive (meaning the first or earliest – 'prime' means 'one' – not undeveloped or retarded) Christian communism."[8]

They have lived in communal farms in southern Canada and the north-midwestern United States for more than a century, since emigrating from Eastern Europe to escape religious persecution around 1874. As strict pacifists, that was their only alternative to extermination. Thus, they have no history of collective violence (warfare). An intensive review by medical and social scientists of their well-documented behavioral history and vital statistics during the first 80 years since their arrival in North America reported that "We did not find a single case of murder, assault or rape. Physical aggressiveness of any sort was quite

---

[6] Kaplan and Plaut, *Personality in a Communal Society*.

[7] Ibid., pp. 50 and 30.

[8] P. Miranda, *Communism in the Bible*, Maryknoll, N.Y.: Orbis Books, 1982.

rare."[9] Hostetler,[10] writing 28 years later, reported that there still had not been a single homicide in Hutterite history, throughout the 109 years since the Hutterites immigrated to North America, and only 1 suicide (in a total population that was by then between 40,000 and 50,000). By comparison, if their lethal violence rate had paralleled that of the US as a whole (20 per 100,000 in 1983), they would have experienced 8 to 10 violent deaths in 1983 alone, and 160 to 200 over the 20 years following that, meaning roughly 67–85 homicides and 93–115 suicides – as compared with zero homicides and 1 suicide.

The fact that these estimates are so rough should not blind us to the relevant point, which is that violence can be almost completely prevented. And given how costly violence is in the United States (not to mention the rest of the world), one has to wonder what we value so much more highly than life that we are willing to continue a set of cultural, economic, and political practices that exact such a high cost in death and suffering.

The downside of this culture, for many of the more hedonistic among us, is the high incidence of guilt feelings, which is hardly surprising given the emphasis in this culture on examining oneself scrupulously for any form of sin or violation of their very strict ethical commandments, and their emphasis on blaming themselves rather than others for any problems they experience. Despite that, however, it appears that suicide is almost as non-existent in this culture as homicide – but then, so

---

[9] Eaton and Weil, *Culture and Mental Disorders.*
[10] John A. Hostetler, *Hutterite Life*, Scottdale, PA: Herald Press, 1983.

are unemployment, homelessness, relative poverty, economic inequality, and the many other causes of lethal violence in the dominant culture of the US. If the emotional costs of this culture include a high frequency and intensity of guilt feelings, the benefits include an almost complete absence of lethal violence. The question I am raising is not whether we must become Hutterites. I take it for granted that that is not a realistic option, but I also do not think it is a necessary one. The question I want to ask is: can we learn something from the Hutterites as to how we might transform our own very different culture into a much less violent one?

The most extreme example of a pure and extreme shame culture in modern Western European history was Nazi Germany (and in modern East Asian history, Germany's ally Japan, before and during the Second World War). Hitler, after all, came to power on the campaign promise to "undo the shame of Versailles," that is, the loss of national honor to which he felt the entire German nation had been subjected by the "war guilt" clause in the Treaty of Versailles and the financial reparations that the Allied Powers demanded Germany pay them; and he made it clear that the only way to undo the shame and regain national honor was by means of virtually unlimited violence. Another more recent political example of the link between shame and violence was the first public statement that Osama bin Laden made after 9/11/2001, when he said that the violence that occurred on that day was a way of making the West taste what he called the "eighty years of humiliation and contempt" to which the entire Islamic nation had been subjected by Europe and America. Again, in the shame

114

ethic that provides the value system for a shame-driven personality in a shame culture, shame can only be wiped out by means of violence, and therefore violence is justified and may even be morally obligated when one has been dishonored.

Shame-driven vs. guilt-ridden personalities

People whose lives and personalities are shaped around shame ethics or guilt ethics can be described as having shame-driven or guilt-ridden characters, respectively. Examples of shame-driven characters would include authoritarian personalities and people whose character structure falls within the borderline or narcissistic spectra of personality types, including anti-social (or criminal) and paranoid personalities. Guilt-ridden personalities would include groups that Freud described as "moral masochists" and "those wrecked by success." Most of us, I think, fall somewhere in between those two extremes.

Shame-driven characters are more likely to commit homicides than guilt-ridden characters, although they may also be prone to suicide as well when that is seen as the only way to escape from overwhelming shame. Guilt-ridden characters, on the other hand, with their abhorrence of violence, are much less likely to commit homicide. They may also be less likely to commit suicide than the shame-driven are, although, when they do commit any lethal violence, it is much more likely to be suicide than homicide.

The shame of it all then stems from the observation

that a shame-driven political value system will engender a party concerned with competition for superior status in an honor–shame hierarchy, a party that will move society in the direction of becoming a more hierarchical, unequal shame culture, which is a recipe for violence. A more egalitarian political ideology shields people from shame by diminishing status differences, so that there is no such thing as being either at the bottom or the top of the totem pole because there is no totem pole. If you go out of your way to make sure that people are not going to be exposed to shame or dishonor or degradation or being forced into a low social caste or class, you will lower the level of violence. The history of violence in America during the twentieth century under the two different political parties appears to bear this out.

5

Who Wants To Be Redundant?

In Britain, the unemployed are referred to as "redundant" – which, of course, they are from the standpoint of the employer and the economy. But human beings cannot survive psychologically when they experience themselves as being redundant: unnecessary, unneeded, of no worth or value to any company or employer. It can be very difficult, and for some people impossible, to maintain a sense of self-esteem or self-respect when one is being treated as worthless by a part of the world that we all need in order to remain psychologically healthy: the world of work. The loss of a job is, of course, only one among the several determinants that must be present in order to cause behavior as destructive and costly as homicide or suicide. But when the other determinants are already in place, becoming unemployed can become the last straw that overwhelms a person's shaky defenses against collapse – just as remaining employed may provide just (barely) enough support to neutralize whatever other assaults on self-esteem and self-respect a person is experiencing.

The inextricable relationship between unemployment and shame runs through all the research and writing on the subject, for few experiences in life can cause people to feel so overwhelmingly humiliated and rejected. Thomas Cottle[1] titled one chapter of his book on the psychological effects of being laid-off from one's job "The Shame of Unemployment," and one reader wrote:

> I purchased this title as part of an effort to understand what happened to my family when my father was fired and was subsequently unable to replace his job. The book was almost unbearably sad to read, but it rang absolutely true to the way I remember this crisis and its effects on my father and our family, *especially the overwhelming sense of shame we all lived with* ... [the long-term unemployed] aren't lazy, useless folks to be disposed of but *human beings with souls who have experienced what amounts to a life tragedy.*[2]

As these comments indicate, unemployment does not affect just the person who has lost a job; it also has profound direct and indirect effects on the person's family and community. To shift to another level of analysis, a high unemployment rate not only harms the unemployed, it also harms those who still do have jobs, both objectively and subjectively in that a high unemployment rate drives down wages and increases insecurity, which is in itself painful but also a barrier to effective bargaining for better wages and working conditions.

---

[1] Thomas Cottle, *Hardest Times: The Trauma of Long-Term Unemployment*, Amherst: University of Massachusetts Press, 2001.

[2] L. Major, retrieved from Amazon.com: customer review of ibid., emphasis added.

The "ripple effects" of unemployment thus ultimately damage everyone except, perhaps, employers, who can reduce their labor costs and neglect worker safety, though even they may suffer in the long run if poverty becomes so widespread that their potential customers can no longer afford to buy their products or services.

That is why the individuals who react to increases in the rate or duration of unemployment with homicide or suicide (or both) may not be limited to those who are themselves unemployed. Entire groups of those who are already most socially and economically vulnerable even before the unemployment rate increases can hardly avoid the stresses and frustrations caused by "job insecurity," the palpable and multiple changes that occur in relations between companies and workers, for everyone who lives from paycheck to paycheck, when unemployment increases: lower wages; fewer job opportunities; less bargaining power; fewer grievance procedures; less assurance that one will not lose one's only source of income in the near future, no matter how hard one works; having more and more unemployed relatives and friends who need one's help (and fewer who could be of help to oneself in an emergency), and so on. When these multiple stresses become overwhelming, when added to whatever other stresses people are already experiencing, we should not be surprised when an increasing number of the most psychologically and economically vulnerable individuals, whether they are themselves unemployed or not, attempt to relieve the pressure by resorting to violence of one type or another (suicide, homicide, or both).

Another scholar, Katherine Newman,[3] also draws our attention to the centrality of shame. Writing about the desperation with which ghetto residents avoid the shame of unemployment by working at humiliating poverty-level jobs, she titles her book *No Shame in My Game*. To illustrate her point, she quotes a young woman who "has had to confront the degradation that comes from holding a 'low job'" at a fast-food outlet, but since "her dignity is underwritten by the critique she has absorbed about the 'welfare-dependent,'" she says, "I'm not ashamed because I have a job" – meaning she would be ashamed if she did not have one, even a humiliating one. "Most people don't" have a job (which is actually true in the neighborhood in which she lives), "and I'm proud of myself that . . . I'm not on welfare" (p. 98) – which, of course, implies that she would be ashamed if she had to be on welfare.

Newman identifies the underlying dynamic of shame vs. honor when she reflects on

> why exclusion from the society of the employed is such a devastating source of social isolation. We could hand people money . . . but we can't hand out honor. Honor comes from participation in this central setting in our culture and from the positive identity it confers. Roosevelt understood this during the Great Depression and responded with the creation of thousands of publicly funded jobs designed to put people to work building the national parks, the railway stations . . . Social scientists studying the unemployed in the 1930s showed that

[3] Katherine Newman, *No Shame in My Game: The Working Poor in the Inner City*, New York: Vintage Books and Russell Sage Foundation, 1999.

people who held WPA [Works Progress Administration] jobs were far happier and healthier than those who were on the dole, even when their incomes did not differ significantly. WPA workers had their dignity in the midst of poverty; those on the dole were vilified and could not justify their existence. (p. 104)

All of this is consistent with our analysis of shame. Newman sums up the psychological necessity of work for emotional survival and the devastating effect of being without it:

Given our tradition of equating moral value with employment, it stands to reason that the most profound dividing line in our culture is that separating the working person from the unemployed. Only after this canyon has been crossed do we begin to make the finer gradations that distinguish white-collar worker from blue-collar worker, CEO from secretary . . . We inhabit an unforgiving culture that is blind to the many reasons why some people cross that employment barrier and others are left behind. While we may remember, for a time, that unemployment rates are high, . . . in the end American culture wipes these background truths out in favor of a simpler dichotomy: the worthy and the unworthy, the working stiff and the lazy sloth. . . . In the United States, . . . those outside the employment system are categorized as unworthy and made to feel it. (p. 87)

In short, to be unemployed is to be shamed.

The word "redundant" is not applied to old people, but it is a feeling that old people often struggle with. When Roosevelt proposed the social security plan and succeeded in getting it through Congress, he was speaking to these concerns. The elderly, who had previously had the highest poverty rate of any age group, were to be shielded from abandonment. Since the elderly have the highest suicide rate of any age group, policies that protect the elderly from feeling redundant (forgotten, abandoned, useless) should result in lower suicide rates. This is what happened under Roosevelt and through the New Deal Era. It is noteworthy that some contemporary Republicans are now trying to abolish social security, along with the rest of the New Deal and even earlier progressive reforms going back to Woodrow Wilson and the changes that have occurred in the political and economic institutions of the US since early in the twentieth century, such as income taxes and new regulatory agencies.

6

Red States, Blue States: Honor vs. Guilt

On the morning of November 8, 2000, Americans woke up to see a startling map on their television screens and in their newspapers. The country was divided politically by region and regional culture into "Red States" and "Blue States." In this disputed election, the Red States were those that voted for the Republican, Bush, and the Blue States for the Democrat, Gore. Although it was not immediately apparent, it eventually became clear that this division was not merely political. It was also a division between more violent and less violent cultures within the US.

When we compare the Red States with the Blue, we find that the Republican-dominated states had significantly higher rates of homicide (both legal and illegal) and suicide than the Democratic-majority states, both in 2000 and 2004.[1] At first blush, this may seem

---

[1] In 2000, 30 states were Red and 20 were Blue, and in 2004, 31 states were Red and 19 Blue, though the total populations of the two groups of states were almost identical, since the Blue States, being more urban, had larger populations per state. Between the two elections, only 3 of the 50 states

surprising, given that one would assume that both sets of states include sizeable minorities of members of the losing party. In fact, however, of the 31 Red States in 2004, fully half had 50 percent more Bush voters than Kerry supporters (i.e., the vote margin in Bush's favor was 60/40). The Blue States were much more evenly divided with only 2 of 19 showing that degree of polarization. Looked at another way, the Pew Research Center's post-election "political typology"[2] pointed out that while Bush's margin of victory, 2.4 percent, was the smallest of any victorious incumbent in US history, "in most of the country, the 2004 race wasn't even close to being close ... In the majority of the nation's 3,153 counties, the election was a landslide – with either Mr. Bush or Mr. Kerry winning by a margin of at least twenty percentage points." Many observers of the Red State / Blue State divide have pointed out that there is an increasing tendency throughout the country for people with similar political values and allegiances to congregate together in the same neighborhoods, suburbs, or regions, thus adding to political polarization and reinforcing the differences between partisans of the two parties.

Up to now, I have been examining differences that occur over time (1900–2007) within the same popula-

in the US switched sides: New Hampshire, which had been Red in 2000, became Blue in 2004; and Iowa and New Mexico, which had been Blue in 2000, became Red in 2004.

[2] The Pew Research Center for the People and the Press, "The 2005 Political Typology: Beyond Red vs. Blue: Republicans Divided about Role of Government – Democrats by Social and Personal Values," May 10, 2005. Downloaded from www.people-press.org on 8/30/2007.

tion, that of the US. Now, I want to look at differences between different populations – those of the Red States versus those of the Blue States – that exist at the same time: the year 2000, and again in the year 2004.

Regardless of which way of looking at the relationship between political parties and violence I use, I find the same result: more violence in Republican-dominated *regions* just as there was in Republican-dominated *eras*, and less violence in the regions as well as the eras of Democratic hegemony. However, these two ways of looking at the correlation between party and violence are not identical in every respect. For example, unemployment rates were not significantly different in the Red States from what they were in the Blue States in either 2000 or 2004. Rather, the difference between Red and Blue States seems to reflect a difference in culture and in the voters themselves.

The Red State / Blue State polarization can remind us that the causal arrow runs in both directions: the correlations between Republican majorities in the electorate and higher rates of lethal violence and between Democratic majorities and decreases in violence, may not be due simply to the effects of Republican and Democratic policies on the population. They may also be a result of preexisting attitudes and values of the different population groups that led them to vote for Republicans or Democrats in the first place. It is not merely that the parties' policies affect and influence citizens' feelings and behavior; it is also true that citizens' attitudes and values shape and influence the parties, not least in the sense that it is their values and attitudes that determine whether or not a given party will win an election and come to power. So, by the time either of the two parties triumphs, the voters who elected them may already be primed with the same values and attitudes as the party they voted for. It is true that much research has shown that the leaders of the two parties are, on average, more politically polarized than the voters are. But that does not negate another finding, which is that there are major differences between the regional cultures of the Red States and the Blue, and between Republican and Democratic voters.

Among the many lines of evidence supporting this difference in political culture and personality are studies of the contrasting practices, values, and attitudes concerning guns, militarism, torture, capital punishment, imprisonment, corporal punishment of children and other indices of violence, force, and coercion that differentiated Red States from Blue, and Republican voters from Democratic ones, in the 2000 and 2004 presidential elections. For example, the Pew Research Center interviewed 2,000 adults in the month after the 2004 election and were able to differentiate Republican vs. Democratic voters on a number of dimensions that clearly involve values and attitudes concerning the use of force and violence. On the basis of this, they developed a "political typology" that identified numerous areas in which Republican voters were far more likely than Democratic ones to see the use of violence as both an effective and an acceptable means of resolving social problems and conflicts. For example, they report that "for the most part, *opinions about the use of force are what divides Democratic-oriented groups from the*

126

Republican groups" (emphasis added).[3] This difference appeared in every aspect of life, from personal to political.

The Pew political typology divided voters into several groups based on their social, political, economic, and moral values. The groups whose members were most likely to have voted for Bush were those they called "Enterprisers" and "Social Conservatives." They found that gun ownership was much more prevalent among Republican groups, especially Enterprisers and Social Conservatives, than among Democrats. Solid majorities (56–59 percent) in both of those Republican-oriented groups say they have guns in their home as opposed to 23 percent of the most strongly Democratic group, which Pew calls "Liberals," and barely more among other Democratic sub-groups. This carries over into attitudes toward the National Rifle Association, toward which 80 percent of the Social Conservatives or Enterprisers have a favorable opinion, as opposed to 20 percent of the most solidly Democratic group, the Liberals.

These attitudes also extend to their views of foreign and military policy, so that "foreign affairs assertiveness now almost completely distinguishes Republican-oriented voters from Democratic-oriented voters." At the same time, "beyond their staunch opposition to the war in Iraq, Democrats overwhelmingly believe that effective diplomacy, rather than military strength, should serve as the basis for US security policy." For example, 70 percent of Enterprisers but

---

[3] Ibid., p. 7.

only 8 percent of Liberals believe that "the best way to ensure peace is through military strength," whereas 88 percent of Liberals and only 13 percent of Enterprisers believe that "good diplomacy is the best way to ensure peace." Pew found that 90 percent of Liberals, but only 9 percent of Enterprisers, believe that "relying too much on force creates hatred and more terrorism," whereas 84 percent of Enterprisers believe that "military force is the best way to defeat terrorism," as compared with only 7 percent of Liberals.

> In fact, public values about ... the use of military force are among the *only* value dimensions in which Republican and Democratic groups clearly align on opposite sides. . . . The extreme partisan polarization over the war in Iraq in recent years is interwoven with sharply divided judgments about . . . assertiveness. Asked whether the best way to ensure peace is through military strength or through good diplomacy, the vast majority in all three Democratic-leaning groups choose diplomacy, while those in Republican-leaning groups express more confidence in military strength. While the degree of intensity within partisan groups may differ, there is a significantly greater difference of opinion between parties than there is within either party coalition. This partisan divide is even broader when it comes to people's views on the war on terrorism. Across all Republican groups, most believe that using overwhelming military force is the best way to defeat terrorism around the world, while a clear majority in all Democratic groups believe relying too much on military force to defeat terrorism creates hatred that leads to more terrorism.[4]

---

[4] Ibid., p. 22.

"On many national security issues, especially the war in Iraq, internal partisan fissures," – meaning differences within each party – "are overshadowed by the vast gulf dividing Republicans and Democrats." Nearly 90 percent of Enterprisers believe the pre-emptive use of military force is "often or sometimes" justified, and only 10 percent (as compared with two-thirds of Liberals) believe it is "rarely or never" justified. In general, then, "Support for the use of military force is strongest among groups that are reliably Republican, somewhat less so among centrist groups, and weakest among Democratic groups." When asked whether torture of suspected terrorists can be justified, Enterprisers were three times as likely as Liberals (63 percent vs. 21 percent) to say that it "often or sometimes" can, whereas a solid 77 percent of Liberals said that it "rarely or never" could be justified.

Patterns of violence in Red States and Blue States

So far, I have differentiated Republican from Democratic voters on the basis of their different attitudes toward different forms of violence. But the Red and Blue States also differ in their rates of lethally violent behavior, i.e., suicide and homicide, including the legal form of the latter, capital punishment (the death penalty). With respect to the suicide rate, in 2000 the Red States had a rate of 13 per 100,000 and the Blue States only 10. In 2004, the suicide rate in Red States was 13.9 vs. the Blue States' 10.2. Homicide rates in the Red States were 5.7 in both 2000 and 2004 whereas in the Blue States they were 4.2 and 4.0 in those years. The difference between Red and Blue States in total lethal violence rates (suicide plus homicide) in 2000 was 18.7 vs. 14.2 and in 2004, 19.6 vs. 14.2. The probability that differences of these magnitudes in both of these years were due to chance was less than 1 in 10,000. The capital punishment rate differences are even more startling. Between 1976 (when capital punishment was reinstituted in the US after having been declared unconstitutional in 1972) and 2009, the Red States executed 1,177 people and the Blues States 54: a ratio of more than 20 to1. Of the 14 states with the most executions, every one is a Red State (11 of them Southern states). Of the 14 states with no death penalty, 10 are Blue States. Of the 31 Red States in 2004, 27 have a death penalty.

The significance of this is not only in the deaths of all of the individuals who were killed over those 33 years, but also in what they communicate to the rest of us as a matter of cultural and moral symbolism. The figures on capital punishment tell us that, at the highest and most authoritative levels of the legal and governmental system in the Red States, there is official, public approval of the principle that killing people, or in other words committing homicide (meaning the killing of another human being by a human being), is an effective and morally and legally acceptable way of expressing disapproval of another person, punishing him (because it almost always is him), and achieving justice. What effect does this have on rates of homicide and suicide in the public at large in these states? The late Justice Louis Brandeis wrote in 1928 that "Our government is the potent, the omnipresent teacher. For good or ill, it teaches the whole people by its example." Brandeis went on to explain why it was so important that government officials not break the law, but, where he spoke of crime, I would speak of violence. He said "Crime is contagious. If the government becomes a lawbreaker, it breeds contempt for laws; it invites every man to become a law unto himself; it invites anarchy."[5] In other words, to paraphrase his remarks, violence is contagious. If the government commits homicide, it breeds contempt for non-violence; it invites every man to commit homicide for himself; it does indeed invite anarchy, the breakdown of the very "law and order" in whose name capital punishment is most often defended.

These attitudes toward the use of violence then carry over into approval of corporal punishment of children, gun ownership and use, and approaches to foreign and military policy. There are higher rates of gun ownership in the Red States than in the Blue,[6] and, not surprisingly, higher rates of death from guns by all three means by which guns kill people – homicide, suicide, and so-called "accidents."

The incarceration rate is significantly higher in the

---

[5] Quoted in Charles E. Silberman, *Criminal Violence, Criminal Justice*, New York: Random House, 1978, p. 47.

[6] Philip J. Cook and Mark H. Moore report that the highest prevalence of gun ownership is in the states of the Mountain Census Region, followed by the South and Midwest (which is precisely the geographic distribution of the Red States). They also report that "The prevalence of gun ownership differs rather widely across urban areas, from around 10% in the cities of the Northeast [i.e., Blue States] to more than 50% in the Mountain states [Red States]." See their article, "Guns, Gun Control, and Homicide," pp. 246–23 in M. Dwayne Smith and Margaret A. Zahn, eds., *Studying and Preventing Homicide: Issues and Challenges*, Thousand Oaks, CA, London, and New Delhi: SAGE Publications, 1999, pp. 248 and 255.

Red than in the Blue States. In the year 2000, the average incarceration rate in the Red States was 712 per 100,000 as opposed to 487 in the Blue States. If rates of capital punishment and imprisonment can be seen as indices of punitiveness, it is clear that the Red States lead the Blue States or exceed the Blue States with respect to both their rates of violence and their levels of punitiveness.

To understand why these two groups of states differ as they do, it is necessary both to understand the cultural differences between them – to see the extent to which they represent two contrasting cultures – and to understand how these two groups of voters differ as they do. That is, it is necessary to identify their differences in attitudes and values, the dimensions of personality that go to make up what has traditionally been called "character."

With only slight oversimplification, the Red States can be described as consisting mostly of the "Old South" and the "Wild West," meaning the 11 former slave-owning states plus two border states, Kentucky and Oklahoma, and the Western mountain and desert states and most of the Midwestern Great Plains states – the states most associated with the historical heritage and symbolism of "Cowboys and Indians." The Blue States, by contrast, occupy both coasts – the Pacific and Northern Atlantic coasts and New England – as well as the North Central states with a strong Scandinavian heritage, such as Wisconsin and Minnesota, together with Illinois and Michigan.

There is by now a small library of studies by historians, anthropologists, psychologists, and political scientists describing and documenting these differences.[7] One repeated finding is the identification of the American South or the Southern states as a culture whose salient moral values exist along the polarity from shame to honor. Another recurrent finding is that the sensitivity to shame in this culture is a direct cause of the increased degree of violence. These patterns can be traced back into the nineteenth century, as can the contrast with the relatively less violent New England states of the North, in which guilt and conscience were apparently more central products and engenderers of what has been described as relatively more of a "guilt culture" than the South. For example, as Wyatt-Brown has summarized a great deal of historical evidence, "child-rearing practices in the antebellum South subjected the young to . . . shame and humiliation and the ideals of hierarchy and honor, a mode in sharp contrast to the conscience-building techniques of pious Yankees."[8]

"Honor" in the southern culture of honor is not simply an abstract "brooding omnipresence in the sky" (as Oliver Wendell Holmes said the common law was not) but, rather, a concrete reality that was codified many times in the history of the South in written documents called "Codes of Honor." These written honor codes

---

[7] See the most complete treatment of these subjects, Bertram Wyatt-Brown, *Southern Honor: Ethics and Behavior in the Old South*, Oxford and New York: Oxford University Press, 1982, and an abridged version of the same, *Honor and Violence in the Old South,* Oxford and New York: Oxford University Press, 1986. See also Richard E. Nisbett and Dov Cohen, *Culture of Honor: The Psychology of Violence in the South*, Boulder, CO, and Oxford: Westview Press, 1996; also Edward L. Ayers, *Vengeance and Justice: Crime and Punishment in the 19th-Century American South*, New York and Oxford: Oxford University Press, 1984.

[8] Wyatt-Brown, *Southern Honor*, p. 118.

consisted of detailed sets of rules as to how men could defend their honor by means of violence such as dueling, and the conditions under which they would have to resort to violence in order to save their honor. The codes of honor can be seen as examples as the codification of shame ethics. Where a guilt culture's central moral code, which I have called a guilt-ethic, counsels people who are struck on one cheek to turn the other, the codes of honor prescribe exactly the opposite behavior: fight a duel. Dueling was not unknown in the North, of course, but it was never as widespread, and died out sooner and more completely than in the South. That is one reason why the South became the dueling center of America, a tradition of acceptance and approval of violence that continues to the present day in other forms, as shown by the statistics on violent death and other types of violence.

Another form of socially recognized and accepted violence that occurred publicly and with regular ritual patterns was the practice of lynching,[9] the very name of which is that of a Southern gentleman. Lynching was not simply a private act; it was well known to and condoned by the legal authorities, thus exemplifying the acceptance of violence by the community, including its political leaders. While lynching is now outlawed and dueling has become archaic, the use of violence to settle personal disputes and express moral disapproval of other people continues in the South of today, as indicated by the high murder rates and the disproportionate use of capital punishment.

[9] See Orlando Patterson, *Rituals of Blood: Consequences of Slavery in Two American Centuries*, New York: Basic Books, 1998.

The codes of honor can be seen as the codification of shame ethics, and the interaction between shame and politics in the Southern states can be illustrated by Lyndon Johnson's remark concerning the "Bourbon strategy" that I referred to previously. He said that it was to the political and economic advantage of the Bourbons (the white ruling class) that racial discrimination continue in the South, because, as long as it did, the poor whites would have an even poorer group of blacks whom they could look down upon and to whom they could feel superior.

Indeed, the historical precursor of present-day racial discrimination in the South, slavery, has also been described in much the same terms[10] as a means by which slave-ownership was seen as a source of honor for the masters, a sign of their superiority to an inferior caste (the black slaves) and also to non-slave-owning whites (who were called a variety of demeaning names, from "crackers" and "red necks" – referring to the sunburn they got from working in the fields – to "white trash").

Even when shame and its opposite, honor – rather than guilt vs. innocence – are the central moral emotions and the central forms of moral blame and praise in a society, which is how the term "shame culture" was originally defined by Ruth Benedict,[11] different societies that can be described as belonging to that general

---

[10] See Orlando Patterson, *Slavery and Social Death: A Comparative Study*, Cambridge, MA: Harvard University Press, 1982; and Kenneth S. Greenberg, *Honor and Slavery*, Princeton: Princeton University Press, 1996.

[11] Ruth Benedict, *The Chrysanthemum and the Sword: Patterns of Japanese Culture* (1946), Rutland, VT, and Tokyo: Charles E. Tuttle, 1970.

category can vary enormously with respect to how frequently and severely they subject their members to experiences of being shamed and humiliated, and how successfully they provide those who have been shamed with non-violent means of redeeming their honor. As I mentioned above, on p. 111, some societies, which we might call "mild" shame cultures, such as contemporary (post-World War II) Japan, recognizing how much destruction and violence can be stimulated by shame (and had been, in their not-so-distant past), have evolved codes of etiquette designed to protect people from even inadvertent or unintentional shaming. Other societies, such as the American South, which can be called more "extreme" shame cultures, may also expect people to obey strict rules of etiquette as a way to avoid treating others or being treated by others with disrespect; but they nevertheless have retained some practices that, in both the past and the present, have functioned as recipes for stimulating the emotion of shame and the behavior of violence. One of these is a high degree of social stratification (whether by class, caste, race, gender, age, religion, ethnicity, or any other means by which people are divided into the superior and the inferior). Slavery was perhaps the most extreme version of this, but stratification by race continues by other means in the present,[12] such as the disproportionate imprisonment and disenfranchisement to which African-Americans have been subjected. To condemn some sub-groups in

---

[12] See Alexander, *The New Jim Crow*; also Robert Perkinson, *Texas Tough: The Rise of America's Prison Empire,* New York: Metropolitan Books, Henry Holt and Company, 2010.

the population to a lower place in the status hierarchy is to subject them to feelings of shame and humiliation, for they are treated with contempt as inferior beings. It is thus only to be expected that a higher level of violence would result, as it does in the South.

I have focused on the South because it is clearly the core strategic region that has been most responsible for the resurgence of the Republican party to power, beginning in 1966–8 and continuing in most of the years since then. Since the success of the Republicans' "southern strategy" in 1966 and 1968, the Republican party has consistently received a majority of white votes and has succeeded in blocking virtually all further civil rights legislation; and the Southern states, having become almost completely Republican in their political allegiances, have become the determining factor in Republican electoral victories.

The history, the cultural heritage, and symbolism of the "Wild West" is as well known and palpable as the honor culture of the Old South. As in the South, male honor was dependent, to a much greater degree than in the more established and peaceful culture of New England and the Eastern seaboard, on men's ability and willingness to demonstrate both their courage and their expertise in the arts of violence. Students of honor, such as the British anthropologist Julian Pitt-Rivers,[13] have commented that disputes of honor can only be settled

---

[13] Julian Pitt-Rivers, "Honor and Social Status," pp. 19–77 in J. G. Peristiany, ed., *Honour and Shame: The Values of Mediterranean Society*, Chicago: University of Chicago Press, 1966, pp. 30–1; Julian Pitt-Rivers, "Honor," pp. 503–11 in *International Encyclopedia of the Social Sciences*, 1968, pp. 509–10.

outside the law, between the persons involved. While that is a characteristic of honor cultures in general, as in the extra-legal patterns of violence in the South (duels, feuds, lynching parties), the relative absence of effective law and government in much of the history of the Western states only exacerbated and reinforced and legitimized this tradition. The cultural heritage left by the history of the Wild West is one in which personal honor can be maintained only by personal violence outside the law. Another related similarity between the Old South and the Wild West is that this cultural pattern is dependent on, and predicated on, the private ownership of guns. Thus, it is not surprising that the areas of the US in which guns are most widely valued, owned, and used, and in which the death rates from guns are at their highest, are the Southern and Western states.

Shame cultures have a universal tendency to create not just a class system but also a caste system, meaning a status system of much greater rigidity and impermeability, thus allowing for much less social mobility than a class system. A member of a lower caste can never escape his place in the caste hierarchy, no matter how successful he or she is in other respects. The lowest caste in the Southern shame culture was the African-Americans; in the West, it was the Native Americans. Today the fight in the US over immigration, especially that of Mexican Americans, is the arena in which many of these shame-culture status contests are being fought out. The issue, however, is always the same: namely, how can those who have a need to feel pride, because that is the only alternative to feelings of shame, maintain their pride and avoid shame except by casting some groups in the population as inferiors whom they can therefore look down upon and to whom they can feel superior: the "Bourbon strategy" writ large. Unfortunately, this is also a recipe for violence.

There is always a reciprocity between culture and personality in the sense that different types of cultures produce different types of personalities through their child-rearing, socialization, and educational practices and the conventions of their criminal justice systems, their religious beliefs and practices, and other social institutions, and those personalities in turn reproduce the culture. Shame cultures typically produce shame-driven personalities and guilt cultures typically produce guilt-ridden personalities (hence such phrases as "guilty white liberal" and "bleeding-heart liberal"). Both of these personality types and differences have been studied mostly in terms of their psychopathology, with "borderline," narcissistic, paranoid, anti-social, and "right-wing authoritarian" character structures seen as characteristic of shame-driven people, and "moral masochists," as well as depressive and obsessional personality patterns, seen as more typical of guilt-ridden personalities. For the purposes of this book, however, the relationship between personality and political attitudes is more relevant. This has been the focus of much research in recent decades contrasting authoritarian with egalitarian personalities.[14]

---

[14] The distinctions originally made between shame and guilt cultures by Ruth Benedict (*The Chrysanthemum and the Sword*), and between authoritarian and egalitarian personalities (Theodor W. Adorno, E. Frenkel-Brunswick, D. J. Levinson, and R. N. Sanford, *The Authoritarian Personality*, New York: Harper and Row, 1950), were both called into

The usefulness of these distinctions in the present context stems in part from their explanatory value with respect to figure 1.1 showing the correlation between the two political parties and the contrasting patterns of lethal violence associated with each. The contrast between shame and guilt cultures corresponds in most respects to the contrasts between the Red States and the Blue States as well as the contrasts between the social and economic policies of the Republican and Democratic parties. In tying these contrasts to the

question by critics soon after they were first formulated. One result of that is that these concepts have been refined and are now once again very much in use. There is an extensive and quite sophisticated anthropological literature on cultures of shame and honor in the circum-Mediterranean culture area and the Arab world, as well as in Japan and the American South. See also Pitt-Rivers, "Honor"; Pitt-Rivers, "Honor and Social Status"; J. G. Peristiany and Julian Pitt-Rivers, eds., "Introduction," in *Honor and Grace in Anthropology*, Cambridge: Cambridge University Press, 1992; Peristiany, *Honour and Shame*; Edwin O. Reischauer, *The United States and Japan*, 3rd edn., Cambridge, MA: Harvard University Press, 1965; David D. Gilmore, ed., *Honor and Shame and the Unity of the Mediterranean*, Washington, DC: American Anthropological Association, 1987.

See also Michelle Rosaldo, ed., *Towards an Anthropology of the Emotions: Rethinking Shame and Guilt* (Proceedings of a Symposium of the American Anthropological Association), Washington, DC: American Anthropological Association, 1983. As Rosaldo wrote in this volume, "of all themes in the literature on culture and personality the opposition between guilt and shame has probably proven most resilient" (p. 135).

In the psychological literature, there is also a renewed recognition of the usefulness of an old concept, "right-wing authoritarianism," in part through the work of Robert Altemeyer. See especially his book *The Authoritarian Specter*, Cambridge, MA, and London: Harvard University Press, 1996; also his *Right-Wing Authoritarianism*, Winnipeg: University of Manitoba Press, 1981; and his *Enemies of Freedom: Understanding Right-Wing Authoritarianism*, San Francisco: Jossey-Bass, 1988.

And see Marc J. Hetherington and Jonathan D. Weiler, *Authoritarianism and Polarization in American Politics*, Cambridge: Cambridge University Press, 2009.

data on high and low rates of homicide and suicide, it becomes necessary to consider the differences between people who vote Republican and those who vote for the Democrats, and here the personality distinctions become central. Shame cultures produce shame-driven personalities who are especially vulnerable to suicidal and homicidal behavior when subjected to a degree of humiliation that is greater than they are able to tolerate. But shame-driven personalities reproduce shame cultures, e.g., Republican administrations whose policies tend to create the conditions of inferiority that generate feelings of shame. Thus it is not that Republican voters themselves are necessarily the ones who are committing more acts of homicide or suicide; it is that they are creating a social hierarchy that casts some demographic groups – e.g. African-Americans and in some cases Latinos and Native Americans – into an inferior social status that subjects them to disproportionate amounts of shame and contempt and thereby stimulates increased rates of homicide and/or suicide.

Among whites, suicide rates are highest among white gun-owning males in the Western states, but they are highest of all among Native Americans, many of whom also live in those states. Here again, the culture of shame creates a climate of violence.

Authoritarian personalities have been distinguished from egalitarian personalities with respect to several differences in values and attitudes. For example, authoritarian personalities are more likely to approve of social inequality, hierarchies, and status differences, and to sanction the use of violence by authority figures such as policemen, soldiers, judges, and jailers. They believe not only in dividing people into the opposing categories of superior and inferior, but in regarding their own demographic group as the superior one. Common examples: whites are superior to people of color, the rich are superior to the poor, the old are superior to the young, and men are superior to women. The success of appealing to people by means of such stereotypes can be seen in the fact that, since 1968, Republicans have received a majority of the votes of those who are white, wealthy, older, and male.

As the research on authoritarianism has become more sophisticated in its methodology, one finding has become clearer: namely, that authoritarianism is associated with right-wing political attitudes and values. To speak of right-wing authoritarianism is essentially a redundancy. As Norberto Bobbio, an Italian political scientist, has pointed out in his book *Left and Right,* right-wing political movements place a positive value on social inequality and status hierarchies just as left-wing political ideologies pursue greater social and economic equality. Thus right-wing politics is completely consistent with the value positions of authoritarian personalities. The preference for authoritarian aggression, that is the use of force by government authorities, is reflected in the greater use of capital punishment and imprisonment in the Red States vs. the Blue States. Altemeyer and his colleagues have concluded, from extensive and repeated studies of authoritarian vs. egalitarian attitudes and values over several decades among Republican and Democratic voters and legislators throughout the United States, that there is a remarkably consistent and statistically significant correlation between authoritarianism and membership in the Republican party, and between egalitarian beliefs and Democratic party affiliations, among both voters and legislators. They found a similar correlation between conservative voters and legislators in Canada, who scored high on the "Right-Wing Authoritarianism" (RWA) attitudes and values scale, whereas those affiliated with liberal party politics scored low. Although most of their research in the US was performed before the "Red State / Blue State" distinction was first made, in 2000, what they found reveals some very interesting inter-correlations between all three of these variables: character, party, and state. In eight studies undertaken during the 1990s, they studied the mean scores of state legislators on the RWA scale, by party and state. They found that: (1) all Republicans scored above the mean on the RWA scale, whether they were from Red or Blue States, with the single exception of those from a Blue State, Connecticut – and even their scores were higher than those of any of the Blue State Democrats; (2) Democratic legislators in Blue States all scored below the mean; (3) the only Democratic legislators who scored above the mean were those from Red States. These results would appear to be consistent with the proposition that culture (Red State vs. Blue State), personality (authoritarian vs. egalitarian), and party identification (Republican vs. Democratic) influence and reinforce each other.[15]

---

[15] Robert Altemeyer, *The Authoritarian Specter*, Cambridge, MA, and London: Harvard University Press, 1996, pp. 291–6, and figure 11.2, p. 292.

I can imagine my readers objecting at this point: "Aren't you guilty of doing exactly what you are accusing authoritarian personalities, and by extension Republicans, of doing: namely, dividing the population into a superior in-group vs. an inferior out-group and putting yourself among the superior?" Or, to put it more bluntly, "Aren't you shaming and blaming Republicans, and everyone who lives in a Red State, and thus in effect promoting violence?" My questioner could continue: "Aren't you guilty of doing what those shame-driven people called 'borderline personalities' do, and splitting people into those who are all good (from your point of view, Democrats and Blue States) and those who are all bad (Republicans and Red States), with yourself in the all good camp?"

So let me be as clear as possible about something that up to this point I have felt was too obvious to need to be mentioned: neither the Democrats nor the Blue States are all good, nor do the Republicans and the Red States have any monopoly on evil. For example, even the lowest violence rates achieved under Democrats would be considered epidemics of murder in every other developed nation on earth, and the suicide levels, even at their lowest under Democrats, are still significantly higher than those in many other developed countries of the world.[16] For example, the US in 1998, when it had the lowest lethal violence rates for the past 30 years, still had a rate of 17.3 violent deaths per 100,000 per year, consisting of a homicide rate of 6.9 and a suicide rate

---

[16] The figures cited here are from Etienne G. Krug, Linda L. Dahlberg, James A. Mercy, Anthony B. Zwi, and Rafael Lozano, *World Report on Violence and Health*, Geneva: World Health Organization, 2002, tables A.8–A.9, pp. 308–21.

of 10.4. Comparing the US with the country that is perhaps closest culturally to it, namely, its mother country, the UK, that country's homicide and suicide rates were 0.8 and 6.8, respectively, in 1999, which means a total lethal violence rate of only 7.6 – a homicide rate only 11 percent of that in the US, a suicide rate some 35 percent lower, and a lethal violence rate only about 40 percent of that in the US.

In fact, during the late 1990s, all 19 of the other largest economically developed countries in the world (consisting of Western Europe, the other English-speaking democracies, and Japan) had an average lethal violence rate of 12.7, as compared with the US rate of 17.3. The US murder rate, at 6.9, was more than 6 times as high as the average rate of 1.1 in the other 19 countries. Only their suicide rates (11.5) were close to those of the US (10.4), and the US suicide rate itself had also been 11.5 as recently as 1991, before Clinton became president, and much higher than that (13.3) in 1975.

As for the Red State / Blue State distinction, I lived in one of the bluest of the Blue States, Massachusetts, from 1966, when the white backlash against the civil rights revolution became the national movement that brought the Republicans back into power throughout the US, and found that even that Blue State had enough capacity for overt racial discrimination to put to rest any assumption that Red States had a monopoly on that particular form of authoritarian ethnocentrism.[17]

---

[17] For a prize-winning account of the racial conflicts that occurred in Boston during this era, see J. Anthony Lukas, *Common Ground: A Turbulent Decade in the Lives of Three American Families*, New York: Knopf, 1985.

So let me emphasize that medicine is not in the business of making value judgments except about one thing which is its *raison d'être*, and that is the value – the sanctity, if you will – of human life (and by extension, of other life as well, both for its own sake and because human life is absolutely dependent on the continued existence of other living things – the more different species, the better). The issue I am addressing in this book is lethal violence, the rates of which can be taken as a measure of the psychological, social, and political health of a nation. My job as a physician is to diagnose ill health, to discover its causes, and to prescribe remedies that will cure illness and promote healing. To get involved in blaming or shaming is not such a remedy, but recognizing and publicizing relevant facts are, I hope, even if the facts may at first seem shameful to some. One of the facts that is relevant here is that shaming people stimulates violence. Another is that providing people with the personal, cultural, and economic resources that strengthen their capacity to tolerate experiences of being shamed without resorting to violence is one way to prevent violence. While I have emphasized so far the pathogenic, maladaptive effects that exposure to feelings of shame can have, it is important to notice that shame can also serve an adaptive function, as an emotion that motivates us to overcome our areas of inferiority, correct our mistakes, and mature, develop, learn, acquire skills and accomplish things in which we can take pride and which can elicit respect from others. That can only happen, of course, when people have access to non-violent means of undoing shame and attaining a positive sense of self-worth, such as education and constructive, meaningful work. But when those conditions are in place, one measure of mental health can be defined as the ability to tolerate feelings of shame until one can replace them with feelings of pride by putting them to work in the service of stimulating growth, maturation, and constructive achievements, as opposed to the destructiveness of violence. When people do not have access to education and work, they may feel that the only means left to them by which to undo whatever feelings of shame they experience is violence.

We cannot grow and develop unless we can change, and we cannot change unless we can recognize that our old ways of thinking, feeling, and behaving have been limited, inadequate, or mistaken – inferior, if you will – and that we need to replace them with new ones that can do more to increase both our own ability to live fully and successfully, and that of our fellow human beings – on whom we depend, and who depend on us. One prerequisite for doing that is to develop the capacity to tolerate feelings of shame without resorting to violence as the means of diminishing them, so that we can benefit from the adaptive uses to which shame can be put, such as stimulating ambition, achievement and the acquisition of knowledge and skills.

One of the mistakes that leads to violence, I believe, is the tendency to divide individuals and groups into those that are all-good or all-bad. But my interest is in violence, and there, whether we like it or not, a clear and absolute binary does exist: namely, the difference between life and death. As a physician, I have devoted my life to attempting to save lives by identifying both the causes of death – the risk factors – and the protective factors, and attempting to remove or neutralize the pathogens and maximize the sources of healing. In looking at homicide and suicide rates, I did not expect to find myself engaged in a political and socio-economic analysis. I could explain individual cases of homicide or suicide from my clinical work with homicidal and suicidal individuals, focusing on the factors in their individual lives that predisposed them to kill others or themselves. It was the epidemics of violence that could not be explained simply by differences between individuals, since these changes from non-epidemic to epidemic rates and back again occurred within short periods of time within the same population.

Prisons as sub-cultures of shame and violence

For the past 40 years, I have been able to use prisons and jails as my social-psychological laboratory, so to speak, in which to learn about the causes and prevention of violence wherever it occurs and on whatever scale, in somewhat the same way that microbiology laboratories can enable us to learn about the causes of death as they operate in the community, outside the laboratory. Doctors in the nineteenth century discovered that the only way to end epidemics of infectious diseases was to change the environmental sources of pathogens to which everyone in the community was exposed, by, for example, cleaning up the water supply and the sewer system (and they only knew why that worked because of what they had learned in their laboratories). In my work in the prisons, I discovered that the only way to end the epidemic levels of suicide and homicide that were going on in these confined spaces was to change the culture in which every individual in the prison community was living and to which everyone was exposed.

What my colleagues and I did, first in the prisons of Massachusetts and then in the jails of San Francisco, was to search for ways to change an authoritarian shame culture into an egalitarian culture. This is not the place to take the space to describe the means by which we pursued that goal[18] except to say that the underlying principle was to treat everyone in the environment with respect and expect them to do the same, one means of doing which was to pay close attention to everyone and listen to their story with undivided attention, and to provide everyone with some non-violent means of gaining some greater degree of self-respect, such as education and meaningful work.

I began my violence-prevention work first in the prisons of Massachusetts, and then was able to develop and

---

[18] For a more detailed explanation of this experiment, see James Gilligan and Bandy Lee, "The Resolve to Stop the Violence Project: Reducing Violence in the Community through a Jail-Based Initiative," *Journal of Public Health*, 27(2): 143–8, June 2005; Bandy Lee and James Gilligan, "The Resolve to Stop the Violence Project: Transforming an In-House Culture of Violence through a Jail-Based Programme," *Journal of Public Health*, 27(2):149–55, June 2005; James Gilligan and Bandy Lee, "Beyond the Prison Paradigm: From Provoking Violence to Preventing It by Creating 'Anti-Prisons' (Residential Colleges and Therapeutic Communities)," in John Devine, James Gilligan, Klaus A. Miczek, Rashid Shaikh, and Donald Pfaff, eds., *Youth Violence: Scientific Approaches to Prevention, Annals of the New York Academy of Sciences*, 1036: 300–24, 2004; Sunny Schwartz (with David Boodell), *Dreams from the Monster Factory: A Tale of Prison, Redemption and One Woman's Fight to Restore Justice to All* (with an Introduction by James Gilligan), New York: Scribner, 2009.

refine it further in the jails of San Francisco. Throughout the 1970s, there had been a homicide a month and a suicide every six weeks in one 600–man Massachusetts prison alone, and riots, hostage-taking, and murders of staff, inmates, and visitors were occurring in the other prisons as well. Yet we were able, by the mid-1980s, to go for a year at a time with no lethal violence throughout the entire 12,000-man prison system.

I was then able to apply and test what we had learned from that experience in a more systematic way when the sheriff of the City and County of San Francisco, a lawyer named Michael Hennessey, wanted to replace retributive justice (which I would call a fancy term for revenge) with restorative justice (by giving violent criminals an incentive and a method of becoming agents of violence prevention, and thus giving back to the community something of what they had taken from it). Sunny Schwartz, Sheriff Hennessey's program director and also a lawyer, assembled a team of creative and innovative people, and my research partner, Dr. Bandy Lee, and I worked with them on the design, implementation, and evaluation of an intensive, controlled violence-prevention experiment, which continued from 1997 to 2007.

One of the members of Sunny's team, Hamish Sinclair, had already developed a systematic method of deconstructing and reconstructing what he called the "male role belief system," meaning the whole set of assumptions and values that almost all men in our society are taught in one form or another: namely, that the world is divided into two groups, the superior and the inferior; that in that dichotomy men are superior to women and real men are superior to other men; and that unless they enforce their superiority, if necessary by means of violence, they are by definition inferior and not even masculine. All those assumptions, which made up a type of shame ethic, are of course recipes for violence, which, as I said, was rampant in the prison culture until we worked intensively with the entire population of one dormitory (rather than cell-block) unit at a time to help them deconstruct and reconstruct the moral value system that serves as the ethos of a shame culture, i.e., what some criminologists have called a "sub-culture of violence."[19]

We found that the level of violence within the San Francisco jail, among those who were exposed to this experimental program, dropped to zero for an entire 12 months (whereas violence continued unchanged in a "control group" of prisoners in an ordinary jail, 60 percent of whom in any given year committed assaults that could have been prosecuted as felonies outside the jail); and that, upon release back into the community, the rate of violent recidivism, or reoffending with a new violent crime, during the first year, was 83 percent lower than in a matched control group that had been in an ordinary jail – after no more than 4 months of participation in this program.

From all these experiences, and my work as a consultant on prison violence around the world, I have concluded that it is possible to stop epidemics of violence, but that one can do so only by changing the culture in

---

[19] Marvin E. Wolfgang and Franco Ferracuti, *The Sub-Culture of Violence*, Beverly Hills, CA: Sage Publications, 1982.

which the population is living. Of course, we worked as intensively as we could with as many individuals as we could, and did so at least briefly with everyone, in our effort to enable us and them to understand and end their violence. But the key to ending the epidemic of violence was to change the social system – the cultural ocean, so to speak, in which all the fish swam.

My work in Massachusetts and San Francisco can hardly be said to have constituted more than a couple of isolated "pilot projects" in the prisons of one state and the jails of one city. But the purpose of pilot projects is to learn lessons that can then be applied on a larger scale outside the walls inside which they took place (and we have been replicating these projects in jails and prisons around the world, from New Zealand and Singapore to Poland and New York). I regard my work in these two quite different correctional settings, in Massachusetts and San Francisco, as experimental confirmations of the hypothesis that the value system that I have called here a shame ethic, and the socio-cultural system that I have called a shame culture (both of which valorize and maximize inequality, social status hierarchies, domination, and authoritarianism), stimulate violence of all types; and that dismantling those beliefs and practices and replacing them with an egalitarian, democratic set of social relationships, in which everyone treats everyone with equal respect regardless of their role in the group, is an effective means of preventing violence.

This experiment provided at least provisional confirmation of my hypothesis that when you challenge inequality (the division of a population into those who are superior to others and those who are inferior), you are striking at the violence-provoking heart of a shame culture, its capacity to induce the feelings and fears of inferiority to others that provoke violence (especially when people are deprived of non-violent means by which to attain feelings of pride, self-respect, and self-worth, such as education and work). We saw in the prisons what happened when a population consisting of the most violent men our society produces were given the opportunity to acquire a college education; and we see both in the prisons and in society as a whole what happens when people are deprived of the opportunity to engage in meaningful, remunerative work.

My intention in this book, then, is to extend and apply what we learned from this experiment in those microcosms of murder (and suicide) called prisons and jails to the macrocosm of our society as a whole. The fact that American society is plagued by recurrent epidemics of violence, and that even in its non-epidemic periods it has a level of violence far higher than those of the other developed nations of the world, underscores the urgency of this experiment. The fact that rates of suicide as well as of homicide are affected by the political, economic, and cultural forces I have described makes the results of this experiment more generally applicable.

It is important to stress that neither shame nor guilt is necessarily pathogenic, nor is the behavior they motivate always maladaptive. The challenge we face is to make available to everyone, inside and outside the prisons, the tools and resources they need in order to reduce their feelings of shame and augment their feelings of pride and self-worth by constructive and creative means, such as education and meaningful work, not destructive ones such as violence.

Conclusion: The Mystery Solved: What Is To Be Done?

I began with a mystery: a correlation that seemed to defy explanation. How could the political party of the president be among the causes of murder, whether of oneself or others? In the chapters of this book, I have laid out a causal chain that is capable of explaining the correlation and thus solving the mystery.

It took many years to establish the link between cigarette smoking and lung cancer. There was clearly an association but causation remained in dispute, in part because the cigarette companies invested huge amounts of money in their effort to cast doubt on the research findings.[1] Nevertheless, the International Agency for Research on Cancer has come up with seven criteria that they conclude can establish beyond reasonable doubt whether a given agent (e.g. cigarettes) could be regarded as causing a given outcome (e.g. lung cancer). I will

---

[1] David Michaels, *Doubt Is Their Product: How Industry's Assault on Science Threatens Your Health*, Oxford and New York: Oxford University Press, 2008.

use their seven criteria here to test whether the political party of the president, itself a proxy for a host of different social and economic policies, can similarly be regarded as causing increases or decreases in the level of lethal violence. To use public health terms, I am asking whether Republican administrations are a risk factor and whether Democratic administrations are a protective factor with respect to homicide and suicide.

In adopting the seven criteria laid out for cancer researchers, I follow them verbatim except that where they say cancer I say lethal violence, and where they speak of biological factors I speak of psychological and social factors.

1. The link or association between the exposure and lethal violence is strong. The association between exposure to political parties and violent death rates (suicide and homicide) is strong, consistent, and statistically significant. It is only when Republicans are in the White House that the rates of suicide and homicide increase to epidemic levels, and only when Democrats are in the White House that they decrease below these levels. This association occurs repeatedly and without any significant long-term exceptions over a wide variety of different time frames of differing lengths and social circumstances. Even more to the point, the net cumulative totals of suicide and homicide deaths from 1900 through 2007 show large and statistically significant increases during the years of Republican presidencies, and almost identical decreases during the Democratic administrations.

2. The risk of lethal violence increases with more expo-

sure to the agent. *The greater the number of years* of Republican administrations, the higher *the net cumulative increase* in rates of suicide and homicide. Conversely, *the greater the number of years* of Democratic administrations, the higher *the net cumulative decrease* in rates of suicide and homicide. That is, the higher the dose, the greater the response.

3. Multiple studies by different investigators with different groups of people come to the same finding. Although several of the sub-findings have been reported by other investigators, the main thesis of this book has not been proposed before. It is an original observation and one that I hope and trust others will seek to replicate. For the moment, suffice it to say that investigators in Australia and the United Kingdom have, independently of each other and of me, found that suicide rates increased significantly throughout the twentieth century in both countries when conservative political parties were in power, and decreased under liberal governments; and that the unemployment rate correlated both with the political parties and with the suicide rate.[2]

4. The exposure to the agent came before the violence. The net increases in suicide and homicide to epidemic levels occur only after Republicans are elected

---

[2] A. Page, S. Morrell, and R. Taylor, "Suicide and Political Regime in New South Wales and Australia during the 20th Century," *Journal of Epidemiological Community Health*, 56: 766–72, 2002; M. Shaw, D. Dorling, and G. Davey Smith, "Mortality and Political Climate: How Suicide Rates Have Risen during Periods of Conservative Government, 1901–2000," *Journal of Epidemiological Community Health*, 56: 723–5, 2002.

to the White House, and the net decreases below epidemic levels occur after Democrats are. While this does not prove the hypothesis ("after this" does not entail "because of this"), it is important to remember that the hypothesis could and would have been disconfirmed if the data had shown that the epidemics of violence occurred *before* Republicans came to power, and the resolution of the epidemics *before* the Democrats did. While events that occur *after* some other event are not necessarily caused by it, events that occur *before* some other event cannot be caused by it. Thus, we can say that this analysis represents an attempt to *disconfirm* the hypothesis, as recommended by Karl Popper,[3] and that it failed to do so. Or, to put it another way, the hypothesis as it stands is consistent with the observed chronological relationships between the hypothesized cause and the hypothesized effect.

5. There is a plausible psychological and social explanation for how the agent would cause the violence. Plausible social and psychological explanations for how Republican and Democratic presidencies act as "risk" and "protective" factors, respectively, in the multi-determined etiology of violent behavior have been discussed in previous chapters. To recapitulate, the immediate psychological motive, or cause, of violent behavior in individuals is exposure to overwhelming intensities of shame and humiliation (feelings of failure and inferiority, of being disrespected, rejected, held in contempt, and regarded as

---

[3] *The Logic of Scientific Discovery*, London: Hutchinson, 1959.

worthless, of no value to others, "redundant," etc.); these feelings can be stimulated and exacerbated by many stressors in the social environment, one of the most powerful and common of which is the experience of being fired from one's job, or for any other reason suffering a severe loss of socio-economic status; this experience has been more frequent and prolonged under Republican than under Democratic administrations throughout the twentieth century, and compensatory measures to reduce the intensity of the humiliation (e.g. the WPA under Roosevelt) have been more extensive and effective under Democratic than under Republican presidents.

6. The link is specific and the agent causes a specific type of lethal injury, namely intentional injury. What I am proposing in this book is that the two political parties have diametrically opposite effects on the causation or prevention of specific types of life-threatening or death-inducing pathology, namely, intentional lethal violence, i.e., homicide and suicide. There does not seem to be a similar correlation between the political parties and overall death rates in America from all causes, nor with the parties and the rates of accidental death. Overall death rates tend to fall every year as medicine advances, and since medical knowledge, once acquired, is, in principle, never lost but only accumulates and grows, it does not fluctuate around a mean from year to year as intentional violence does: it almost always moves only in one direction, toward ever-increasing life expectancies. Presidential elections are therefore likely to have only the most remote connection, if any, to the everyday practice

of medicine and medical knowledge. Also, any given research project of the type that is responsible for the growth of medical knowledge often takes years to complete and can easily overlap with more than one president without being affected by which party they belong to. Similarly, the yearly incidence of lethal unintentional injuries – the so-called "accidental" deaths – has tended to fall in almost all years since those rates began being measured in 1900. What this demonstrates is that, if there is one thing that is not accidental, it is so-called "accidents," most of which are preventable – so they in fact have been prevented progressively more effectively, and the preventive techniques, such as automobile seat belts, motorcycle helmets, and so on, once adopted, tend not to be abandoned. Rather, they continue to be preserved and make a permanent contribution to safety, so that, as with medicine, there tends to be cumulative progress in preventing "accidental" deaths, rather than the wide fluctuations in death rates that one sees with intentional injuries.

7. The link fits together with what we know from other studies. Every link in the causal chain presented here fits together with findings from other research studies. Both the correlation between political parties and violent death rates, and the interlocking chain of causal mechanisms that explain that correlation, fit together with what we know from other studies of: (a) the association between political parties and numerous forms of *socio-economic stress, distress, and inequality* – including rates and duration of unemployment; depth, duration, and frequency of

economic contractions, recessions, and depression; inequalities of wealth and income, i.e., relative poverty and deprivation – all of which have been shown in social-scientific studies to increase statistically under Republicans and decrease under Democrats; (b) the association between *relative economic stress*, deprivation or inferiority, including economic inequality, unemployment, economic growth, and *lethal violence*, which has been confirmed and reconfirmed in multiple published studies, and is indeed one of the most robust findings in the social-scientific literature; (c) the fact that the experience of becoming *unemployed* or suffering any other major sudden loss of socio-economic status (e.g. being rejected, and defined as worthless and valueless by one's employer) and thereby subjected to a lowering of one's socio-economic status, leads to increased intensities of *shame and humiliation*; (d) the causal association between feelings of overwhelming *shame and humiliation* and *violent behavior* – suicide and homicide – has been reported and replicated in every branch of the behavioral sciences, and has indeed, for centuries and millennia, been one of the most ancient and widely repeated observations about human behavior.

As cigarette smoking has been shown to increase the rates of lung cancer, so the presence of a Republican in the White House increases the rates of suicide and homicide. And as regular exercise and drinking red wine in moderation have been shown to increase longevity, so the presence of a Democrat in the White House decreases the incidence of lethal violence. Not everyone who smokes gets lung cancer; not every Republican president presides over an epidemic of lethal violence. Not everyone who exercises lives a long and healthy life; not every Democratic president presides over a decrease in violence. What I have demonstrated here is a highly significant link between the party affiliation of the president and the rate of lethal violence in the society, and I have solved the mystery posed by this correlation by identifying a chain of evidence that can explain what is otherwise an inexplicable association.

I want to discuss the larger implications of these findings both for American politics and for the understanding of violence, but, first, I can sum them up with two syllogisms, the premises of which are based on empirical evidence.

The first syllogism is the psychological syllogism:

Major premise: Feelings of shame and humiliation motivate, and hence increase the rates of, both suicide and homicide.

Minor premise: Socio-economic distress and suffering in the form of unemployment, relative poverty and the sudden loss of social and economic status stimulate feelings of shame and humiliation.

Conclusion: Therefore, socio-economic distress and suffering, in the forms just mentioned, increase the rates of suicide and homicide.

(Empirical evidence in support of the major and minor premises and the conclusion are summarized in chapters 4, 5, and 2, respectively.)

The second syllogism is the political syllogism:

Major premise: Republican administrations increase the level of socio-economic distress and Democratic administrations reduce them.

Minor premise: Economic and social distress increase rates of homicide and suicide.

Conclusion: Therefore, suicide and homicide rates can be expected to increase during Republican administrations and decrease under Democratic ones.

(Empirical evidence in support of the major and minor premises and the conclusion are summarized in chapters 3, 2 and 1, respectively.)

Implications for the future of American politics

By now, it should be obvious that it is not the party label as such that causes changes in the rates of lethal violence. Instead, the party label is merely a proxy for thousands of policies and practices carried out by thousands of people who come to power in any given administration. But, beneath all the variability from one president and one party to another, it turns out that there is enough continuity and consistency associated with each party label for certain statistical regularities to emerge. Or, to vary the metaphor, each party and each administration can be seen as a package containing many different ingredients, some toxic and some salubrious for public health, social and mental (as measured by rates of suicide and homicide), just as cigarettes are a package containing a variety of ingredients that add to

163

their lethality, and regular exercise is a package containing a variety of ingredients that prolong life.

The implication of the research reported here for American politics is rather stark: the Republican party functions as a risk factor for lethal violence and the Democratic party functions as a protective factor.

Having said this, I want now to broaden the lens and make a distinction between political democracy and social democracy. Political democracy, which is common to the United States and all other developed countries, has been shown in many studies to prevent international violence between democracies. However, social democracies, which exist in every developed country except the United States, have been shown in virtually all studies of this subject to decrease the form of intranational violence called homicide. The United States stands alone in maintaining a rate of murder that would be considered, even at its lowest levels, an epidemic in every one of the other developed countries. The way I understand this is in terms of the continuing prevalence and political influence of a shame ethic and shame cultures within the United States, which determine political and economic values and assumptions.

Looking at the current state of American politics, the antagonism between Republicans and Democrats and the divisions between Red and Blue States, we can see a polarization that has never been higher. To those who say, as Ralph Nader did from the left and as George Wallace did from the right, that there is no difference between Republicans and Democrats, I would respond that the data presented in this book show that things are not quite that simple. In this book I am concentrating almost exclusively on domestic policy because I am attempting to understand a domestic outcome – intranational violence, not international. So I will not even comment here on comparisons between the Democrats' and the Republicans' foreign or military policies. But even when looking only at domestic actions, I have to admit that, yes, it is true that Democrats often do the will of their corporate masters – how else could they persuade them to donate the campaign funds without which they could not win any elections? For example, under Clinton, economic inequality continued to increase, which it had been doing since – and only since – the Republicans ended the 37–year period of Democratic hegemony that had lasted from 1933 until Nixon took office in 1969. But this inequality was increasing only about a third as fast under Clinton as it had been under Reagan and Bush Sr.[4] And there were many other indices of economic equality, which I have mentioned before, that did improve during Clinton's terms in office. But most importantly, for the purposes of this book, lethal violence rates during Democratic administrations going back to the beginning of the twentieth century had fallen, not risen (as they had done under the Republicans). In that respect, the two parties were not merely *different*, they were *opposite* to each other! The same applies to the rates and duration of unemployment, both of which have, like the rates of suicide and homicide, also increased during Republican

---

[4] Jared Bernstein, Lawrence Mishel, and Chauna Brocht, "Any Way You Cut It: Income Inequality on the Rise Regardless of How It's Measured," Briefing Paper, Economic Policy Institute, n.d. Downloaded from http://epinet.org.

administrations and decreased under Democratic ones. Again, not merely different – opposite.

And since the two parties have diametrically opposite effects on the rates of lethal violence, the choice between electing Republicans and Democrats to the White House is a choice between life and death, and not just one death but thousands of them, year after year.

The fact that lethal violence is the bell-wether directs our attention to the role of shame. Although it is not usually cast in these terms, the polarization rending US politics reflects a clash between an authoritarian shame ethic and a more egalitarian ethic that, at its highest stage of development, may have more to do with love, equal respect for self and others, and what Albert Schweitzer called "reverence for life," than with either shame or guilt.

And now I would like to turn to considering the implications the data presented in this book might have for the way we think about politics.

How to think about politics

The US Declaration of Independence states in its famous preamble that "All men are created equal," that "Governments are instituted among Men" in order to secure their "unalienable Rights" to "Life, Liberty and the pursuit of Happiness," and that "whenever any Form of Government" (or, by implication, any political party) "becomes destructive of these ends, it is the Right of the People to alter or to abolish it, and to institute new Government such . . . as to them shall

seem most likely to effect their Safety and Happiness."
The Constitution of the United States stated its purpose
(and, by implication, the purpose of forming this new
nation) was to "insure domestic tranquility . . . promote
the general welfare, and secure the blessings of liberty to
ourselves and our posterity."

If the data presented in this book are correct, it would
seem difficult to avoid the conclusion that they constitute empirical evidence that, from 1900 through 2007,
the Republican party has impeded and the Democratic
party has facilitated our ability to achieve every single
one of those goals for whose attainment the American
government was created. For the effect of the Republican
party has been to reduce, not maximize, the amount of
equality, life, liberty, happiness, safety, domestic tranquility, and general welfare enjoyed by the American
people. The Democratic party, through its leadership
and policies, has had the opposite effect.

Jefferson issued a litany of charges against George
III and the British government he headed. Following
Jefferson's example, I will describe the Republican party
in terms not dissimilar from those he used to character-
ize the British king.

1) *Equality.* They have increased – whereas the
   Democratic party has decreased – the degree of economic inequality among the American people. They
   have also increased, not decreased, racial inequality
   through a "Southern strategy" that resulted in their
   finally returning to power in 1969 by winning votes
   through appealing to the racial prejudices that are
   still widespread in the former slave states, and among

many whites in the rest of the country as well; by supporting discriminatory drug laws, law enforcement practices, and prison sentencing policies that have resulted in the disproportionate imprisonment of African-Americans; and by depriving millions of African-Americans, for the rest of their lives, of the right to vote, once they were convicted of any felony (for example, one violation of the drug laws, for which they are prosecuted far more often than whites, even though the rate at which those laws are broken by members of the two races is essentially the same). I cannot see how this pattern of interrelated policies can be understood except as the re-imposition of white supremacy by the Republican party, whether that was its conscious intention or not, after slavery, lynching, disenfranchisement by means of poll taxes and "literacy tests," and racial segregation had all been legally abolished at various different times over the past century and a half, and after the civil rights movement, Supreme Court decisions, and Kennedy's and Johnson's civil rights legislation threatened to undo the old patterns of racial inequality, once and for all.

2) *Life.* The Republican party has been a force destructive to life, to the extent that the effect of its governance has been to increase the rates of suicide and homicide, including capital punishment, not to decrease them as the Democrats and the Democratic majority Blue States have done.

3) *Liberty.* The ultimate deprivation of liberty is, of course, death, including by means of the death penalty, as well as murder and suicide; the second

greatest, imprisonment; the third greatest, the inability to travel where you want and do what you want without the fear of being assaulted or even killed. Republicans have reduced liberty to the extent that the "war on crime" initiated by President Nixon in 1968 led not only to the greatest increase in violent crime since the last previous period of Republican hegemony that culminated in the Great Depression, but also, and on a scale far greater than the increase in rates of crimes and violence, to a historically unprecedented explosion in the rate of incarceration, beginning in the mid-1970s. As a result of this, the US imprisonment rate is now higher than that of any other nation on earth, including such police states as China and Iran, and six to seven times higher than it was in the US at any time before the Republicans returned to power in 1969.

4) *The pursuit of happiness.* On the principle that actions speak louder than words, one of the most accurate measures of the degree of happiness in a society is its suicide and homicide rates. They are the tips of the icebergs of two types of unhappiness – with oneself and one's own life, as in suicide, and with other people and their lives, as in homicide. Thus, the Republican party's effectiveness in increasing the rates of both of these forms of lethal violence can be seen as empirical evidence of the degree to which they defeat rather than advance the pursuit of happiness (in contrast to the Democratic party's record in this regard).

5) *Safety and domestic tranquility.* If the degree of safety and domestic tranquility in a society can be

measured by the degree to which its citizens are free from the threat and reality of lethal violence, then it would be difficult to avoid the conclusion that the Republican party moves the US further from that goal also, in contrast to the Democratic party's record in that regard.

6) *The general welfare.* If the general welfare can be gauged in part by the degree to which people are economically secure (employed, with access to good education, housing, and health care, with incomes and wealth sufficient to shield them from both absolute and relative poverty and deprivation "from cradle to grave," and with the opportunity to live in a society with a flourishing economy), then the data presented in this book would seem to offer empirical evidence that it is the Democratic party that improves the chances of achieving every one of those goals, whereas the Republican party diminishes them. But perhaps the greatest irony is that the political rhetoric common to Republican politicians serves to distract people from awareness of those facts by accusing the Democrats of aiming at a European-style social democracy or "welfare state," and then claiming that that in turn would lead to Soviet-style communism, poverty, and tyranny. This argument represents an egregious distortion of reality, in that all the nations of Western Europe, without exception, since shortly after the Second World War, have formed themselves into remarkably non-violent, peaceful, prosperous welfare states with the same degree of political democracy and civil liberties as in the US but with much less poverty, homelessness, murder,

and imprisonment, no capital punishment, longer life spans, greater leisure, less infant and maternal mortality and morbidity, greater access to free, high-quality child care, health care, and higher education, and greater economic security than the people of the United States are able to enjoy.

In conclusion, I want to take up three questions: first, are there any other social, political, or economic variables that could explain away the data reported in this book? That is, could there be other causes of the changes documented here that would show that the correlations between the two political parties and the two violent death rates are spurious? Have we exhausted all possible attempts to disconfirm the hypothesis that there is a causal relationship between the nature of the two political parties and the violent death rates observed under each?

Did prisons bring down our lethal violence rates?

For example, was it the social engineering experiment called mass incarceration that actually brought down the rates of lethal violence under Clinton during the 1990s? If so, the Republicans should be given credit, since the policy of mass imprisonment occurred in response to Nixon's call in 1968 for a "war on crime" and a "war on drugs." And was it the "zero tolerance" and "broken windows" policing policies pursued by New York's Republican mayor Giuliani (during the years Clinton was president) that brought down the rates of suicide and homicide in New York City during that time? Was

New York unique among the major cities of that time, and a demonstration that only Republican political leaders know how to prevent violence and that they do it better than their Democratic rivals?

We can easily show that mass incarceration is not the explanation for the dramatic decrease in lethal violence that occurred only after Clinton was elected. The US suffered an epidemic of suicide and homicide that began in Nixon's second year in office (1970) and lasted without interruption throughout four Republican administrations and one Democratic one (Carter's). When Clinton took office in 1993, he inherited from his Republican predecessor, Bush Sr., a suicide rate of 11.3 and a homicide rate of 10.4 per 100,000 per year. By 1997, both of those rates had dropped below their epidemic "floors" (which, as I mentioned above, could be considered as 11 for suicide, 8 for homicide), thus bringing an end to the epidemic levels of violence that had been going on for the previous 27 years. By Clinton's last year in office, 2000, the homicide rate had declined from 10.4 to 6.4, the lowest level since 1966; and the suicide rate had dropped from 11.3 to 9.6, the lowest level since 1902.

Could that dramatic decrease in lethal violence have been caused by the equally dramatic increase in our imprisonment rate? If the increase in our prison population, beginning in the mid-1970s during Nixon's second term in office, were responsible for the ending of our epidemic of violence, why did it take until 1997 to bring the epidemic to an end?

Our national imprisonment rate had been essentially constant throughout the first three-quarters of the twentieth century at roughly 100 (plus or minus 20) per 100,000 population. It was only in the mid-1970s that it began increasing steadily and rapidly year after year so that today it is over 700 per 100,000. Is there any evidence that this prison-building and prison-stuffing binge was even indirectly responsible for ending the epidemic of violence? Here is some relevant evidence that it was not:

1) Since our epidemic of violence involves suicide as well as homicide, it is worth noticing that not even the most avid supporters of mass imprisonment claim that there is any reason to believe that increasing our incarceration rate would have in any way contributed to the decline in the suicide rate that occurred following Clinton's election. In fact, imprisonment is well known as a major precipitant of suicide, not as a preventer of it.

2) Two Democratic presidents, Woodrow Wilson and Franklin Roosevelt, both inherited epidemics of lethal violence from their Republican predecessors (in 1913 and 1933, respectively), and succeeded in ending those epidemics without making any major increases in the incarceration rate. That is consistent with the conclusion that increasing the imprisonment rate is not a *necessary* prerequisite for ending an epidemic of violence.

3) The series of Republican presidents from Nixon to Bush Sr. (1969–92) began by inheriting a non-epidemic rate of lethal violence from their Democratic predecessors, Kennedy and Johnson, and turned it, from 1970 on, into the longest uninterrupted epidemic of lethal violence in the twentieth century, despite increasing the imprisonment rate from

173

roughly 100 to 700 per 100,000, for the first and only time in the twentieth century. That increase did not have the slightest effect on the homicide rate, which remained continuously at epidemic levels. That is consistent with the conclusion that increases in the imprisonment rate are not *sufficient* for ending an epidemic of violence.

4) A Democratic president, Bill Clinton, inherited the epidemic of lethal violence left him by his Republican predecessors in 1993, and ended the epidemic without ending the ongoing yearly increase in imprisonment rates.

5) Wilson, Roosevelt, and Clinton all inherited epidemics not only of violence but also of unemployment (and other indices of socio-economic inequality, stress, and deprivation) from their Republican predecessors, and ended those epidemics as well.

6) The net implication of all the empirical evidence cited in the above five paragraphs would seem to be that increasing the imprisonment rate (as the Republicans did) is neither necessary nor sufficient for either preventing or ending epidemics of lethal violence; but that ending epidemics of unemployment and relative deprivation (as the Democrats did) is both necessary and sufficient for preventing and ending epidemics of lethal violence.

As the National Academy of Sciences' review of this question concluded in 1993:

What effect has increasing the prison population had on levels of violent crime? Apparently, very little. . . .

If tripling the average length of incarceration per crime had a strong preventive effect, then violent crime rates should have declined. . . . Analyses suggest that a further increase in the average time served per violent crime would have an even smaller proportional incapacitation effect than the increase [in time served] that occurred between 1975 and 1989. . . . This analysis suggests that *preventive* strategies may be as important as criminal justice *responses* to violence.[5]

In fact, I must turn the question around and ask whether our policy of mass incarceration might have had exactly the reverse effect. After all, prisons have been known throughout the centuries as "schools for crime" – in fact, graduate schools in crime and violence, or, as my colleague Sunny Schwartz[6] has called them, "monster factories." We have only been able to fill all the prisons we have built, to the point of severely over-crowding them, by sentencing an ever larger number of people to them for non-violent crimes. And, as I have repeatedly observed over the past 40 years and as all recidivism statistics demonstrate, the most effective way to turn a non-violent person into a violent one is to send him to prison. So we have to ask whether putting more and more non-violent people into prisons for longer and longer times might actually have had the effect of prolonging and exacerbating our epidemic of violence, rather than of mitigating or ending it; and whether

[5] Albert J. Reiss Jr. and Jeffrey A. Roth, eds. (Panel on the Understanding and Control of Violent Behavior, National Research Council, National Academy of Sciences), *Understanding and Preventing Violence*, Vol. I, Washington, DC: National Academy Press, 1993.

[6] Schwartz, *Dreams from the Monster Factory*.

the dramatic and rapid reduction in lethal violence rates that occurred during the Clinton administration (1993–2000) occurred *despite* the continuing orgy of mass incarceration, rather than because of it.

One last piece of evidence that the policy of mass incarceration had no demonstrable effect on the murder rate is the fact that, in 1970, when our national incarceration rate was about where it had been for the first three-quarters of the twentieth century – 100 per 100,000 population – the murder rate was 8.3 per 100,000. By 15 years later, in 1985, the incarceration rate had doubled to about 200 per 100,000. What was the murder rate? Still 8.3. By another 11 years after that, in 1996, the imprisonment rate had doubled again to more than 400 per 100,000. What was the murder rate that year? Still 8.3. It does not appear that the doubling or even quadrupling of the imprisonment rate over a 27–year period made even the slightest dent in the murder rate, which came down below the epidemic "floor" of 8 (in fact, reaching a low of 6.4 by 2000) only after President Clinton had instituted the economic reforms described in this book; following which, with the election of another Republican president, Bush Jr., the murder rate immediately stopped declining and reversed itself, drifting upward even though (or perhaps because) the imprisonment rate also continued to climb upward.

Is Giuliani the one?

But what about New York's Mayor Giuliani? Didn't he bring New York's epidemic of violent crime under control by getting "tough on crime" with his no-nonsense, "zero tolerance" policy for any violations of the law, even ones as trivial as failing to pay a subway fare? Let me begin by referring to what I said above: not even Giuliani's most avid supporters would claim that "getting tough on crime" could have had any noticeable effect on the suicide rate, which also declined, not just in New York but also throughout the nation, during Giuliani's years in office. Clearly, something more was going on in every major city in the country than just Giuliani's policy of a more inflexible punitiveness toward the most trivial of crimes – and in many cases what was going on was the opposite of Giuliani's policies, which was nevertheless followed by comparable reductions in both homicide and suicide.

Giuliani was the mayor of New York during 1994–2001, almost exactly the same years during which Clinton was president of the United States (1993–2000), and, as I have said, the murder rate throughout the country began declining dramatically year by year, from 10.5 during Clinton's first year in office, to 6.4 by his last. During those years, the murder rate declined equally dramatically in every one of the 25 largest cities in the United States – not just New York, but every one. And they did this while pursuing policies that were in some cases the opposite of New York's. San Diego, California, for example, the fifth-largest city in the country, had a decline in its homicide rate that was not significantly different from New York's, but their police, rather than getting "tougher" on their citizens, enlisted them as allies by forming a cooperative working relationship with neighborhood "crime watch" groups.

While New York's murder rate decline was the largest in percentage terms of the largest cities, the percentage increase in its murder rate during the previous 35 years had been among the highest. For example, between 1960 and 1990, the national homicide rate increased by 117 percent, whereas New York City's increased by 368 percent. New York's murder epidemic began and ended on approximately the same schedule as the nation's, with the non-epidemic period lasting until the late 1960s, epidemic levels from 1970 on, and a year-by-year decline back down to normal levels during the Clinton years of the 1990s. It both increased and decreased at faster rates than the nation's did, but it did so on essentially the same schedule, as did the murder rates in all of the largest cities. So, despite the enormous positive publicity Mayor Giuliani succeeded in gaining for himself, a review of the actual history of what happened leaves one reminded of the rooster who thought it was his crowing that made the sun rise. As the criminologist Andrew Karmen put it, "It appears that New York's [police] commissioners have pointed to forces beyond their control when the situation was deteriorating [i.e., when the homicide rate was skyrocketing, during the years of national Republican hegemony] and have accepted full responsibility when conditions were getting better." And the same appears to be true of the city's mayor.

To summarize, then, another reason for doubting that it was mass imprisonment rather than the election of a Democratic president that helped end our epidemic of lethal violence is the fact that all three epidemics of lethal violence in the twentieth century ended not with the introduction of mass imprisonment, but with the election of a Democratic president: Woodrow Wilson in 1912, Franklin Roosevelt in 1932, and Bill Clinton in 1992. All of those presidents inherited epidemics of lethal violence from their Republican predecessors, and all three epidemics ended without changes in the imprisonment rate (or, in Clinton's case, without changing the pattern of ongoing year-by-year increases in the imprisonment rate that had already been going on throughout the previous quarter of a century without any decline in rates of either homicide or suicide, and continued even after Clinton left office). All of those Democratic presidents did, however, undertake many policies that had the effect of reducing economic inequality, for example substantially increasing the progressivity of income and other taxes (e.g. increasing the highest marginal income tax rates), reducing the rate and duration of unemployment, increasing the social-welfare "safety net" for the poorest and most vulnerable members of the population, and increasing general prosperity and economic growth and expansion.

The resemblance between the Roosevelt and Clinton records with respect to lethal violence rates is especially close. Rates of both suicide and homicide began declining dramatically and steeply, year after year, beginning with the first year of their administrations for suicide and the second year for homicides, and both brought those rates below epidemic levels by the beginning of their second term in office, with the decreases continuing right up to their last year in office. It is well known how active Roosevelt was in sponsoring innumerable policies, laws, and agencies to undo the Great

Depression that began under the Republicans. One result was that the economy reversed from one of contraction to one of expansion, beginning in Roosevelt's first year in office (as the National Bureau of Economic Research has shown), so that, while it took World War II to bring a definitive end to the Depression, the fact is that Roosevelt began mitigating and undoing it right from the beginning. But, perhaps just as important with respect to matters like suicide and homicide, he also succeeded in enabling millions of people throughout the country who were in despair and felt abandoned by their government and the other institutions of their society to feel cared about and to become capable of a renewed sense of hope.

While all that is well known about Roosevelt, it is not as well known that the rates of suicide and homicide reached the lowest levels in 30 years by Clinton's fifth year in office (1997) only when the unemployment rate had also reached the lowest level in 30 years; both median and minimum wages had increased in real terms for the first time in 30 years (despite Republican Congressional leaders' opposition to the latter); the "negative income tax" (the Earned Income Tax Credit), which most economists believe is the most effective poverty-prevention tool in our economic arsenal, was given an unprecedented increase (thus undoing the Republican attempt to abolish it entirely); and the proportion of families in two of the demographic groups most vulnerable to homicidal violence – African-Americans and Latinos – whose incomes were below the poverty level declined to the lowest percentages since those indices first began being measured. Clinton has often been depicted by liberal Democrats as a "Republicrat" and has been accused of having compromised with the Republicans to the point where there was little difference left between the two parties (as when he agreed to "dismantle the welfare system as we know it" and to make work a precondition for some forms of welfare). But the US president whom he most resembles with respect to the matters that are the subject of this book is Roosevelt, the only other president who did as much as Clinton to undo both an epidemic of Republican-caused violence, and an economic structure of Republican-caused inequality and relative poverty.

Thus I find it difficult to conclude that the policy of mass incarceration that was initiated under a Republican president, Nixon, can plausibly be believed to have ended the epidemic of lethal violence that also began during his administration. By contrast, there are multiple reasons for believing that the very different policies pursued by a Democratic president were responsible for ending that epidemic, because there are multiple causal mechanisms, at the level of social and economic affairs and at the level of individual emotional and psychological health and welfare (the restoration of pride, hope, confidence, and the sense that one lives in a society that cares about one's welfare), that can plausibly be seen as mediating between the two variables whose correlation we are studying here – the rate of lethal violence, and the political party that is in power.

I have now presented you with my candidate for a solution to the murder mystery by uncovering the causal links connecting the political party of the occupant of the White House to the rates of lethal violence. But I have also discovered why it is a mystery, or rather needs to be a mystery: i.e., why these facts have been hiding in plain sight for the past century. It becomes clear now that the "divide and conquer" strategy extends to the division between homicide and suicide – because "they" commit homicide and "we," or at least the more unfortunate of us, commit suicide instead. We can now see why it seems so important not to see the violence in suicide, and thus to place killing oneself in the universe of mental illness and killing others in the universe of crime and violence. For this keeps us from making the connection between both forms of lethal violence and the political and economic system. In the end, it is no mystery why this murder mystery has been a mystery.

I began this journey by looking at data that were of interest to me as someone invested in uncovering the causes of violence. The data themselves are arcane – statistics compiled by the National Center for Health Statistics. The fact that suicide and homicide rates rise and fall together was of interest to me, as were the mountain peak and valley patterns of their distribution across the twentieth century – the fact that there were periods when these rates rose to epidemic levels and other times when they returned to what might be thought of as "normal." When I spotted on the correspondence between these peaks and valleys and the presidential election cycle, I literally could not believe my eyes.

And even now, some years since I first observed the association and found it to be a statistically significant correlation, I have a sense of crossing a boundary in moving from the consideration of violent deaths, whether self-inflicted or inflicted by others, to issues of political parties and social justice. And I wonder if others share this sense of transgression. Not only in seeing something that is not meant to be seen, but also of crossing categories.

It is painful enough to think about suicide or about murder when it occurs not on the movie screen but in somebody's life. The categories we have set up for thinking about these tragic events are those of mental illness and criminology, respectively. In this book, the murder and suicide rates became flags, like nautical markers showing a channel that led not into the heart of the despondent individual or murderer but into the White House and the economic policies that differentiate our two major political parties. Some politicians are more dangerous than others, not because they are bad people or because they never do good, but because the policies they pursue cause death.

Is it the president or the party?

One of the most important and perhaps most surprising implications of the data presented in this book is that the party of the president appears to be an even more powerful predictor and determinant of the rise and fall of lethal violence epidemics, and such closely associated economic phenomena as unemployment, inequality, and overall prosperity (the rate of economic growth), than the personality of the individual president himself. I emphasize that because most presidential election campaigns seem to me to be treated by the candidates, the mass media, and the general voting public as a kind of "beauty contest" or "horse race" between two individuals who just happen to be the candidates of one party or the other – as though it is the difference between the personalities or the biographies of the two individuals that is the most important basis for deciding whom to vote for. That may be especially true for those voters who regard themselves as "independents," rather than those who already have a firm partisan identity and always vote for "their" party's candidate. On the other hand, it is usually the independent swing voters, as well as those who switch their vote from the candidate of the party they usually support to that of the other party, who determine the outcome of many elections. Thus, I believe it is important to emphasize the fact that, despite the rather large differences in personality between the 12 Republican presidents and the 7 Democratic ones who served between 1900 and 2007, it was the party label that predicted their effect on lethal violence far more clearly than did any identifiable differences between the individuals. After all, who could be more different from each other than the flamboyant Teddy Roosevelt and the phlegmatic William Howard Taft, or the dour Richard Nixon and the sunny-dispositioned Ronald Reagan, or the patrician Franklin Roosevelt and that commonest of common men, Harry Truman? And yet the party affiliation clearly overrode each of those individual differences, and united the most disparate of personalities under the banner of a common party.

So it is important for voters to remember that when they vote for a presidential candidate, they are not voting for an individual nearly as much as they are voting for a political party, and for all the associated baggage, for good or for ill, that goes with that party. I realize that may sound like the father who thinks he is giving good advice when he advises his child that you don't marry an individual, you marry a family (advice that, in my experience, those who are in love with an individual do not want to hear, since they are in love with the individual, not his or her family). But whether or not that is good advice regarding marriage, I think that it is valuable for voters to remember, when deciding whom to vote for, that it is, with extremely rare exceptions (only Eisenhower, among the 12 Republican presidents from 1900 to 2007, and Carter, among the 7 Democrats, had records that were even slightly atypical for presidents from their party), more important to notice the difference between the parties of the candidates than the difference between the individual candidates themselves. Indeed, one purpose of framing an election campaign as a purely individual contest between the two candidates may be to distract the voting public from noticing what the actual policies of their parties are, so that the debate is over two individuals and whatever personal accomplishments or scandals they are associated with, rather than over the consequences of their parties' policies and political and economic records.

Another implication of the data presented here is that much – if not most – political rhetoric, both during an election campaign and during the actual governing and legislative process that follows the election, is so much hot air, since it consists of speculations, predictions, and unsupported opinions as to which party's policies are going to be more effective in increasing life, liberty, happiness, safety, domestic tranquility, prosperity, and welfare – in the future, after a particular bill is passed, or a particular individual elected. But what the data presented here show is that, with regard to most issues, we do not need to speculate about the future, for we already know what the past has shown us – namely, that it is Republican policies that have repeatedly, regularly, and with remarkable consistency brought us large increases in the rate and duration of unemployment, in the frequency, depth, and duration of recessions and depressions, in socio-economic inequalities in wealth and income, and in rates of suicide, homicide, and (since the mid-1970s) imprisonment and capital punishment; and it is Democratic policies that have brought us equally large decreases in all of those destructive phenomena (even in imprisonment and capital punishment, as the contrast between the Red and Blue States shows).

What surprised me most in writing this book was the discovery that the rates of lethal violence were like a string hanging out of a maze, and that, by following the string, I was led through a series of turns past the economic and social policies of Republican and Democratic administrations, the psychology of shame and guilt, the association of shame with unemployment (redundancy) and socio-economic inferiority, and the polarization of American politics into Red and Blue States.

I am a physician, not an economist or political scientist. My interest, training, and experience have focused on matters of life and death, not recessions and elections – and especially on the causes and prevention of violent death, which I have approached as problems in public health and preventive medicine, including preventive psychiatry. I was as surprised as anyone when my investigations of the causes and prevention of the deaths caused by violence led me, quite unexpectedly, to the discovery that certain political and economic phenomena could play an etiological role in the pathogenesis of life-threatening behavior, functioning as "risk factors"; and that certain others could play a preventive or even therapeutic role, as "protective factors."

In the end, I arrived at the realization that the association of rates of lethal violence with the party to which the occupant of the Oval Office belonged could be explained by the nesting of Republican and Democratic parties with social and economic policies that fostered or alleviated inequality, respectively, with the contrast between shame and guilt ethics, and the contrast between authoritarian (shame-driven) and egalitarian personalities and cultures.

In the end, then, I began to think that the maze itself tends to keep people from seeing this. However, by examining the rates of lethal violence we open a window into our political and economic system that makes it difficult for us not to see what we are doing. What I would ask you, my reader, is not to close this window too quickly, but rather to join me in thinking about two final questions.

What has made it so difficult or seemingly impossible for the Democrats to free themselves from Republican campaign rhetoric's reversal of the truth and take credit for their success in ending epidemics of lethal violence in this country for over a century? They, and they alone, have done this. Could this be the downside of being ruled by a guilt ethic and inhibiting their aggression so much that they, the Democrats, often fail to defend themselves strongly enough to undo both the misinformation and the damage caused by their Republican adversaries?

Second, following Thomas Jefferson's statement that it is "the Right of the People," whenever "any Form of Government becomes destructive" of the ends of life, liberty, and the pursuit of happiness, "to institute new Government such . . . as to them shall seem most likely to effect their Safety and Happiness," what actions might we now take with respect to our political parties in the service of this creative endeavor and in the interest of achieving "domestic tranquility" and advancing the "general welfare?" In the mid nineteenth century, the Republican party's predecessor, the Whig party, simply imploded and was replaced by a Republican party whose first and greatest president, Abraham Lincoln, achieved the most radically progressive, egalitarian and liberalizing reform in America's social and political history, the eradication of slavery. And the Republican party, after Lincoln's death, followed its great success in advancing democratic ideals by gradually reversing itself from being the party of progress and equality to being the party of reaction and inequality, from its egregious pandering to the "Robber Barons" which led to what Mark Twain called "the Gilded Age" at the end of the nineteenth century, to the "Southern strategy" through which the Republican party returned to power in 1969, at the cost of making itself the party of racial discrimination rather than racial equality.

The great question that confronts us now, I believe, is this: can we find non-violent means of replacing the

Republican party, which has become the main source of a degree of inequality and violence that the Democratic party has only partially reversed even when it was in power, with a party that could succeed in reducing inequality, relative poverty, and violence as much as has been done by the social-democratic parties of every other Western democracy? From Western Europe to Canada and Australasia, the rates of murder, imprisonment and relative poverty have been only 10–20 percent as high as in the US for most of the past 40 years. What would the United States look like if the Republican party went the way of its Whig predecessor and simply imploded, and the Democratic party's "loyal opposition" came from its left rather than from its right? Could the US finally become as humane and civilized as other Western democracies? To accomplish this would require confronting the shame ethic that renders social democracy a threat to those with a need for social stratification and hierarchy, and makes it shameful and politically risky for Democrats themselves to endorse more egalitarian social policies.

Another implication of the data summarized here is that, insofar as we are trying to prevent lethal violence, by reducing the rates of suicide and homicide on a nationwide scale, it is far more important to identify, also on a nationwide scale, the risk factors in our social, economic, and political environment that elevate, and the protective factors that reduce, the frequency with which individuals commit those actions, than it is to merely identify which specific individuals are at greater or lesser risk of doing so, and offer them therapy (or imprisonment) only after they have already become exposed to those risk factors, or attempted or committed violent acts. Clinical medicine focuses on getting doctors and hospitals and medicines to heal individual patients after they have become sick. And while we will always need that option, since even the best preventive medicine is almost never 100 percent successful, what we need to emphasize far more strongly is approaching our epidemics of lethal violence from the orientation of public health and preventive medicine. In the nineteenth century we discovered that cleaning up the water supply and the sewer system is far more effective in preventing deaths than all the doctors, medicines, and hospitals in the world. In the twentieth century we learned that it is both less expensive and more effective to assure that food is uncontaminated than it is to treat salmonella infections after they occur.

In the same spirit, what we need to learn in the twenty-first century is that cleaning up our political and economic system, by reducing the inequality, humiliation, and despair that are directly involved in the pathogenesis of epidemics of suicide and homicide, is far more effective in preventing or reversing those epidemics than investing our limited resources on treating or punishing people after they have been exposed to those risk factors. The US Public Health Service's Centers for Disease Control and Prevention have already established a Division of Violence Prevention. As two of their principal officers have written:[7]

---

[7] James A. Mercy and W. Rodney Hammond, "Preventing Homicide: A Public Health Perspective," pp. 274–94 in Smith and Zahn, eds., *Studying and Preventing Homicide*, p. 290.

The majority of existing violence prevention resources are spent trying to modify individual factors thought to contribute to violent behavior. Much less scientific and programmatic attention is given to addressing the social factors that may contribute to violence. . . . Yet scientific research suggests that marked social and economic disparities contribute to the etiology of violence in fundamental ways. . . . Poverty and the lack of real employment opportunities can promote violence by generating . . . low self-esteem, hopelessness about the future, and family instability. Racism and sexism exacerbate social and economic disparities. . . . More attention should be given to research and policy development that will guide us on how we might reduce violence through addressing larger social and economic issues.

One final implication of the data presented in this book is that they provide an empirical basis for evaluating different political parties and their social and economic policies and achievements – an assessment grounded in the human sciences, such as public health, preventive medicine, and economic and epidemiological statistics. These can serve as fact-based alternatives to the much more frequent opinion-based assertions and predictions concerning political parties, candidates, and policies. At a time when every knowledgeable person is calling for evidence-based medicine, isn't it time we also had evidence-based politics?

My point is that we will save more lives if we replace moral and political value judgments that are neither proveable nor unproveable with an empirically based set of findings that can be confirmed or disconfirmed. I offer this as a method for basing political thought and decision-making on factual knowledge concerning the social, political, economic, and psychological forces and processes that support, promote, and sustain human life, as opposed to those that lead to death, rather than basing political conclusions on assertions, opinions, or social and political ideologies as to what is fair or unfair, or what people "deserve" or do not "deserve."

One of the theoretical models and inspirations of this book, on many of whose insights the basic assumptions of this book are founded, was one of the greatest physicians of the nineteenth century, Rudolph Virchow (1821–1902).[8] He is perhaps most famous as the man who is credited with having made as many contributions as any one person in history to the project of transforming medicine from a crude set of practices based on tradition and superstition as often as on evidence – and which often did more harm than good – into the modern applied science that it has become, based on the empirical and theoretical foundations provided by both the natural and the human sciences. He is widely regarded as among the most important founders of the medical specialties of cellular pathology (it is largely due to him that everything from biopsies to autopsies are so central in modern medicine), public health, and preventive and social medicine (from improving housing and nutrition for the poor, to designing the first hygienic, pollution-free water supply and sewer system for Berlin), and as one of the pioneers of the social science called anthropology; and he made equally important contributions

---

[8] See L. Benaroyo, "Rudolf Virchow and the Scientific Approach to Medicine," *Endeavor*, 22: 114–17, 1998.

to the progressive politics of his time, an activity that he regarded as indissolubly one with functioning as a physician and healing diseases. In his "Report on the Typhus Outbreak of Upper Silesia" (1848), for example, he wrote that the outbreak could not be solved by treating individual patients with drugs or with minor changes in food, housing, or clothing laws, but only through radical action to promote the social and economic advancement of an entire population of (mostly) poor people. This conclusion is identical to what I am saying in this book about the epidemics of homicide and suicide from which the US periodically suffers. As a young man, Virchow fought in one of the revolutions of 1848, and later served for many years as one of Bismarck's main parliamentary adversaries in the Reichstag in Berlin. It was Virchow who proclaimed, in a series of bold and ringing statements, a set of conclusions that I will quote as the coda with which to conclude this book:

> The improvement of medicine will eventually prolong human life, but improvement of social conditions can achieve this result more rapidly and more successfully.[9] [That is why] physicians are the natural attorneys of the poor, and social problems fall to a large extent within their jurisdiction. As the science of man, medicine has

---

[9] Quoted in Howard Waitzkin, "One and a Half Centuries of Forgetting and Rediscovering: Virchow's Lasting Contributions to Social Medicine," *Social Medicine*, 1(1): 5–10, February 2006. Also quoted in Erwin H. Ackerknecht, *Rudolf Virchow: Doctor, Statesman, Anthropologist*, Madison: University of Wisconsin Press, 1953, p. 127, and in Leon Eisenberg, "Rudolph Ludwig Karl Virchow, Where Are You Now That We Need You?" *American Medicine* 159(19): 524–32, Sept. 1984, p. 527.

a duty to perform in recognizing these problems as its own and in offering the means by which a solution may be reached. Medical statistics will be our standard of measurement: we will weigh life for life and see where the dead lie thicker. . . . Medicine is a social science, and politics is simply medicine on a larger scale.[10]

---

[10] These were mottos of the weekly journal he founded, *Die Medizinische Reform (Medical Reform)*. The last sentence is in Rudolph Virchow, *Disease, Life, and Man* (trans. by L. J. Rather), Stanford: CA: Stanford University Press, 1958, p. 6, some of the essays from which also appeared in *Bulletin of the History of Medicine*, 30: 436–49, 537–43, 1956. These remarks are also quoted in George Rosen, "What Is Social Medicine? A Genetic Analysis of the Concept," *Bulletin of the History of Medicine*, 21: 674–733, 1947, p. 676, and in Eisenberg, "Rudolph Ludwig Karl Virchow," p. 525. See also D. Pridan, "Rudolf Virchow and Social Medicine in Historical Perspective," *Medical History*, 8: 274–84, 1964.

Appendix A

How Accurate and Complete Are the Data?

Although the US began publishing vital statistics data on a yearly basis in 1900, these data were not derived from all 48 of the then-existing states until 1933. The first report, in 1900, was based on only 10 states, mostly from New England. Additional states were added year after year, until by 1933 all 48 states were included. By 1912, the first year in which there was an electoral realignment from a Republican to a Democratic administration (when Woodrow Wilson replaced Taft), there were 22 states included; by 1920, the year of the next electoral realignment (from Wilson to the Republican Warren Harding), there were 34; and by 1932, when Roosevelt was elected, only 1 of the 48 states (Texas) was not included.

The fact that so many states were not included at first is not, however, as great a handicap to the research program I am presenting in this book as might at first appear, for several reasons. First, violent death rates have been reported separately for each of the three groups of states that constituted the death-registration area in 1900, 1910, and 1920, respectively, from the times when they were first included to 1933, when all states were included, and continuing on to 1940. When we examine those records, we find that all three groups of states showed the same pattern: net cumulative increases in violent death rates when Republicans were in power (1900–12 and 1921–32), and decreases when a Democrat was (1913–20). So it appears that the two parties were, so to speak, equal-opportunity employers – they increased or decreased violent death rates, no matter how many states were involved: whether it was a small sample, a larger one, or the whole country. In that sense, each "sample" of states was representative of the country as a whole, at least with respect to the larger question we are asking here: do violent death rates increase during Republican regimes and decrease during Democratic ones?

Second, if we examine only the data available from 1933 on, when all the states were being studied, we still have a huge database – 78 years' worth – and we again find the same result: massive increases in violent death rates under Republicans, and equally large decreases under Democrats. That is, we do not have to go back to 1900 in order to demonstrate this pattern, although that is no reason not to learn whatever we can from the data we do have prior to 1933.

A third alternative is to take advantage of the fact that the different states have been remarkably stable over time in the proportion to which they have contributed to the national violent death rates. For example, the Southern states have been known to have the highest homicide rates in the country, by far, whenever those rates were measured, ever since the first half of the nineteenth century, and they still do. The New England states, by contrast, have always had among the lowest homicide rates; the Western states, the highest suicide rates; and so on. And we know what the actual violent death rates were for each of the 48 states from 1933 on, and for an ever-increasing sample of the states from 1900 on. Finally, we know the size of the population for each state in any given year, and the age-distribution within each state.

Since we know that the murder rates in the New England states have always been lower than in the country as a whole, it is only reasonable to assume that a murder rate based on figures from the New England states alone, as in 1900, would almost certainly be lower than what the actual nation-wide murder rate was in that year. So the only question is: how do we correct for the missing data from the other states? By means of a sophisticated econometric statistical methodology that had proved successful in predicting future trends in various types of economic data, Eckberg[1] performed a rigorous "postdiction" of our national murder rates from 1900 through 1932 which has been accepted by most criminologists and epidemiologists as the "gold standard" for correcting for the missing homicide data for that era.[2]

---

[1] Eckberg, "Estimates of Early Twentieth-century U.S. Homicide Rates."

[2] Margaret A. Zahn and Patricia L. McCall have published a graph displaying Eckberg's corrected data for the period 1900–32, together with the data originally published by the US government's *Vital Statistics* reports, and comment that, although Eckberg's estimates of the pre-1933 homicide rates are higher than those enumerated in the original *Vital Statistics* reports, "the general trends are comparable. Both series display rates that fluctuate through time but show a general increase, peaking in 1906,

Since I do not know of any comparable recalculation of the reported suicide data, I devised a similar method of performing the same task for them (although we have every reason to believe that the reported suicide data during the early years of the century are not as discrepant from the true national rates as the homicide data were, since the discrepancy between the suicide rates in New England and the rest of the country is not nearly as great as it is for the homicide rates). We know what the ratio is between the complete national suicide rates, and those for each of the smaller samples of states (the 10 states whose rates were calculated in 1900, the 22 that were counted in 1912, and the 34 states that were registered in 1920), from 1933 on. Assuming that those samples of states contributed the same proportion to the total suicide rate throughout the times being studied (an assumption that is confirmed by all the data we do have), it is easy to calculate how much lower the actual national suicide rate is likely to have been from 1900 through 1932 than the reported rates indicated.

1921, and 1931" (Margaret A. Zahn and Patricia L. McCall, "Homicide in the 20th-Century United States: Trends and Patterns," pp. 10–30 in Smith and Zahn, eds., *Studying and Preventing Homicide*, p. 16, commenting on figure 2.1, p. 15). In other words, the shape of the two charts shows the same pattern, with lines that essentially parallel each other, but with Eckberg's data higher in both the peaks and the troughs, and with the difference gradually narrowing as more and more states were included in the government's data pool. For my purposes in this book, there is little relevant difference between the two charts, in that both show the same pattern: increases in the homicide rate during Republican administrations, and decreases during Democratic ones. I do believe, however, that Eckberg's data are very probably more accurate than those originally published, and I am happy to use them for purposes of calculating the differences attained under each political party.

Also, the suicide rates in the first ten (mostly New England) states (the 1900 sample) were higher than the national suicide rates, just as their homicide rates were lower than the true national rates. As a result, the uncorrected figures for total lethal violence rates (suicide plus homicide) are not as discrepant from what we can assume the true national rate would be as the suicide rates alone or the homicide rates alone would be. That is, the excess in the suicide rates and the under-estimate in the homicide rates partially cancel each other out, so that the total lethal violence rates are a closer approximation to the true rates than the suicide or homicide rates alone presumably are.

Since we have every reason to think that the corrected homicide and suicide data are more accurate than those reported by the government's own vital statisticians from 1900 through 1932 (and the revised figures are, after all, based on the more accurate data that we have from the time we had a complete sample of all 48 states from 1933 on), those are the figures that I refer to. Since the data that first caught my eye were the uncorrected data published in Holinger, I have included these data in figure B1 (which appears in appendix B). But since I was responsible for one of the data corrections (for suicide), let me immediately emphasize that Eckberg's and my corrected data both give results that are more favorable to the Republicans than the uncorrected government statistics are. That is, if I relied only on the uncorrected figures, the Republican record on lethal violence in America prior to 1933 would look even worse than it does with the corrected data. As a comparison between the uncorrected data (figure B1) and the corrected data (figure 1.1) shows, the figures that were originally published by the government's vital statistics branch before 1933 indicate that there were cumulative totals of 0.9 more suicides, 2.8 more homicides and 3.7 more total violent deaths per 100,000 per year during Republican administrations than the corrected data show; and that the discrepancy between the total violent death rates observed under the two parties was only 19.9 according to the corrected data, as compared with the uncorrected data, which would tell us (incorrectly) that the difference between the two parties was substantially greater, at 23.1. Thus, we would be unfair to the Republicans not to use corrected data for the period from 1900 through 1932. The results of their political actions were not as deadly as the original data would seem to indicate – although both sets of data are absolutely consistent with each other in showing that all three violent death rates (suicide, homicide, and the sum of suicide and homicide) increased during Republican administrations and decreased when Democrats were in power; and also in showing that there were significantly larger cumulative increases under Republicans, and larger cumulative decreases under Democrats, the longer the time-period being measured (what I have referred to as the "dose-response curve").

In order to be as fair and comprehensive as possible, I examined and compared all four groups of data:

• the uncorrected (originally reported) violent death rates, 1900–2007, which from 1900 through 1932 were based on an ever-enlarging but incomplete sample of states (figure B1),

- the violent death rates, 1900–2007, with the data for 1900–32 corrected to compensate for distortions created by the fact that not all states were yet included during those years in the national death registration area (figure 1.1),
- the death rates from the ever-increasing samples of states, as recorded from the presidential election year in which they were first included in the death-registration system (1900–40, 1912–40, 1920–40, and 1933–40), and
- the violent death rates for all 48 (and, later, 50) states from 1933 to 2007.

What I found was that all four of those groups of data come up with the same results: suicide and homicide rates both show net cumulative increases during Republican administrations, and net decreases during Democratic ones, and all of these differences are statistically significant. That remarkable fact in turn suggests that these correlations between party in power and death rate are in fact quite powerful and robust. No matter how you slice and dice the data in order to make sure you get the most accurate, comprehensive, and undistorted set of data possible, you keep getting the same results – net cumulative increases in rates of suicide, homicide, and the sum of the two during Republican administrations, and net decreases in all three measures during Democratic ones.

In order to clear up another possible misunderstanding, I should also reiterate that the death rates examined in this book are "age-adjusted." That is important since violence, like most other causes of death, is so strongly

age-dependent, with higher murder rates (for both perpetrators and victims) among the young, and highei
suicide rates among the elderly. As a result, changes in
the proportion of the population that is of an age that is
more or less vulnerable to a particular type of violence
would create arbitrary changes in the resulting death
rates that might appear to be related to some external
event in the environment, such as a change in the ruling
political party, but would in fact be merely an artifact of
the "baby boom" or some other transient demographic
variation. "Age-adjusting" is a way of holding the
age-distribution of the population constant, for statistical purposes, so that that distortion will not happen.
That is how we can be sure that the swings in violent
death rates that are reported in these tables are not just
reflections of swings in the percentage of people in the
population of the nation as a whole who have reached
a particular age.

Perhaps the principle involved will be most easily
comprehended if one compares it to holding the value of
the dollar constant in order to adjust for inflation, when
one is comparing financial data for a series of different
years, as when we speak, for example, of "1980 dollars." Clearly, for purposes of relative comparisons, it
makes no difference whether one is using the year 1980,
1990, or 2000 as the basis for holding the purchasing
power of the dollar constant; the important thing is
merely to choose one year, and then stick with that one
consistently.

The year I have chosen as the standard for age-adjusting is 1940. While that may seem rather remote from
2007, it is, I think, the best thing to do, for several rea-

sons. First, it was the year that the National Center for Health Statistics recommended using until 1999, and it is the year on which all previous vital statistics had been based up to that point, going back to 1900. Second, it is closer in time to most of the years under study here than the year 2000. But third, and most important, it actually makes no difference to the questions I am asking in this book: that is, it is not going to distort the results of this investigation of the relationship between political parties and violent death rates throughout the twentieth century (and the beginning of the twenty-first). If death rates are increasing or decreasing under one party or the other, we will still be able to see the proportion by which those changes are occurring just as clearly using 1940 as the standard year for age-adjustment as we would if we used 2000. It is as easy to download the figures for the same years age-adjusted to 1970 or 2000 as to 1940, which I have also done, and it makes no difference to the question we are asking here: the three violent death rates all show a net cumulative increase under Republicans and a decrease under Democrats regardless of the year chosen as the standard for purposes of age-adjusting. So, while the particular year chosen is arbitrary and irrelevant, what would not work would be to use 1940 for part of the study and, say, 2000 for another part, so I have not done that when comparing changes in death rates from year to year.

Why have I not used the FBI's statistical publication, the *Uniform Crime Reports* (*UCR*), as the source for my homicide data? The answer is very simple: it is not nearly as complete or accurate as the vital statistics data compiled by the National Center for Health Statistics

(NCHS), since it relies on police reports and does not even receive data from all of the law-enforcement agencies in the country, and, furthermore, it does not provide age-adjusted data. The purpose of the *UCR* is mostly to provide such information as we have (incomplete though it is) about the perpetrators of various crimes (many of which are not reported to the police, if they were non-lethal, and many of the perpetrators of which are never apprehended), whereas I am asking questions about all known victims of lethal violence, all of whom are counted. Finally, the FBI's *UCR* is not even attempting to provide information about suicides, since those are no longer considered to be crimes, as they used to be in previous centuries.

The NCHS, by contrast, is counting victims, and thus it counts every death that is known to have occurred in this country, whether violent or non-violent, and has data available to it from every coroner, inquest, autopsy, and death certificate pronouncing the cause of death. While it is not perfect, as nothing human ever is, it is incomparably more trustworthy, comprehensive, and accurate than the *UCR* is about death rates, and is the only source of data that is sufficiently accurate to be useful for scientific purposes, in my opinion. If you merely want information about perpetrators, however, the *UCR* is the most extensive source of data we have, incomplete though it is, and that is the purpose it should be used for.

Appendix B

Figures and tables

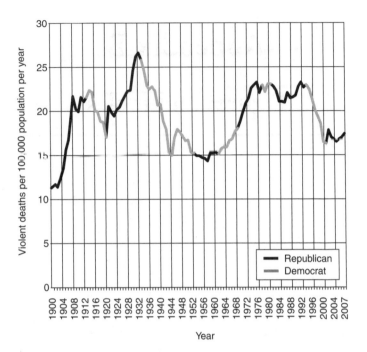

Figure B1   1900–2007 Violent Death Rates Age-Adjusted to
Standard Year 1940 with Data from 1900–1932. Not Corrected to
Adjust for the Non-Inclusion of Some States Prior to 1933

Source: Holinger, *Violent Deaths in the United States*

Table B1: Rates of unemployment under Democratic vs. Republican presidents, United States, 1900–2008

Party	President	Years	Unemployment rate, beginning of term	Unemployment rate, end of term	Increase/ decrease
Republican	McKinley, T. Roosevelt, Taft	1900–12	5.0	5.9	+0.9
Democratic	Wilson	1913–20	5.9	5.2	−0.7
Republican	Harding, Coolidge, Hoover	1921–32	5.2	22.9	+17.7
Democratic	F. D. Roosevelt, Truman	1933–52	22.9	3.0	−19.9
Republican	Eisenhower	1953–60	3.0	5.5	+2.5
Democratic	J. F. Kennedy, L. B. Johnson	1961–8	5.5	3.6	−1.9
Republican	Nixon, Ford	1969–76	3.6	7.7	+4.1
Democratic	Carter	1977–80	7.7	7.2	−0.5
Republican	Reagan, Bush	1981–92	7.2	7.5	+0.3
Democratic	Clinton	1993–2000	7.5	4.0	−3.5
Republican	Bush Jr.	2001–8	4.0	5.8	+1.8

Net change: Republicans: +27.3%; Democrats: −26.5%.
Net cumulative difference between the two parties: 53.8%.
Source: Bureau of Labor Statistics, US Department of Labor.

Table B2: Duration of unemployment under Democratic vs. Republican presidents, Post-war United States, 1948–2003

Party	President	Years	Average weeks unemployed, beginning of term	Average weeks unemployed, end of term	Increase/decrease
Democratic	Truman	1948–52	8.6	8.4	−0.2
Republican	Eisenhower	1953–60	8.4	12.8	+4.4
Democratic	J. F. Kennedy, L. B. Johnson	1961–8	12.8	8.4	−4.4
Republican	Nixon, Ford	1969–75	8.4	15.8	+7.4
Democratic	Carter	1977–80	15.8	11.9	−3.9
Republican	Reagan, Bush	1981–92	11.9	17.7	+5.8
Democratic	Clinton	1993–2000	17.7	12.6	−5.1
Republican	Bush Jr.	2000–3	12.6	19.6	+7.0

Net Change: Republicans: +24.6 *weeks*; Democrats: −13.6 *weeks*.
Net cumulative difference between the two parties: 38.2 weeks (9 months.)
Source: Bureau of Labor Statistics, US Department of Labor.

Appendices

Table B3: Red States vs. Blue States

Violent death rate differences according to state voting patterns,
Democratic vs. Republican, 2000 and 2004

2000	Red States (*n* = 30)		Blue States (*n* = 20)		Significance	
Death rate						
(per 100,000)	Mean	SD	Mean	SD	T	p
Homicide	5.70	2.85	4.23	2.43	1.90	0.064
Suicide	13.0	2.89	10.0	2.95	3.57	0.001*
Total	18.7	3.80	14.2	4.02	4.01	0.000*

2004	Red States (*n* = 31)		Blue States (*n* = 19)		Significance	
Death rate						
(per 100,000)	Mean	SD	Mean	SD	T	p
Homicide	5.70	2.67	4.01	2.15	2.38	0.021*
Suicide	13.9	3.19	10.2	2.70	4.28	0.000*
Total	19.6	4.04	14.2	2.90	5.16	0.000*

* = significant

Source: National Center for Health Statistics, Centers for Disease Control
and Prevention, U.S. Public Health Service. Retrieved from: "CDC – Injury
– WISQARS (Web-Based Injury Query and Reporting System)"

Bibliography

Adorno, Theodor W., E. Frenkel-Brunswick, D. J. Levinson, and R. N. Sanford, *The Authoritarian Personality*, New York: Harper and Row, 1950

Alexander, Michelle, *The New Jim Crow: Mass Incarceration in the Age of Colorblindness*, New York and London: The New Press, 2010

Altemeyer, Robert, *Enemies of Freedom: Understanding Right-Wing Authoritarianism*, San Francisco: Jossey-Bass, 1988

Altemeyer, Robert, *Right-Wing Authoritarianism*, Winnipeg: University of Manitoba Press, 1981

Altemeyer, Robert, *The Authoritarian Specter*, Cambridge, MA, and London: Harvard University Press, 1996

Ayers, Edward L., *Vengeance and Justice: Crime and Punishment in the 19th-Century American South*, New York and Oxford: Oxford University Press, 1984

Bartels, Larry M., *Unequal Democracy: The Political Economy of the New Gilded Age*, New York: Russell Sage Foundation, 2007

Benaroyo, L., "Rudolf Virchow and the Scientific Approach to Medicine," *Endeavor*, 22: 114–17, 1998

Bernstein, Jared, Lawrence Mishel, and Chauna Brocht, "Any Way You Cut It: Income Inequality on the Rise Regardless of How It's Measured," Briefing Paper, Economic Policy Institute, n.d. Downloaded from http://epinet.org

Blumenthal, Sidney, "Crime Pays," *The New Yorker*, May 9, 1994, p. 44

Chiricos, Theodore G., "Rates of Crime and Unemployment: An Analysis of Aggregate Research Evidence," *Social Problems*, 34(2): 187–212, April 1987

Cook, Philip J., and Mark H. Moore, "Guns, Gun Control, and Homicide," pp. 246–73 in M. Dwayne Smith and Margaret A. Zahn, eds., *Studying and Preventing Homicide: Issues and Challenges*, Thousand Oaks, CA, London, and New Delhi: SAGE Publications, 1999

Cottle, Thomas, *Hardest Times: The Trauma of Long-Term Unemployment*, Amherst: University of Massachusetts Press, 2001

Eaton, Joseph W., and Robert J. Weil, *Culture and Mental Disorders*, Glencoe, IL: The Free Press, 1955

Eckberg, D. L., "Estimates of Early Twentieth-century U.S. Homicide Rates: An Econometric Forecasting Approach," *Demography* 32: 1–16, 1995

Emerson, Ralph Waldo, *Journals*, ed. E. W. Emerson and W. E. Forbes, Boston, 1909–14, Vol. IV

Ford, Henry Jones, *The Rise and Growth of American Politics*, New York: Macmillan, 1898

Galbraith, James K., *Created Unequal: The Crisis in American Pay*, New York: The Free Press, 1998

Gilligan, James, *Preventing Violence*, London and New York: Thames and Hudson, 2001

Gilligan, James, "Shame, Guilt and Violence," *Social Research* 70 (4): 1149–80, 2003

Gilligan, James, "Spare the Rod: Why Are More American Children Victims and Perpetrators of Violence than Those

of Any Other Developed Country?" in James Garbarino,
ed., *A Child's Right to a Healthy Environment*, New York:
Springer, in press, 2010

Gilligan, James, "The Last Mental Hospital," *Psychiatric
Quarterly* 72(1): 45–61, 2001

Gilligan, James, *Violence: Our Deadly Epidemic and Its
Causes*, New York: Grosset/Putnam, 1996 (also pub-
lished in paperback as *Violence: Reflections on a National
Epidemic*, New York: Vintage Books, 1997)

Gilligan, James, and Bandy Lee, "Beyond the Prison Paradigm:
From Provoking Violence to Preventing It by Creating
'Anti-Prisons' (Residential Colleges and Therapeutic
Communities)," in John Devine, James Gilligan, Klaus
A. Miczek, Rashid Shaikh, and Donald Pfaff, eds., *Youth
Violence: Scientific Approaches to Prevention, Annals
of the New York Academy of Sciences*, 1036: 300–24,
2004

Gilligan, James, and Bandy Lee, "The Resolve to Stop the
Violence Project: Reducing Violence in the Community
through a Jail-Based Initiative," *Journal of Public Health*,
27(2): 143–8, June 2005

Gilmore, David D., ed., *Honor and Shame and the Unity
of the Mediterranean*, Washington, DC: American
Anthropological Association, 1987

Greenberg, Kenneth S., *Honor and Slavery*, Princeton:
Princeton University Press, 1996

Hetherington, Marc J., and Jonathan D. Weiler,
Authoritarianism and Polarization in American Politics,
Cambridge: Cambridge University Press, 2009

Hojman, Daniel, and Felipe Kast, "On the Measurement of
Income Dynamics," Harvard University, Kennedy School
Working Paper, Oct. 2009

Holinger, Paul C., *Violent Deaths in the United States*, New
York: Guilford Press, 1987

Hostetler, John A., *Hutterite Life*, Scottdale, PA: Herald Press, 1983

Hostetler, John A., *Hutterite Society*, Baltimore, MD: Johns Hopkins University Press, 1974

Hostetler, John A., and Gertrude Enders Huntington, *The Hutterites in North America*, Fort Worth: Harcourt Brace, 1996

Hsieh, Ching-Chi, and M. D. Pugh, "Poverty, Income Inequality, and Violent Crime: A Meta-Analysis of Recent Aggregate Data Studies," *Criminal Justice Review*, 18: 182–202, 1993; reprinted as pp. 278–96 in Ichiro Kawachi, Bruce P. Kennedy, and Richard G. Wilkinson, eds., *The Society and Population Health Reader*, Vol. I: *Income Inequality and Health*, New York: The New Press, 1999

Juergensmeyer, Mark, *Terror in the Mind of God: The Global Rise of Religious Violence*, 3rd edn. (Comparative Studies in Religion and Society, 13), Berkeley: University of California Press, 2003

Kaplan, Bert, and Thomas F. Plaut, *Personality in a Communal Society: An Analysis of the Mental Health of the Hutterites*, Lawrence, KS: University of Kansas Press, 1956

Kaplan, Justin, gen. ed., *Bartlett's Familiar Quotations*, Boston: Little, Brown, 1992

Karmen, Andrew, *New York Murder Mystery: The True Story behind the Crime Crash of the 1990s*, New York: New York University Press, 2000

Kauffman, Kelsey, *Prison Officers and Their World*, Cambridge, MA: Harvard University Press, 1988

Krug, Etienne G., Linda L. Dahlberg, James A. Mercy, Anthony B. Zwi, and Rafael Lozano, *World Report on Violence and Health*, Geneva: World Health Organization, 2002

LaFree, Gary, and K. A. Drass, "The Effect of Changes in Intraracial Income Inequality and Educational Attainment on Changes in Arrest Rates for African Americans and Whites, 1957 to 1990," *American Sociological Review*, 61: 614–34, 1996

Land, Kenneth C., Patricia L. McCall, and Lawrence E. Cohen, "Structural Covariates of Homicide Rates: Are There Any Invariances across Time and Social Space?" *The American Journal of Sociology*, 95(4): 922–63, Jan., 1990

Lee, Bandy, and James Gilligan, "The Resolve to Stop the Violence Project: Transforming an In-House Culture of Violence through a Jail-Based Programme," *Journal of Public Health*, 27(2): 149–55, June 2005

Lukas, J. Anthony, *Common Ground: A Turbulent Decade in the Lives of Three American Families*, New York: Knopf, 1985

Major, L., customer review of Thomas J. Cottle, *Hardest Times: The Trauma of Long-Term Unemployment*. Downloaded from Amazon.com: Books

Mercy, James A., and W. Rodney Hammond, "Preventing Homicide: A Public Health Perspective," pp. 274–94 in M. Dwayne Smith and Margaret A. Zahn, eds., *Studying and Preventing Homicide: Issues and Challenges*, Thousand Oaks, CA, London, and New Delhi: SAGE Publications, 1999

Messner, Steven F., and Richard Rosenfeld, "Social Structure and Homicide," pp. 27–41 in M. Dwayne Smith and Margaret A. Zahn, eds., *Homicide: A Sourcebook of Social Research*, Thousand Oaks, CA, London, and New Delhi: SAGE Publications, 1999

Michaels, David, *Doubt Is Their Product: How Industry's Assault on Science Threatens Your Health*, Oxford and New York: Oxford University Press, 2008.

Miller, Michael, "A Suicide Map of the U.S.," *Boston Globe*, August 22, 2004

Miranda, P., *Communism in the Bible*, Maryknoll, NY: Orbis Books, 1982

Neustadt, Richard E., *Presidential Power and the Modern Presidents: The Politics of Leadership from Roosevelt to Reagan*, New York: The Free Press, 1990

Newman, Katherine, *No Shame in My Game: The Working Poor in the Inner City*, New York: Vintage Books and Russell Sage Foundation, 1999

Nietzsche, Friedrich, "Beyond Good and Evil" and "The Genealogy of Morals," in *Basic Writings of Nietzsche*, trans., ed., and with an Introduction and notes by Walter Kaufmann, New York: Random House, 2000

Nisbett, Richard E., and Dov Cohen, *Culture of Honor: The Psychology of Violence in the South*, Boulder, CO, and Oxford: Westview Press, 1996

Page, A., S. Morrell, and R. Taylor, "Suicide and Political Regime in New South Wales and Australia during the 20th Century," *Journal of Epidemiological Community Health*, 6: 766–72, 2002

Patterson, Orlando, *Rituals of Blood: Consequences of Slavery in Two American Centuries*, New York: Basic Books, 1998

Patterson, Orlando, *Slavery and Social Death: A Comparative Study*, Cambridge, MA: Harvard University Press, 1982

Peristiany, J. G., *Honour and Shame: The Values of Mediterranean Society*, Chicago: University of Chicago Press, 1966

Peristiany, J. G., and Julian Pitt-Rivers, eds., "Introduction," in *Honor and Grace in Anthropology*, Cambridge: Cambridge University Press, 1992

Perkinson, Robert, *Texas Tough: The Rise of America's Prison Empire*, New York: Metropolitan Books, Henry Holt and Company, 2010

215

Pew Research Center for the People and the Press, "The 2005 Political Typology: Beyond Red vs. Blue: Republicans Divided about Role of Government – Democrats by Social and Personal Values," May 10, 2005. Downloaded from www.people-press.org

Pitt-Rivers, Julian, "Honor," pp. 503–11 in *International Encyclopedia of the Social Sciences*, 1968

Pitt-Rivers, Julian, "Honor and Social Status," pp. 19–77 in J. G. Peristiany, ed., *Honour and Shame: The Values of Mediterranean Society*, Chicago: University of Chicago Press, 1966

Ponnuru, Ramesh, *The Party of Death: The Democrats, the Media, the Courts, and the Disregard for Human Life*, 2006

Popper, Karl, *The Logic of Scientific Discovery*, London: Hutchinson, 1959

Reiss, Albert J. Jr., and Jeffrey A. Roth, eds. (Panel on the Understanding and Control of Violent Behavior, National Research Council, National Academy of Sciences), *Understanding and Preventing Violence*, Vol. I, Washington, DC: National Academy Press, 1993

Rochlin, Gregory, *Man's Aggression: The Defense of the Self*, Boston: Gambit, 1973

Rosaldo, Michelle, ed., *Towards an Anthropology of the Emotions: Rethinking Shame and Guilt* (Proceedings of a Symposium of the American Anthropological Association), Washington, DC: American Anthropological Association, 1983

Sabini, John, "Aggression in the Laboratory," pp. 343–371 in Irwin L. Kutash, Samuel B. Kutash, and Louis B. Schlesinger, eds., *Violence: Perspectives on Murder and Aggression*, San Francisco: Jossey-Bass, 1978

Schlesinger, Arthur Jr., *The Imperial Presidency*, Boston: Houghton Mifflin, 1989

Bibliography

Schwartz, Sunny (with David Boodell), *Dreams from the Monster Factory: A Tale of Prison, Redemption and One Woman's Fight to Restore Justice to All* (with an Introduction by James Gilligan), New York: Scribner, 2009

Shaw, M., D. Dorling, and G. Davey Smith, "Mortality and Political Climate: How Suicide Rates Have Risen during Periods of Conservative Government, 1901–2000," *Journal of Epidemiological Community Health*, 56: 723–5, 2002

Silberman, Charles E., *Criminal Violence, Criminal Justice*, New York: Random House, 1978

Thomas, Herbert E., "Experiencing a Shame Response as a Precursor to Violence," *Bulletin of the American Academy of Psychiatry Law*, 23(4): 587–93

Tomkins, Silvan S., "Ideology and Affect," pp. 109–67 in E. Virginia Demos, ed., *Exploring Affect: The Selected Writings of Silvan S. Tomkins* (Studies in Emotion and Social Interaction), Cambridge: Cambridge University Press, 1995

Tomkins, Silvan S., "The Right and the Left: A Basic Dimension of Ideology and Personality," pp. 389–411 in R. W. White, ed., *The Study of Lives*, New York: Atherton Press, 1963

West, Donald J., *Murder Followed by Suicide*. Cambridge, MA: Harvard University Press, 1967

Wilkinson, Richard, "Why is Violence More Common Where Inequality Is Greater?" pp. 1–12 in John Devine, James Gilligan, Klaus A. Miczek, Rashid Shaikh, and Donald Pfaff, eds., *Youth Violence: Scientific Approaches to Prevention, Annals of the New York Academy of Sciences*, 1036, 2004

Wilkinson, Richard, and Kate Pickett, *The Spirit Level: Why Greater Equality Makes Societies Stronger*, New York: Bloomsbury Press, 2009

Wilson, William Julius, *When Work Disappears: The World of the New Urban Poor*, New York: Vintage, 1996

Wolcott, James, "Red State Babylon," *Vanity Fair*, Nov. 2006, p. 162

Wolff, Edward N., *Top Heavy: The Increasing Inequality of Wealth in America and What Can Be Done about It* (An Expanded Edition of a Twentieth Century Fund Report), New York: The New Press, 1996

Wolfgang, Marvin E., and Franco Ferracuti, *The Sub-Culture of Violence*, Beverly Hills, CA: Sage Publications, 1982

Wolfgang, Marvin E., *Patterns in Criminal Homicide*, New York: Science Editions, John Wiley & Sons, 1966 (original publication: Philadelphia, PA: University of Pennsylvania Press, 1958)

Wyatt-Brown, Bertram, *Southern Honor: Ethics and Behavior in the Old South*, Oxford and New York: Oxford University Press, 1982; abridged version: *Honor and Violence in the Old South*, Oxford and New York: Oxford University Press, 1986

Zahn, Margaret A., and Patricia L. McCall, "Homicide in the 20th-Century United States: Trends and Patterns," pp. 10–30 in M. Dwayne Smith and Margaret A. Zahn, eds., *Studying and Preventing Homicide: Issues and Challenges*, Thousand Oaks, CA, London, and New Delhi: SAGE Publications, 1999

Index

Page numbers in *italics* denote a graph

Index

Index

Index

Index

Index

and prisons/imprisonment
171–6, 179, 181
reasons for not noticing
correlation between
political party and 35–7
and recessions 48
Red State / Blue State
differences 123–4, 125,
129–30, *209*
Republicans and rise in 3–4,
7, 8, *12*, 13, 14, 17–18, 19,
20–2, 23, 24, 25, 26–31,
34–5, 36, 38, 48, 69,
156–8, 161, 163, 168, 169,
196, 201
and the rich 80
and shame 97–8, 115, 162
and unemployment 41–4, 46,
48, 49, 66–7, 117
and wealth inequality 47, 48
liberty
Republicans and reduction of
168–9
Lincoln, Abraham 188
Loayza, Norman 46
longitudinal studies 45
lung cancer
and smoking 26, 34, 155,
161
lynching 134

McCall, Patricia L. 46
male role belief system 150–1
marijuana 87
Marx, Karl 51
mass media 94
master morality
distinction between slave
morality and 108
Mexican Americans 138
Miller, Michael 36n

morality 104–5
distinction between master
and slave 108
murder *see* homicide rates;
lethal violence

Nader, Ralph 164
National Academy of Sciences
174–5
National Bureau of Economic
Research 54, 57
National Center for Health
Statistics (NCHS) 5, 182,
203–4
National Rifle Association 93,
127
Native Americans 138, 141
Nazi Germany 114
Neustadt, Richard E.
*Presidential Power and the
Modern Presidents* 71
New Deal 21, 68, 122
New Deal Consensus 47, 65, 73
New England states 132, 133,
137, 195, 197
New York
Giuliani and lethal violence in
171, 176–8
Newman, Katherine
No Shame in My Game
120–1
Nietzsche, Friedrich 106, 108–9
Nixon, Richard 22, 47, 184
and increase in lethal violence
rate 17–18
"war on crime" 76, 84, 169,
171
"war on drugs" 87, 171

Obama, Barack 60, 74–5, 104
Orwell, George 83–4, 92

224

Index

Index

Index

227

Index

Index

It's the Sun, Not Your SUV
CO$_2$ Won't Destroy the Earth

Jᴏʜɴ Zʏʀᴋᴏᴡsᴋɪ

Foreword by Peter Dietze

Sᴛ. Aᴜɢᴜsᴛɪɴᴇ's Pʀᴇss
South Bend, Indiana
2008

Manufactured in the United States of America.

1 2 3 4 5   13 12 11 10 09 08

Library of Congress Cataloging in Publication Data
    Zyrkowski, John, 1945–
       It's the sun, not your SUV: CO_2 won't destroy the Earth / John
    Zyrkowski; foreword by Peter Dietze. – 1st ed.
         p. cm.
       Includes bibliographical references and index.
       ISBN-13: 978-1-58731-376-9 (hardbound: alk. paper)
       ISBN-10: 1-58731-376-6 (hardbound: alk. paper)
       1. Solar radiation – Observations. 2. Solar radiation – Environmental
    aspects. 3. Global temperature changes. 4. Carbon dioxide – Absorption
    and adsorption. I. Title.
    QC911.8.Z97 2008
    363.738'74 – dc22   2008006674

∞ The paper used in this publication meets the minimum requirements of the American National Standard for Information Sciences – Permanence of Paper for Printed Materials, ANSI Z39.48-1984.

ST. AUGUSTINE'S PRESS
www.staugustine.net

Contents

Acknowledgments

To my wife, Nancy and my son Casey for all of their support while I neglected them and family projects to complete this book.

To my mother, who treasured the earth and its flora and fauna and delighted in her garden; my sisters Mary Jo and Kate, who continue to preserve it; and my niece Lily, who continues the garden.

To my nephew Joe, who led me on this search for scientific information.

To Bruce Fingerhut, who is not only a friend, but a publisher with a keen vision of what is good and right.

To Peter Dietze, who has been graciously supportive in time and efforts even though I was a complete stranger when we started. To Dr. Palle, and Dr. Willson for their kindness in answering my requests for information. Their helpfulness is a strong affirmation that scientific people are intelligent and caring. They together demonstrate that there is a vibrant unseen social structure that supports and advances our global civilization. The new aspect is that this structure is taking place in cyber space.

Foreword
by Peter Dietze

This book is an excellent presentation of the truth about the changes in temperature over the past 125 years. Increases in solar activity along with reduction of cloud coverage and thus Earth albedo (reflectivity) are the primary reason temperatures have increased. Greenhouse gases are to a lesser extent involved in the temperature changes. This book brings a fresh new set of information that provides the undeniable truth that the IPCC report's focus upon Greenhouse Gases is fatally flawed. It also puts to rest as to whether there is any need for action on this overly politicized issue.

The book starts discussing the subject in easily understandable language and later offers the ability for the average person to review the computer models that "explain" and forecast the changes in temperature. It begins with easy to understand basic information, then turns to clearly explaining the science involved in this most important and complicated ecological and political subject.

As a natural scientist, known Climate Skeptic, and reviewer of the IPCC 2001 report, basically graduated as electrical and control engineer, I congratulate the author for this excellent piece of work. Not alarmism and disinformation but realism and sound science are required to resolve the true energy-related and ecological problems that we are encountered worldwide.

I have been intensively working for 18 years, analyzing the scientific background of climate models and the global warming hype. The IPCC models not only underestimate the carbon sequestration of oceans and biomass – they indeed vastly exaggerate the radiative CO_2 effect whereas the effect of solar activity has been underestimated almost by a factor of 5. I have also presented my findings in the U.S. Capitol building in 2000 to help the U.S. avoid the devastating economic effects that the Kyoto Treaty would have upon its economy. It is fortunate that President George Bush has decided not to support the Kyoto Treaty. Even Prime Minister Tony Blair recently joined the opinion that the Kyoto Treaty would slow economic growth for Britain.

My Web papers have been reviewed by scientists around the world, and they helped many to understand the true science behind climate change, the carbon cycle and radiation physics. The number of critical people impacted by these writings has grown each year. An amazing number of people across the world have responded to me with appreciation for resolving misunderstandings and providing information to them so that they understood the true science of climate change. This has helped them form their own informed judgment about climate modeling and the solar impacts upon temperature.

Over the years, there have been continued conflicts with IPCC principles over key elements of the report on climate change. The most recent was the so-called Hockey Stick or the assertion by the IPCC report that the late 20th century was the hottest period in history. This was discredited by researchers, who found that the original work in tree rings – which are indeed questionable temperature proxies — would yield a similar increase in temperature from random numbers. It was also revealed that the peer review effort did not test the basic mathematical computations for this key assertion and has led to demands that publicly funded research has to provide open access to the data used and computer programs. This is a major improvement in the cause of science.

Other areas of disagreement included the true amount of radiative energy that increasing levels of CO_2 are absorbing. The original IPCC reports attributed more temperatue increment to CO_2 absorption and vapor feedback than the science would suggest, though some changes were made in the 2001 report. The next area of contention was the mean residence time of emitted CO_2 in the atmosphere. Here the IPCC report asserted 120 years (whereas 55 years should be the correct value derived from observation), though it was proven that their published diagrams with future CO_2 increments apply more than 500 years. This conflict continues even to today.

This book makes the proper adjustments to the IPCC approach and finds that the extraordinary forecasts of temperature increases are improbable.

Additionally, new sets of actual measured data from several sources show that the reflectivity of the Earth's clouds has changed remarkably over the years. The data also demonstrate that the solar and other natural forces have changed direction since 1998 at the same time the global temperatures followed those changes. This data support the earlier data that my associates and I used in our research effort, but was discounted in the 2001 IPCC report. This new data provide a more definitive way to demonstrate that the effects of Greenhouse Gases are overly portrayed in that IPCC report by showing that Greenhouse Gases concentrations have not changed direction as the temperature record has shown. This is fundamental to any study of an elusive process. It is at the changes in direction that the true driving forces can be separated from other lesser important forces.

More research is needed on the physics behind the formation of clouds as well as how they influence light reflectivity and the Earth's infrared radiation budget. The research in this area has not been well founded, since the principles of the IPCC report did not consider reflectivity to be an important subject for research. Fortunately, others were more insightful, and we have gained substantial success with the data that we do have.

As is the case with science and the search for truth, it takes very dedicated people who are highly trained in sciences and mathematics to arrive at the truths about the natural order. This book provides the basis for individuals to increase their own knowledge of how the climate changes from a scientist's point of view and will help each person make an informed decision about the need or lack of need for action on the climate and the debate about it.

I want to thank John Zyrkowski for his persistence in working and writing on this subject. He has certainly created a valuable book that shatters a lot of myths of a large number of scientists.

Sincerely,
Dipl.-Ing. Peter Dietze
IPCC TAR Reviewer
Langensendelbach, Germany

Preface

The discussion about ecological problems began in the early 1960s. There are very good reasons for the need to address the problem of pollution. As time has passed, a clear understanding has been developed within the ecology, government, and business communities that ecological solutions and economic realities must be balanced to be effective.

The central points for establishing that balance are the foundations of science that support the solutions to any ecological problem that our society confronts.

At a time when the ecology movement was beginning to raise concerns about insecticides, herbicides, and fertilizers, I was in the Peace Corps in Guatemala, working with some of the poorest people in the world in the middle of what used to be a jungle.

Public-health workers were protecting the people in the area from malaria, using insecticides that were sprayed in every house or thatched-roof hovel in the area to control mosquitoes.

Along with other volunteers we taught small farmers to use insecticides, herbicides, and fertilizers under U.S. Department of Agriculture guidelines with the goal to raise their corn-crop yields by almost 10 times. The yields many were receiving from using these products were equal to those in the best farms in Iowa or Illinois. These poor farmers also could receive two to three crops a year because of the climate, when the farmers in the U.S. can only get one crop of corn and about 25% of the same yield in winter wheat.

I also worked with a foundation developed by Guatemalan businessmen to create training facilities for dairy cattle. With support from the World Bank, Pan-American Bank, and Heifer Project, a training center was completed. In the first year, the number of head of dairy cattle per acre was 16 times higher than the best dairy farms in the U.S. We used insecticides, herbicides, and fertilizers within the guidelines of the U.S. Agriculture Department and in a climate that provided a year-round growing season.

During this time, I was heart-broken when I attended the funerals of many children who died of malnutrition or common diseases such as measles. The primary reason they died in a country capable of three growing seasons was economics – not enough money for food or medicine, or even potable water. Poverty kills, and the skills I needed to teach their parents could have prevented their gruesome premature deaths.

It is obvious that the poisons of pollution kill people. It is less obvious that ecological solutions with dramatic negative impacts on the economic incomes of groups of poor people also kill. Many times those killed are the least known in society.

Later, I was the senior executive leading five different manufacturing facilities to increase productivity and improve processes sufficiently so that the facilities would not be closed. Their problems included competitiveness problems but also needed to balance U.S. ecological requirements. Some of the facilities were part of Fortune 500 companies such as Alcoa. The need for clear science directing ecological regulations was apparent on multiple occasions.

State Occupational, Safety and Health Agency (OSHA) representatives at times had unclear directives about the requirements to meet environmental regulations. Many times our own internal environmental officers were clearer about what and how to measure and how to comply. An enormous amount of time was needed to help the State OSHA representatives understand that we were complying with the rules. Or we spent an enormous amount of money studying problems that, at the end, we found the State OSHA inspectors had already seen easily solved, with minimum investment.

The loss of time and the lack of scientific knowledge were very costly to those operations that were struggling to compete in a global market, where companies in countries with no environmental regulations had $0.25 per hour labor. While we were successful in continuing to be able to provide U.S. jobs for union and non-union factory workers, the threats to their jobs could have been avoided if the lost time and costs associated with understanding the science behind the requirements were clearly understood.

The climate discussion presents us with another balancing question. The foundation of that question again comes back to the science. If there is a scientific basis to the assumption that "greenhouse gases" (GHG) are truly affecting the livability of the earth, then the costs to remediate the problem are worth the investment. This should be more important than the good of solving poverty issues such as world hunger or avoiding the default of the Social Security system. More people would be killed by a global ecosystem collapse than would be killed by hunger or poverty.

If, on the other hand, the science does not support the theory that GHG at elevated levels portend an ecosystem collapse and or has little or nothing to do with human actions, our priorities can remain focused upon the good that comes from solving other important problems, such as world hunger and avoiding the default of the Social Security system. Fewer people would be killed by the lack of basic medical services and food from these poverty forces.

If we do not clearly understand the science of the GHG issue, and take action to solve a non-problem, then we will waste time and money, leaving us without the resources to do the good we could have done with those resources addressing other, better issues.

As a consultant, I have worked with some of the largest producers of alternative energy to improve the processes and productivity with the goal to reduce production costs sufficiently to make these alternative-energy sources commercially viable. The cost per kilowatt hour of energy from these sources is enormously more expensive than from current fossil fuels and atomic reactors. It is quite unlikely that they will become a commercially viable alternative even with the most efficient manufacturing processes known today. That is why we do not see them being used unless they are subsidized or have extraordinary applications.

Assuring we have employed science correctly to answer this question is the only solution to the question of GHG. That is the point of this book.

Data sources and model approaches

To the extent possible, datasets used in the IPCC report and also available from regularly updated sources have been used throughout this book.

Complex models with user-defined adjustment variables are not used to develop the results of this book. Every effort has been made to permit the measured data to select the model used. All models are readily available from the website referred to in this book.

Chapter 1

Right or Wrong, We Need the Weather Forecasters

There are a lot of jokes and discussions about weather forecasters. A recent commercial showed a series of situations where people followed the advice of the weather forecaster. We see people holding umbrellas on sunny days. After a few seconds, we see a teenager dressed in shorts, standing in deep snow, throwing a snowball at a man in a suit. The nerve of the delinquent! A few seconds later we find out that the man in the suit is the weatherman, and while we emotionally do not condone the delinquent's actions, we are a bit more understanding of him.

Many weather forecasters are Climate Scientists. They have skills that are focused upon improving the accuracy of weather forecasts two to three days from now. The global climate system is not a willing participant, to say the least. The effort these scientists employ to improve their forecasting is almost heroic given how difficult it is to get good data readings. That is because everything is in motion! Winds move in different directions at various heights above the earth. Moisture builds over fields, forests, oceans, and lakes at different rates due to the amount of sun that strikes each area based on the amount of cloud cover. This changes the amount of potential rain that Cleveland or Moscow can expect in the next few days.

We are enthralled with the weather forecasts, especially during hurricane season. In 2005, we spent weeks watching hurricanes as they hit the southern U.S. coastline and New Orleans. A gray-haired gentleman gravely looked at us on our televisions and showed us a big red comma with the tail touching the hurricane's position on the global map and the wide other end covering the possible points of landfall. We were amazed that he can forecast to within 1000 miles three to four days out. What an improvement since the 1940s, when there was no warning system.

As the comma narrowed over the next several days, people in the affected 400 miles were told to pack up and leave. Many in Houston, Texas, got into their cars and started driving toward areas outside those 400 miles. They braved highway parking lots to get out of the way. Some, though, decided to wait out the storm because the storm's destructive impact is only 10% to 15% of what the weathermen indicate is the probable area that would be affected. Some people waited it out and didn't even have a roof shingle disturbed. Many in New Orleans who were in the affected areas were at risk, and many actually were killed by the storm or the levy failures and storm surge. The wind in these areas can make a branch or coconut into a lethal weapon. Later, as if to prove the point, we saw news footage of a 2-by-4 sticking through a palm tree.

We know that the deaths are not the fault of the weather forecasters, but we also understand the lack of faith that many have in their forecasts. Governments find it difficult to pass laws that force people to leave the probable affected areas because they know that the forecasts have a high degree of inaccuracy.

The deaths from tornadoes and hurricanes spur climate scientists to improve their forecast accuracy by a few more hours. These improvements will save lives and reduce property damage through preparedness. New advances in forecast accuracy are presented as major events on Discovery Channel and in magazines, news shows, and newspapers. We all want this to work.

We have, though, developed ways to check on whether the forecast for our area is accurate . . . *we look out the window!* It's raining. Gee, the forecast was accurate because they said yesterday it would rain. Three days ago, they said to expect partly cloudy, but that's OK, because one day is all I need. Or we look outside and it's cloudy, but no rain. That's OK, because I was ready for rain, but cloudy is better.

But if we look outside and they said it was going to rain and it's sunny each day for a week, we'd probably stop listening for a while. News programs would lose sponsorship because the traffic and weather are among the few reasons we have to listen to the news, since it's depressing to hear all the bad things going on in the world.

So we have a checking system for the weather, *we look out the window.*

There are a group of climate scientists who have taken the bold step of trying to forecast 50 to 100 years out. Back in the '60s, a group of climate scientists were predicting we were heading into an ice age because data from around the world showed the average temperature was going down. The temperature data they were using were missing reports from large areas of the world, but they boldly predicted the ice age on the basis of "IF" the current trend continued.

Well, it was hard to put our heads out the window and check to see how accurate this forecast was, since the predictions were 50 to 100 years ahead. But the important thing was that we only had to listen to these reports on the TV news as fill-ins from grave-looking reporters and climate scientists between the traffic, weather, murders, and political shenanigans going on then. We didn't have to do anything, and it didn't cost us anything.

Then came a day in which the temperature information being collected from across the world stopped declining and increased a bit on average. Even though the temperature data weren't available from 70% of the planet, with complete gaps from areas such as the Amazon, the Congo, the Sahara or either pole, and most of the oceans, a group of climate scientists from across the globe started predicting that we were going to broil now. Carbon dioxide and other "greenhouse gases" (GHG) were holding on to sunlight and were going to increase temperatures so high that it would bring devastation to every living creature and ecosystem on the planet.

In fact, they said, the total temperature on the globe has increased to the highest levels since the pre-industrial ages prior to 1880. This statement is made with an added point that their forecast assumed that the sun's radiation is a constant, meaning it doesn't change. (Chapters 2 and 3 have the references.)

Also, *it was now our fault.* We humanoids were causing this 50-to-100-year-out catastrophe because we are doing unspeakable things, such as driving SUVs or other gas-guzzling cars, heating our houses from electric, coal, gas, or oil, and using and disposing of plastic products, to name a few things. We also couldn't get our electricity from atomic plants because they could cause another Three Mile Island or Chernobyl.

No explanation has been given for the shift from ice age to broil. But, hey, we've been there every day. Look out the window – check the forecast. Chances are 50/50. Not a worry because we always carry a hidden umbrella just in case. We're used to inaccuracies. Let the climate scientists keep working. They have made progress. With more time, they could get their accuracy up. That's a good thing. Keep going!

OK, so now we had a different fill-in where grave-looking reporters and climate scientists projecting a warming global catastrophe and demanding immediate remedies to stem the GHG increases. This we hear between the traffic, weather, murders, and political shenanigans going on nowadays. But now there is a twist. Before, it wasn't going to cost us anything, just the time to watch TV news. Now the immediate remedies are very costly.

This group of scientists had formed the Intergovernmental Panel on Climate Change (IPCC) and stated their case for CO_2 as the primary driver of temperature increase. They have given two reports, one in 1995 and another in 2001. Updates are made every six years. Another update is due in 2007–8.

Using the IPCC information, the United Nations started talking about reducing CO_2 and other "greenhouse gases" (GHG) under the Kyoto Treaty. This treaty was signed initially in 1997, but could not take effect until enough countries signed the agreement. Russia finally approved their participation in 2005, not for ecology reasons, but for economic reasons and to gain membership to the World Trade Organization. [R1.1] Part of the treaty was the commitment to reduce the amount of CO_2 going into the atmosphere by conservation and converting to alternative energy sources.

These alternative sources are wind-powered generators, solar (photovoltaic) cells, and hydrogen-generation units coupled with fuel cells. Fusion atomic energy or coal gasification with CO_2 sequestration could be possible. Fusion atomic energy does not produce long-lasting dangerous radioactive dust if they explode. And the present research designs are not likely to explode.

CO_2 sequestration means taking the CO_2 out of the air and storing it someplace else. A lot of pilot tests have been made to contain CO_2, including dissolving it into the oceans below 10,000 feet deep. The oceans contain more than 60 times more carbon (as dissolved ions) than the atmosphere and have enormous amounts of calcium and other salts to stabilize any fears of increasing acidity. Other ideas include placing the gases as well as other harmful products, such as mercury, back into the coal seams after the coal is extracted and burned. The last two would cost us the same or less, but the science does not support them yet.

Changing over to alternative energy sources would only slightly reduce our dependency on the Middle East and all its political complexities.

The reports said that these sources would cost us more, but we'd be saving the planet. OK, but how much more? We haven't been given any numbers for over 10 years. Various governments have sponsored all of these alternative sources with subsidies in the hundreds of millions of dollars. That's small compared to the trillions now spent on energy, but we still don't have any numbers to compare. Some efforts with wind, fuel cells, and solar have had questions about commercial viability, but that is because they are so much more expensive.

There are varying reports of costs for solar cells, hydrogen-generation units coupled with fuel cells, and wind generators. These reports include consumer costs for homeowners to install these systems. The range of data is from three to 25 times more expensive than current producer costs. Inside-industry sources hold that solar cells sold today have a producer-installed large-unit-generation cost of about 12 cents per kW hour. This is over three times more expensive per unit of energy to the producer than present fossil-fuel energy and provides energy only part of the day. Fossil-fuel or atomic generation is needed for energy in the dark hours as well as to some extent on cloudy and rainy days.

Hydrogen-generation units coupled with fuel cells, according to industry sources, have an installed producer electric-generation cost of about 23 cents per kW hour. That is almost six times more expensive for commercial energy producers than the current cost to producers. The only reason that there is a need for these hydrogen fuel cells is because of the need for surge electric power in downtown areas or applications in rural government special-purpose sites. The justification for the commercial applications, according to these sources, is that the cost of digging trenches, laying more electric cables, and the additional investment of surge capacity to meet the demand in high-rise office complexes is extremely high in crowded streets.

Wind generators, while a relatively lower-cost alternative source, has a very high cost of investment as well as installation and maintenance of the units plus the electric grid cables to collect all the electricity. This comes from 2005 reports from German researchers, who contend that doubling Germany's wind capacity will push the cost of electricity beyond $0.12 per kW hour. Germans pay almost two times more for electricity than we do in the U.S. The costs of wind generation, then, are about four and a half times or more than producer cost of fossil fuels. Additionally, fossil fuel or atomic generators are needed during wind lulls. [R1.2]

To summarize, the range for alternative energy sources is three to six times more expensive than current U.S. producer costs. There are reports of up to 20 times higher cost for solar cells in Europe than the U.S. [R1.2a] Atomic (and possibly fusion) generators produce energy at about half of today's U.S producer costs for fossil fuels. Coal gasification with sequestration is about equal to today's costs with higher oil and gas prices, though higher than costs a few years ago. Adding over three to six times more energy costs to a product made in the U.S. could destroy its manufacturing viability especially if other countries do not have to meet these treaties, such as China and India.

Now other scientists contend that the increase in temperatures since 1880 is more complex than just being related to "greenhouse gases" (GHG). (Chapters 4, 6, and 7 will discuss in detail.)

These scientists contend that the sun has had large increases in two energy forces. The actual light that the sun releases, called total solar irradiation (TSI), has increased at about the same rate as temperature. Also, the strength of the solar magnetic field has increased over the past 125 years as well as the number of sun spots, which eject high-energy particles called cosmic rays (CR). The two forces interact to increase or decrease the amount of high-energy CR that strike the earth, forcing changes in cloud cover. Drs. Marsh and Svensmark found that CR effects upon cloud cover absorbed four to five times the actual solar radiation changes in energy to the atmosphere. [R5.5] Other research from Dr. Palle, et. al, at the Earthshine project demonstrates greater enhancement of solar forces upon the climate. We will discuss in greater detail in Chapter 5.

Additionally, the forces that change the wind patterns and cause the effects called El Niño and La Niña have strong relationships to the 11- and 22-year cycles of solar peaks in the above two forces. [R1.3] As a result, most of the temperature increases come from solar-force increases, leaving much lower percentages to be explained by increases in GHG. (Chapters 4 and 5 will discuss in detail.)

That also means that CO_2 is not as dangerous as the IPCC group says. In fact, it probably means that we don't need treaties or to spend more on energy than we are today. In other words, since **IT'S THE SUN AND NOT YOUR SUV**, it will not cost us anything more than the economic forces on price can demand.

Several of the skeptical scientists were also instrumental in helping the U.S. Congress decide not to sign the Kyoto Treaty because of its "economic consequences," to quote President Bush. Tony Blair has also joined this point of view, saying in September 2005 that the British could not meet the demands of Kyoto because it would have "economic consequences" that would be too high.

Their point of view differs from the daily media fill-ins presented by CBS,

ABC, and CNN, where they quote the Sierra Club or other environmental groups on various subjects. Sometimes the presentations are difficult to believe because they do not present much data.

Well, we can't look out the window to check this one. We're talking 50 to 100 years out and the window check only works for the next several hours. What about checking out the historic temperature data and relating those changes to the sun's impacts and "greenhouse gases" (GHG)? We will be able to determine how important each force is on changing temperature.

Many of us learned how to relate variables in high school or college. Most modern spreadsheets have all the statistical packages we need, and it is just point and click.

What about the raw data? The web has government sites that our tax dollars pay for that have all the information. It's free!

Chapter 2

Why Buy This Book?

Caveat: This chapter is the only one in the book that is not a proof, that isn't filled with information. It's meant as a guide, rather than a destination and, let us hope, will answer the ultimate question in the mind of readers everywhere: "Why should I buy this book?"

The answer to this question is partly subjective and partly objective, and this chapter can deal with the objective only. It intends to address three questions that, together, should give you an answer whether putting aside the money and time to read and understand the argument in this book is important for you:

1. What will I learn?
2. How do I learn it?
3. What does it mean?

What will I learn?

Surface temperature on the earth has changed. We all know this. In fact, it is ever changing, and humans have recorded relatively cold periods and relatively warm periods for centuries. The amount of change in atmospheric temperature is open to question. There are primarily two large organizations, one in America (the National Oceanographic and Atmospheric Administration, NOAA) and the other in England (Hadley), that track earth temperature. Tracking is done on land and sea, and, in the case of NOAA, also includes among other methods, use of balloons and satellites. While these two organizations had slightly divergent data from 1940s to the 1970s, from 1975 to 1997 they have largely been in agreement for ground-based global temperatures. However, both the Hadley and the satellite data differ, only recording about 60% from 1979 to 2006 of the NOAA ground-based change. NOAA also publishes a Land-Ocean index for temperatures that attempts to resolve the differences between satellite- and ground-based measurements. This index realizes a 1979 to 2006 88% change in temperature vs. NOAA's ground-based data.

The earth's atmosphere is primarily impacted by the sun's energy. There are two components to the sun's influence: light energy and high-energy particles, the latter released in greater numbers during solar storms. The sun has been viewed and measured for centuries. Solar eleven- and twenty-two-year cycles and sunspots have been counted for many centuries, though high-energy-particles measurement has been active only since 1951.

Solar cycles have been estimated back into history by several scientists, and their estimates show wide swings in temperature since the ninth century. For example, the mid-twelfth and early nineteenth centuries had surface temperatures that were equal to or higher than our own, (see Chapters 5 and 6), but mini-ice ages occurred in the late eleventh, mid-fifteenth, mid-sixteenth, and early eighteenth centuries.

The amount of sunlight striking the earth has been measured with any degree of accuracy for only a few centuries, though very accurate measurements of solar-light energy have been available since 1970 from satellites. Since 1970, scientists differ on the amount of light that is emitted by the sun, but the larger question is, how is solar radiation converted to temperature? There are two primary approaches to this conversion: one focuses on greenhouse gases (GHG) with natural sources secondary, and the other on solar and natural sources primarily, with GHG secondary. It's clear that to decide *how* to do this, we must first discuss the energy sources that drive temperature changes.

Every day a certain amount of the sun's energy strikes the earth. Some of it is absorbed and some reflected away (usually about 31 percent, changing about 10%, or about 3 percentage points, in recent years). Changes in absorption have been linked to changes in cloud formation and changes in the light reflected from the earth. Current research is focused upon furthering the understanding of cloud formation. Yet the Intergovernmental Panel on Climate Change (2001), whose work formed the basis for the creation of the Kyoto Treaty, rejected the possibility that reflectivity of the earth changed. This is contradicted by incontrovertible facts that will be shown in later chapters of this book. Once this data are incorporated into the book's models, we can see how changes in radiative impacts have a definite correlation to known historic temperature changes, even taking into account the minor influences of greenhouse gases, as well as aerosols and other man-made influences.

The IPCC Report did not recognize the changes in the earth's reflectivity and assumed a much-higher influence of greenhouse gases than from natural sources. For these and other reasons, using the IPCC Report as a model for back-predicting historic temperature ranges has no validity, whereas the numerous tests made that take reflectivity into account correctly show high validity.

These validity test failures, using the IPCC data and assumptions, prove that the global-warming-theory hypothesis is false and that a solar-warming theory (the sun and not CO_2) is the most probable explanation for the climatic influences we are witnessing upon our planet.

How do I learn it?
Don't take the book's word for it. This book is filled with charts and graphs from irrefuted and irrefutable sources. Most sides of issues are shown, and you are directed on how to access both the data available now and the relevant data that

will be offered in the future. Moreover, a number of models were developed in Windows Excel™ that you can use to track and prove for yourself what has been driving the climate change we experienced, how it came to pass, and what is the likely future. A website, www.itsthesunnotyoursuv.com, has been established that will aid you in your quest and link you to other websites with continuing data on climate change and earth temperature. You need not be limited to repeating the arguments in this book, but will instead have the knowledge and wherewithal to prove to yourself that the sun and not global warming has been causing the changes in our climate.

What does it mean?
For nearly two decades now, it has been generally known that there has been a slight change in temperature on the earth over the past century. Although it's almost never mentioned this way, higher temperatures are by no means a one-sided disaster. Higher temperatures usually mean higher farming yields, for example. But the news is typically told in catastrophic, even apocalyptic, terms, replete with stories of large population centers inundated by rising sea levels, entire groups of species summarily extinguished, and cataclysmic climate changes. Moreover, the entire tenor of the reporting of these changes has always had a strong moral tone to it, since reporting on climate change nearly always emphasizes man's actions as being the cause of these changes. Thus only a radical change in man's bad behavior, it is asserted, will avert a calamitous future for our children and for the earth itself.

While global-warming information is supported by network news and political parties, a "smoking gun" proof of the impending devastation has not appeared after all these years. It is hard for scientists to develop clear evidence, since the global temperatures peaked in 1997–1998 and have been generally lower during the ensuing years.

Peak temperatures have been focused upon when they occur, while record low temperatures have been ignored. For example, Houston, Texas, had record low temperatures in February 2006, and Florida's and California's citrus crops have been destroyed by unusually cold weather in 2007, facts generally not reported or used as a counterpoint to global warming. The network news and political pundits who emphasize global warming find it difficult to detach themselves to demonstrate a "fair and balanced" discussion of this subject.

Recently, though, several climate scientists have resigned from participation in the primary global-warming organization, supported by the U.N., called the Intergovernmental Panel on Climate Change, or IPCC. As a result, interestingly, several news organizations have started to offer an alternative view by these well-known scientists to the global-warming view. In general, though, these alterative views are not included in reports.

This book shows that, at best, this is a gross and intellectually suspect exaggeration. The proof that the earth's climate is changing at a rate that endangers human and animal life in general is not validated, and the assertions that man's actions alone can revert all the climate change that has taken place is not valid on a scientific basis.

Chapter 3

Where Do We Start?

First we need to understand the problem.

The average global surface temperature has changed 0.53° to 0.7° Kelvin since 1880 (Kelvin is the same as Celsius, but it measures to absolute zero, when atoms stop moving. Its short form is "K").

Imagine being on the space shuttle. You want to know whether your space suit will hold up when you go out to repair a satellite. You would want to know what temperature the space suit will experience in the light and in the dark. In the light, it would experience 394° K. In the dark, it would have to be flexible to as low as 116° K, or 3° K if in deep space. So your space suit has to be able to support 250° Fahrenheit (short form: F) in the light and -250° F in the dark near earth. This is quite a range, which would require special material. [R3.1]

Why do we need to know those numbers? The sun, balanced by the atmosphere, maintains the earth at an average of 288.4° K. That varies 10° to 20° K or 3.5% to 7% when measured in K from night to day. The range changes, depending on the location on the earth. If there were no sun, the earth would be equal to deep space, -454° F.

At those temperatures, the oceans would be solid and nothing would live as we understand it. Though scientists believe the moon of Saturn, Europa, might have some life forms under its frozen water mantle, it's probably not a climate fit for shopping malls.

The 1880-to-2000 change is 0.6° K, only 0.2% in 120 years, according to the IPCC report. That is about the first fifteen to thirty minutes of temperature change at sunrise. Or it's about the first four seconds of temperature change just before a severe thunderstorm.

This might lead you to stop reading, since the issue is quite small. There is a case to be made for saying there is "no problem," and thousands of climate scientists offer that point of view. However, if you need to talk to others about the issue, it is strongly recommended that you continue building your knowledge. What we, the electorate, fail to understand could cost us a lot of money unnecessarily.

Below is charted the total change in surface temperature, along with the sea surface, since it is another database that is maintained. Sea-surface temperature has changed 0.5° K since 1880. There is another well-maintained temperature database from England. It is called the Hadley and is also included in Chart 3.1. This is how the IPCC report likes to look at these small changes.

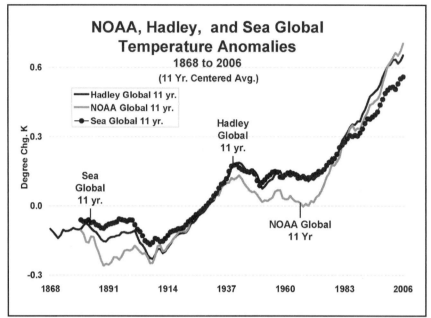

Chart 3.1: The data comes from the National Oceanographic and Atmospheric Agency (NOAA). The data site is located at: http://www.giss. nasa.gov/data/ update/gistemp/graphs/ then click on your choice of chart or data file. Sea-surface temperatures from NOAA at www.ncdc.noaa.gov/oa/ climate/resesarch/1998/anomalies/annual_ocean.ts.; 2001–2006 not currently available. Hadley Source to 2005: http://www.cru.uea.ac.uk/ftpdata/tavegl2v.dat; 2006: change in http://www.cru.uea.ac. uk/cru/ data/temperature/hadcrut3vgl.txt.

There seems to be some difference between the U.S. and U.K. data especially during the years from 1942 to 1976. Notice that the Global Sea and Hadley track together until 1980. We will discuss this further in a few paragraphs.

Not only do we have different databases that raise questions about the accuracy of the data. We also have issues with the reporting locations. The surface temperatures are from reporting sites across the globe. The historic information has less coverage than current data, which you may wonder about. Does the historic data represent a good base for evaluating temperature change? Do the gaps in data from around the world today represent a clear picture of the current changes?

Chart 3.2 is from the IPCC report, and it shows the reporting sites across the globe today. Notice any gaps?

Not hard to see! Seventy percent is ocean and that is a big area of contention.

Also, over time, ground-based equipment has been upgraded to eliminate the need for humans to record data, a key source of errors in the past. The ground-based historic stations were in areas that have experienced greater urbanization. As cities grow, more energy is expended by surrounding buildings and fewer trees

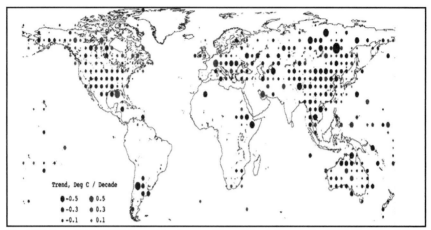

Chart 3.2: From IPCC 2001 Report http://www.grida.no/climate/ipcc_tar/wg1/054.htm. The stations represented are non-urban stations only. An all-stations chart is not shown in the report.

or plants are available to cool through evaporation of water in the area around the recording sites in the urban areas. These factors increase the readings from these sites. However, this is not representative of the surrounding areas. The increases are misrepresentations of the true temperature.

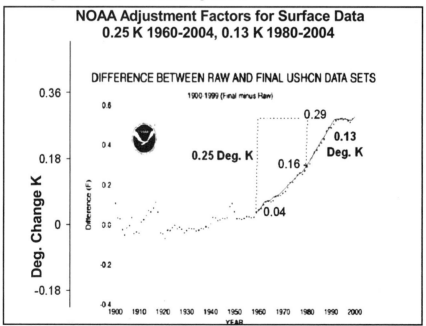

Chart 3.3: In IPCC 2001 Report and available at www.ncdc.noaa.gov/img/climate/research/ushcn/ts.ushcn_anom25_diffs_urb-raw_pg.gif.

As a result, NOAA has had to adjust the raw data with a factor they developed so they could link the temperature from earlier years when humans wrote down the temperature (1880 to 1960) to the present when temperatures are recorded electronically. In fact, the total temperature change recorded is about 0.5° K from 1960 to 2000 and the adjustments to the data equal 0.25° K or 50% of all of the increases registered by ground-based temperature. Chart 3.3 is from NOAA, showing the adjustments made to the actual recorded temperatures since 1960 to the U.S. dataset. The website also contains explanations of the adjustments. There are reports that adjustments were made to the global data using these adjustment factors, though it is difficult to find literature references.

The human adjustments from 1980 to 2000 equal 0.13° K or 33% of the change in temperature recorded. Is there a better source of data?

Those weather satellites we spend so many tax dollars on have only been available since late in 1978 to measure temperature and other atmospheric data. The value of satellites is that they cover most of the globe.

The satellite data are called the "MSU" data and are an important dataset to learn about. It is the principle satellite dataset that everyone refers to and compares to surface station data. The dataset is prepared by the Global Hydrology and Climate Center (GHCC) at the University of Alabama. This center is a joint project with NASA. GHCC scientists have compiled more than two decades of data, showing how atmospheric temperature has behaved over the entire globe. The data are derived from microwave radiation from atmospheric oxygen that varies with temperature, among other factors. Microwave sensors on weather satellites take oxygen temperature measurements in the atmosphere, from the surface to the top of the atmosphere. The data we will use in this book are from the lower troposphere, from 5 to 25,000 ft., generally.

Some climate scientists say that satellites are not useful to compare to surface temperatures, because they are measuring higher altitudes starting at 5,000 feet, but are usually measuring higher altitudes. There has also been some question about the adjustments needed to the satellite data. The satellites drift a bit from expected orbits. These issues have been addressed over time, the latest in August 2005 [R3.2], but not all scientists are satisfied.

The value of a satellite database is that it covers the globe, even the Amazon and Congo Jungles, the Sahara and Gobi Deserts, most of the Polar Regions, and especially the ocean.

Proponents of the satellite database point out that the ground-based data have too many gaps to be useful. They also remind us that urbanization was discovered from the satellite data.

Knowing that the satellite data have been adjusted, we can see in Chart 3.4 an increase in the trend of 0.3° K from late 1978 to present. The El Niño of 1998 was especially strong, though there were others in 1983 and 1988. The dips in 1983 and 1991 occurred at the time of two major volcano eruptions, El Chichon

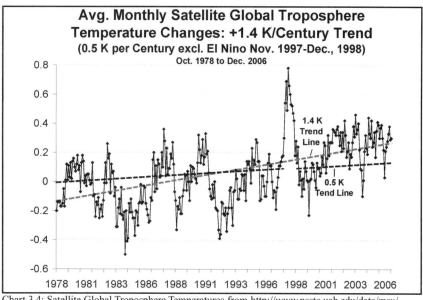

Avg. Monthly Satellite Global Troposphere Temperature Changes: +1.4 K/Century Trend
(0.5 K per Century excl. El Nino Nov. 1997-Dec., 1998)
Oct. 1978 to Dec. 2006

Chart 3.4: Satellite Global Troposphere Temperatures from http://www.nsstc.uah.edu/data/msu/
t2lt/uahncdc.lt.

and Pinatubo. The 1998 El Niño did raise the trend to 1.4° K per century, but as we see, the temperatures returned to lower levels in 1999. If the 1998-year data are left out, the temperature increases are only 0.5° K per century. Prior to 1998, the trend was a slight negative.

The reason the 1997–98 El Niño is focused upon is that the waters of both the Pacific and Atlantic had strong increases, while it is usually the Pacific that experiences the temperature rise. This was shown very graphically on the global maps generated by NASA from the MSU satellite data. An average month might look similar to November 1998 as shown in Chart 3.5. Notice that some areas in white/light gray are below-average temperature, and some areas in black/dark gray are above. In this case the northern polar region is quite a bit warmer and the southern polar region is quite a bit cooler. Also notice the Ross Ice Sheet area of Antarctica (circle) was warmer, and news reports were talking about it splitting from the continent. Notice also that another area close by was unusually cold (arrow), but not reported.

The U.S. is above average and Europe and Russia are much colder. If we had used the "look out the window" test, we would have said, "Yes it is warmer," but friends in Europe would have been saying just the opposite.

Chart 3.5 shows what the map looked like at the peak of the 1998 El Niño. Notice that the temperature in the Pacific and Atlantic were much above normal. The Arctic is much warmer, and Antarctica is much colder. But by November, the temperature had returned to the normal variations of Chart 3.6.

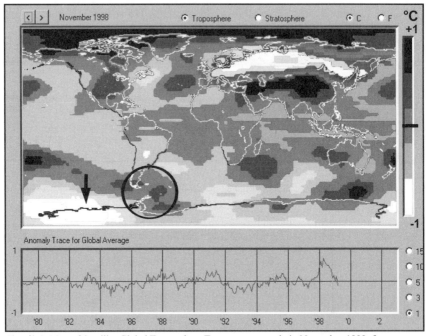

Chart 3.5: Map of Satellite Global Troposphere Temperatures made in November 1998, from
http://wwwghcc.msfc.nasa.gov/temperature, currently not available. Trend data offered at
www.climat.uah.edu.

The area in Chart 3.6 around the Ross Ice Sheet is much warmer than the rest
of Antarctica. This region is talked about quite often. It floats in the ocean,
attached to Antarctica, but at times pieces about the size of a small state in the
U.S. break off. News programs report these events with some reference to global
warming. Generally, the pieces break off and return back to where they were,
which is usually not reported. In fact, during a recent period of localized warming one piece broke off that was comparable to the size of Rhode Island. At the
same time, the scientists at the South Pole were reporting the lowest temperature
ever recorded on the earth, -100° F. This last point was not reported in the news.
Information channels and scientific journals did report that fact.

To continue the discussion about the temperature databases, let's create a new
chart, 3.7, that has the satellite data plotted into the Global Temperature Chart 3.1.

Wait, the satellite data and the ground data don't agree. In fact, there seems
to be a major difference between them since 1979.

What's happening? Are the satellites wrong or are the ground and sea surface
temperatures wrong?

Chart 3.8 is a comparison of the global surface temperature data and the
satellite data for the period of 1979 to 2006. There is a difference of almost 0.15° K
over this period of time

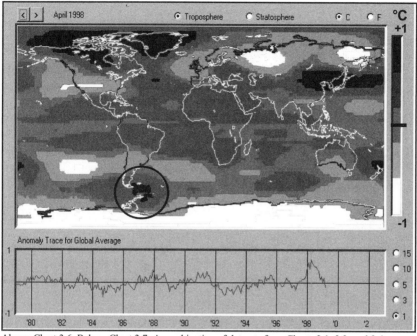

Above: Chart 3.6. Below: Chart 3.7: A combination of datasets from Charts 3.1, 3.3, and 3.4.

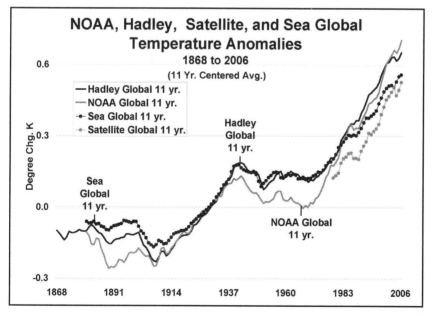

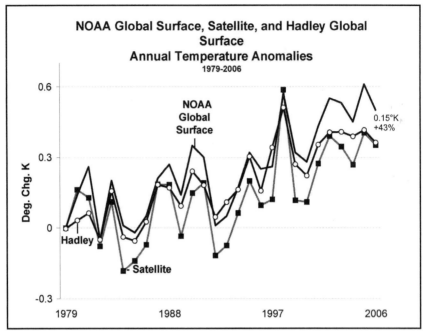

Chart 3.8: A combination of datasets from Charts 3.1, 3.7.

The differences between satellite/Hadley and NOAA ground have not been reconciled. But if we take out the NOAA U.S. adjustments from the NOAA global
surface data, they are plotted in Chart 3.9.

In all the literature about the climate, this author has not seen this chart
developed by any other source, though it is simple to complete. Recent correspondence from NOAA indicates that global data are created after local national databases are adjusted according to their own factors. Therefore there is no
published index of global NOAA adjustments. Since the satellite and Hadley
data are consistent, it is not important to use the unadjusted NOAA data later in
the book.

There are a lot of other articles on the subject of satellite vs. NOAA ground
temperatures. They might be worth reading. A very good article is in the reference section that talks about the trends in the data. This article was written by a
group of climate scientists. One was the director of the NOAA satellite program
for many years [R3.3]. The focus of much of their criticism between ground-
based and satellite-based data is over the oceans. There seems to be a major discrepancy between the two.

It seems that the NOAA surface data and satellite data are trending in opposite directions when we review the data by latitude, as we see in Charts 3.10 A, B,
and C. The primary areas of divergence are in the tropics and to some extent in

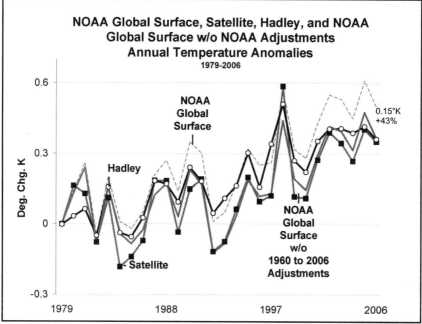

Chart 3.9.

the northern latitudes, especially from 1979 to 1996, as shown by trend lines for that period.

Because of all the gaps in data, especially from the oceans in the tropics, NOAA has recognized that the sea-surface data have critics. The data for the sea surface are collected from the water intakes from ships on the ocean and from weather buoys floating in the water that are sparsely place across the oceans.

When the satellite data collected over the oceans were compared to the sea-surface temperature, the sea surface was rising much more rapidly than the satellite ocean data. Over time this gap has grown and NOAA developed the Land-Ocean Index, which uses surface land data and satellite ocean data shown in Chart 3.11. This adjustment does not resolve the differences between the satellite/ Hadley/unadjusted NOAA global surface. However, it does lower the total change in temperature below the Hadley (Chart 3.12). An unadjusted Land-Ocean seems also to close the gap, as shown in Chart 3.13. Let us hope that future research will resolve this very interesting issue.

To further complicate the discussion, when the surface-station and satellite data are compared to different datasets, such as weather balloons and other atmospheric temperature measurement methods, the trend in temperature supports the satellite data, not the global surface data. Here is a comparison of the various temperature sources in Chart 3.13.

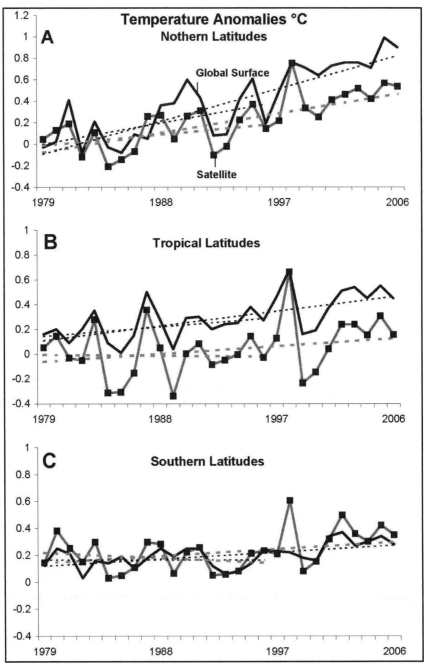

Chart 3.10. All data come from the dataset used in Chart 3.4.

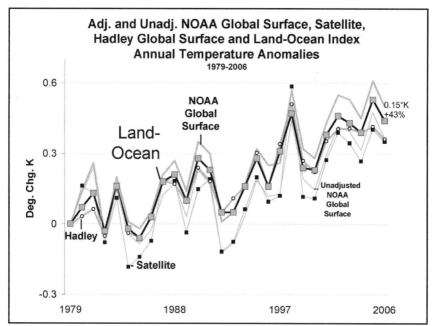

Above: Chart 3.11: Land-Ocean Index from NOAA at http://www.giss.nasa.gov/data/update/
gistemp/graphs/. Below: Chart 3.12: A combination of datasets from Charts 3.1, 3.3, 3.4, and 3.11.

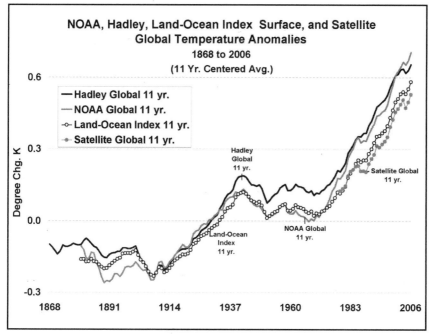

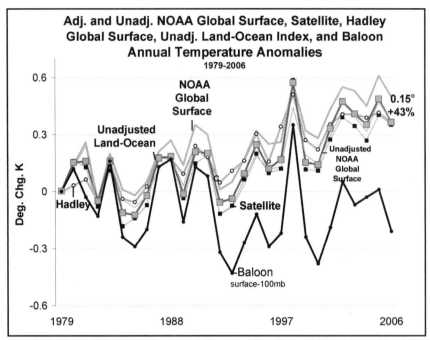

Chart 3.13: Weather Balloon data from: http://cdiac.esd.ornl.gov/ftp/trends/temp/angell/global.dat
but see [R3.4] for latest information.

Notice that the data for satellite and balloon return to lower trends after the
1997–98 El Niño. The NOAA surface temperature does not seem to return.

There are corrections to the balloon data that were proposed by Sherwood,
S., J. Lanzante, and C. Meyer, 2005 in "Radiosonde daytime biases and late 20th
century warming. August 11, online at http://www.scienceexpress.org" [R3.4].
The data from the official balloon web site has not been changed.

There are strong opinions about each set of data without a lot of science to
help settle this issue, though there seems to be considerable activity during the
spring and summer of 2005 in addressing the issues of these databases. Will this
hurt our ability to check out how much the sun or CO_2 are affecting us? It might
not. What if we looked at each set of data and found out how much of the change
in temperature was caused by the sun or GHG?

So let's compare the data regarding what could be forcing the change in temperature. The temperature chart is very busy; therefore, we need to focus on key
temperature records. Let's begin with the Hadley (Chart 3.14).

What is forcing the temperature to change?
1. Sun: any combination of the following:
  a. Total solar irradiation (TSI or sun light) as well as a surrogate for sunspot
     intensity.

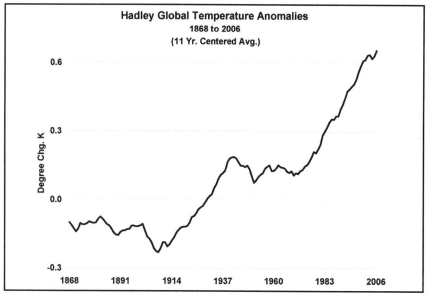

Chart 3.14 Data from Charts 3.1, 3.3, 3.4, and 3.12.

    b. Magnetic flux impacts on cosmic rays (CR).

    c. 11-year and 22-year cycles that trigger El Niño and the reverse called La
       Niña.

2. GHG possibly interlinked with Solar impacts.

    Let's start with the sun.

Chapter 4

Solar Radiation Data

Where do we get sun data? Solar radiation numbers are the first datasets we need. The same website at NOAA has data on solar radiation, except the data are located in a file called "Paleo." That's the same file that was referred to in the movie, *The Day After Tomorrow.* Bet you didn't know it was free and available through point-and-click.

By the way, look out the window. Do you see the signs of a catastrophic ice age coming your way, brought on by global warming from all the CO_2? If you can't understand the logic, it's probably because only a clone of Stephen King could have come up with this one.

If we open the files, we find Chart 4.1 on solar radiation.

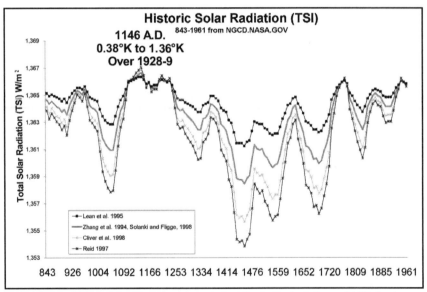

Chart 4.1: From NOAA at ftp://ftp.ngdc.noaa.gov/paleo/climate_forcing/solar_variability/bard_irradiance.txt.

Several different types of scientists have gone back in time and put together the possible solar-radiation numbers back to pre-Christian times. The more recent data are from solar observatory sources, and the earlier data are from evaluations of tree rings, and [14]Carbon (Carbon 14) and [10]Beryllium (Beryllium 10) isotopes.

Scientist have found through statistical correlations that specific Beryllium isotopes are created in larger numbers when the solar radiation and magnetic field (flux) are at higher levels, and lesser amounts are formed when these solar forces are at lower levels. [R4.1]

Tree rings have been used also, but it is difficult statistically to assure that the results agree with the historic conditions written about by people who lived during those periods. A key problem is that tree rings grow faster in wet periods and slower in dry periods, unrelated to relative temperature changes. Therefore, tree rings are an unreliable indicator of temperature change. However, they were used and caused a major controversy in the IPCC 2001 report. Their results showed that the temperature has increased sharply in the past 50 years to the highest levels since 1500. Other reviewers audited the tree-ring data and found that the statistical-sampling methods used would reproduce the same spike in temperature from random numbers. They also found that the actual data would have shown much higher temperatures in the 1400 and 1500 period, demonstrating that the current period is not unusual. This has led to a lot of discussion about the validity of tree-ring data to provide substantiation to the claim that this century has been the hottest ever. It also raised major concerns about the lack of review by "peer reviewed" magazines. [R4.2]

The ^{14}Carbon and ^{10}Beryllium isotope data had to be calibrated to earlier periods in time. Several periods in history have been used as benchmarks to adjust the data. One of those periods is called the Maunder Minimum of 1640 to 1700, when the people of the time wrote about experiencing unusually low temperatures. There are reports that the Thames River froze over during these years, and shopkeepers were able to sell their wares on the ice. Basically, the reports sound as if they experienced the first shopping mall, au natural.

We now consider the conditions described to have been a mini-ice age and led to the ice-age forecasts of the late 1960s. There were also other mini-ice ages and warm periods. The most recent time that the Thames froze over was in 1910. This period of cold followed the meteor that exploded over Siberia in the Tunguska region. The current data show this period to be the lower points in the datasets for this book. The most recent warmest is probably in the 1100s. Some literary historians refer to this period when Norse explorers wrote that Greenland was "green." There are others who say it was written this way to divert explorers away from Iceland. Based upon models in Chapters 5, 6, and 8, the temperatures were probably 1.36° K above 1928–1929, as shown in Chart 4.1. Current peak is 0.65° K. The IPCC report shows 2000 temperature being 0.6° K +/- 0.1° K higher than about 1930.

With a certain level of speculation, it appears that solar radiation has varied historically from 1355 watts per square meter (W/m^2) to 1368.5 W/m^2.

How do we relate these data to today? Several scientists have also extended this data until 1978, when satellite data became available. Two of these datasets are presented in Chart 4.2. They are from Dr. Lean in 1995 and Drs. Hoyt and Schatten in 1993. Dr. Lean of NOAA has updated the numbers in 2000. It is important, though, to note that the trend up is significant. There is a difference in the timing of the rises, though. Drs. Hoyt and Schatten's data seem to match to the temperature data more closely the rise from 1938 to 1948 and the slight decline from 1948 to 1970.

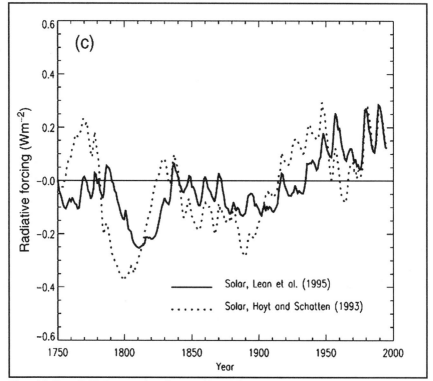

Chart 4.2: From IPCC Report at http://www.grida.no/climate/ipcc_tar/wg1/fig6.8.htm.

Why did scientists have to use isotopes and tree rings? Why did they not just measure the amount of light that strikes the earth? Here is the struggle for scientists on the ground when they measure solar radiation. This data come from the observatory on Mauna Loa in Maui, Hawaii, the oldest consistent database for surface solar-radiation measurements. There are only 26 of these sites on the globe, though some 200 other sites also collect less precise data.

There are huge gaps in data which introduce a lot of uncertainty in sorting out the cloud and dust from the changes in solar radiation. Do you see how the atmospheric changes affect temperature (thin line under the arrow)? (See Chart 4.3.)

Neither can most people.

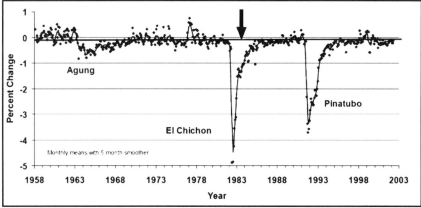

Chart 4.3. Adapted from earlier version of Mauna Loa chart currently available at:
http://www.mlo.noaa.gov/programs/esrl/solar/img/img_solar_radiation_transmission.jpg.

An article in *Science* magazine on May 6, 2005, by Dr. Martin Wild, et al., titled "From Dimming to Brightening: Decadal Changes in Solar Radiation at Earth's Surface" studies the relative changes in the above charts from places around the globe and finds that the period in the 1950s was dimmer than the current times. [R4.3]

To gather data about the levels of solar radiation, it is necessary to measure

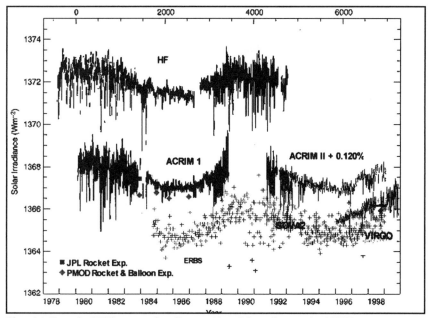

Chart 4.4: From the IPCC report at http://www.grida.no/climate/ipcc_tar/wg1/244.htm.

above the atmosphere. Now it is easier to understand all the money spent on satellites. However, this raises another issue. Multiple satellites have been in orbit, each one built with increasingly more sensitive instrumentation (Chart 4.4).

Linking these datasets together is somewhat questionable, since they each have a "native" range. One way to link them is advocated by a Dr. Willson and the ACRIM team of NASA. (Chart 4.5):

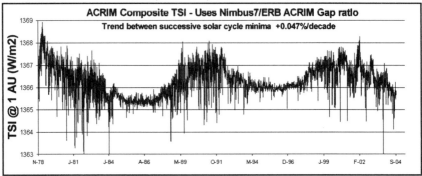

Above: Chart 4.5: adapted from the ACRIM website at: http://www.acrim.com/RESULTS/Earth% 20Observatory/earth_obs_fig26.pdf. Below: Chart 4.6 Lean 2000 from: ftp://ftp.ncdc.noaa.gov/pub/ data/paleo/climate_forcing/solar_variability/ lean2000_irradiance.txt. This data are used from 1860 to 1980. The Max Planck estimates from http://www.mps.mpg.de/projects/sun-climate/papers/ iscs2003.pdf, Figure 6 is used from 1981 to 2006, and the ACRIM data are from Chart 4.5 from 1984 to 2006. The actual datasets are available at the website referred to in Appendix C.

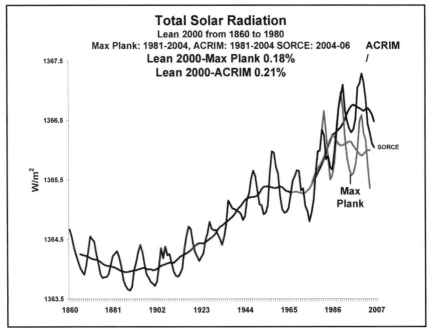

Another way was completed in November 2004 by the Max Planck observatory in Switzerland. They linked the various satellite datasets together using the Paleo surrogate Lean 2000 for solar cycles. [R4.4]

Now what does that mean? If we connect the satellite solar data to the Lean 2000 database surrogate, we get this chart. The ACRIM data from Dr. Willson's ACRIM team constitute the upper line. The lower line is the Max Planck interpretation of the satellite W/m^2 data (Chart 4.6).

How do we relate the solar radiation data to the global temperatures?

Chapter 5

Linking Temperature to Solar Radiation

As reported in the IPCC report, climate scientists agree that not all the solar radiation is able to get through the atmosphere to the surface. The solar radiation at the top of the atmosphere since 1880 is 1365 W/m^2 (watts per square meter) plus or minus 2 W/m^2 as measured at noon. According to the IPCC report, a geometry factor of 0.25 needs to be applied to reflect a 24-hour average and 31% of the light is reflected (called Albedo). This results in about 235.5W/m^2 and 168 W/m^2 are all that are absorbed by the surface. It is important to know to which timeframe the watts-per-square-meter number is referring.

The earth's reflectivity is called the earth Albedo. That is a strange, but important word and one that we need to learn. There are only a few new words in this book.

Albedo is the ratio of light reflected by the earth versus the total energy striking the top of the earth's atmosphere. The light energy not reflected is the amount of energy absorbed. The IPCC report says the earth reflects 31% of the light and does not discuss any change in this reflectivity. Therefore their models do not have to account for any changes in reflection. We'll discuss this important issue with the IPCC report a bit later. [R5.1]

Full daylight lasts only for a portion of the day. The 168 W/m^2 is close to measurements made at Mauna Loa and other locations at the surface, but is higher by 14 W/m^2, than the average of these ground-based measurements. The IPCC-report number is assumed not to change. The surface measurements have changed over time. This difference in numbers will be addressed in the next chapter. Either number still means that only about 12% of the watts in space affect temperature at the surface when we measure on an average of 24 hours. Not all of the light filters to the surface; some is absorbed in the atmosphere at the various levels – the stratosphere, the troposphere, as well as near ground. The total radiation change on the ground from the solar irradiance changes from the lowest point near 1880 to 2004 is about 0.18% to 0.21%. When we multiply these percentages times 168 W/m^2, we have an ACRIM change of 0.38 W/m^2 and a Max Planck change of 0.3 W/m^2. (Calculations are available at the website.)

How do we relate this change in watts to a change in temperature? This is a very critical subject for us to understand. If the sensitivity factor we use is too high, then we will predict too much temperature for a small amount of energy. If the sensitivity rate we use is too small, then we might understate the possible changes in global temperature.

Physicists have established laws for the amount of energy from light that is needed to raise the temperature of any object the light strikes. The famous physicists, Drs. Stefan and Boltzmann, established a mathematical formula to calculate the amount of temperature increase that could be expected if light energy of various intensities illuminated an object called a "black body." This formula is called the Stefan Boltzmann factor.

However, the IPCC report assumes that climate temperature is affected differently from this famous physics formula. The IPCC report has various sensitivity factors of the amount of total solar radiation energy (called solar irradiance) that it takes to calculate an increase or decrease in temperature. In fact, there is very little agreement about the sensitivity factor of energy (from any source) to temperature.

Chart 5.1a shows the sensitivity factors from the IPCC report for the scenario from the same report called B2. The chart shows the ratio of degrees of temperature change that are assumed to take place due to a change in the number of watts of energy. Added to Chart 5.1a are the statements of one of the key contributors to the report, a Dr. Hansen of NASA. He has stated in an article in 2003 that the equilibrium sensitivity is 0.75 K per Watt/m^2 in the IPCC report, though not revealed in the report [R5.2 and Chart 5.1a and b]. This factor was just reduced to 0.67 K/W/m^2 by Dr. Hansen in a recent article (April 2005) because of newly discovered higher energy absorption by black carbon particles that float in the atmosphere and are part of the group of atmospheric substances called "aerosols"

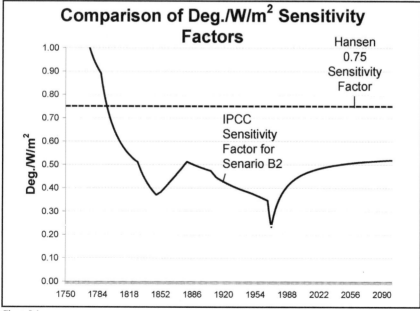

Chart 5.1a.

[R5.3a]. Not all research published at the same time agrees with the importance of black carbon particles. Additionally, in June 2005, Dr. Hansen, et al., printed research results indicating that the oceans were absorbing 40% of the solar energy trapped by GHG since 1880 or 0.91 W/m². No adjustment was made to the sensitivity factor of the total energy budget shown in Chart 5.1a. [R5.3b] The 40% absorbed in the oceans is about half of the 1.71 W/m² associated with aerosols. No discussion of the apparent conflict has been discovered at the date of publication, though one would presume there is some explanation offered. This book will offer an explanation in the next few pages.

The reason mentioned in the IPCC report for the variety of sensitivity factors is that there are "feedbacks" from atmospherically absorbed energy that are released from the atmosphere and heat the surface. The actual data showing this "feedback" are difficult to obtain. Many times climate scientists use the term "feedback" to fill a gap they cannot explain from the actual data.

Peter Dietze is a reviewer of the 2001 IPCC report. He suggests that the equilibrium sensitivity rate should be 0.24 near ground for a black body whose emission is restricted to 77% as defined by the Stefan Boltzmann sensitivity factor for light absorption characteristics by an object such as the earth. His point is that this is one of the key difficulties of the IPCC report. Because this factor is not properly used, it aided researchers in ignoring other key factors that force temperature change. And because the other factors were ignored, the report's extraordinary forecasts were a logical extension. The Dietze calculation of the sensitivity factor is plotted in Chart 5.1b.

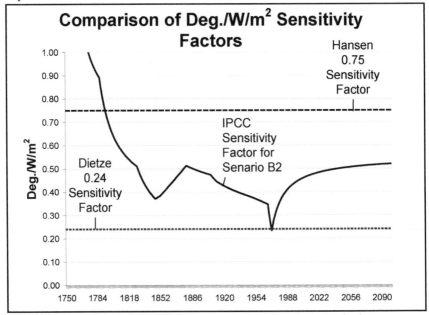

Chart 5.1b: Sensitivity factor explained at http://www.john-daly.com/forcing/moderr.htm.

Perhaps you have been wondering what is so important about these factors. Their importance becomes evident when we try to see how well the solar-radiation data fit to the temperature data using the Hansen sensitivity rate and the Dietze sensitivity rate. This is easy. We can plot the ACRIM solar radiation lines we just created multiplied by the IPCC factor (Hansen) (Chart 5.2).

It would seem that the higher IPCC sensitivity factor provides the basis for explaining a lot of the change in temperature because of increasing solar radiation. There is less for CO_2 or other GHG to explain in the change in temperature. This higher sensitivity factor almost refutes the IPCC report because actual temperature change would have to have been much higher to utilize all energy forces identified in the IPCC report! The Dietze approach, based upon the scientifically based heat absorption by an object such as the earth, would require other energy sources to explain the changes in temperature than just solar irradiation.

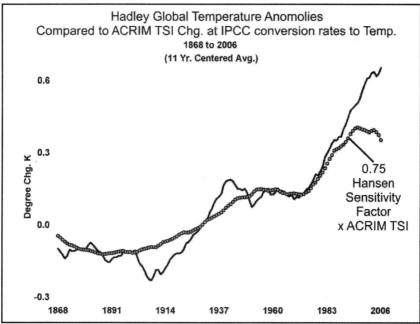

Chart 5.2: Solar effects only using the Hansen factors from Chart 5.1b.

Other Solar Forces

Most solar scientists contend that the magnetic flux or magnetic field from the sun changes, and they have developed an index for the amount of change in strength of the magnetic flux or field of the sun. The index is titled the AA Index. This index loosely follows the solar-radiation cycles. They also have found that as the magnetic flux changes during the 11- and 22-year solar cycles, the amount of cosmic rays (CR) that strike the earth change. The CR are measured at mountain-top observatories at different points on the globe; one in the U.S. is called Climax.

The dataset is called the Climax Neutron Index. (Data references are in [R5.4] and Chart 5.6.)

Drs. Marsh and Svensmark of the Danish Space Research Institute published a paper in 1998 that found that as the magnetic flux changes, CR or high-energy solar and galactic particles that strike the earth also change the amount and type of cloud cover. It is surmised that the high-energy particles split atoms, creating nuclei that collect water vapor, forming ice crystals. The research data were limited, but indicated that as the solar-magnetic strength increases, the amount of CR striking the earth decrease and the low, thick clouds retain more radiation, thus decreasing the earth's reflectivity. The W/m^2 of change in reflectivity was equal to four to five times the change in solar-radiation change. [R5.5]

The IPCC report considered this information in Chapter 6.11.2.2 "Cosmic rays and clouds" (Full text at R5.6). It concluded that: "At present there is insufficient evidence to confirm that cloud cover responds to solar variability" because it was unclear at that time how CR or high-energy particles affect cloud cover. Satellite imaging has difficulty differentiating between snow, low clouds, mid-level clouds, and high clouds. Also, the satellite that generated these results was not functioning correctly after 1995.

While Drs. Marsh and Svensmark have not published on this subject since an update report in 2001, scientists at the California observatory at Big Bear had been working on a project called "Earthshine."

In a magazine article titled, "Changes in the Earth's reflectance over the past two decades," Drs. E. Palle, P.R. Goode, P. Montanes Rodriguez, and S.E. Koonin (*Science*, 28 May 2004) stated that they had measured the amount of reflection from the earth on the *Dark Side of the Moon* for several years. It is quite interesting to realize that the earth reflects into space and that these researchers were able to measure the change in the earth's light reflection during those periods when the moon is a sliver in the sky. [R5.7a] The data was updated in January, 2006. [R5.7b]

The data they generated were able to confirm the published reports by Drs. Marsh and Svensmark that the reflectivity of the earth changed. They additionally found a relationship between changes in the amount of CR and the amount of clouds at various levels, especially low clouds as a ratio to high/middle clouds.

However, both research groups have been unable to clearly define the relationship between high-energy particles and cloud formation.

The Earthshine team was also able to relate the amount of change in radiation energy they measured on the dark side of the moon from 1999 to 2004 to the number of watts per square meter of change for the years 1984 to 2004. The number of watts per square meter had changed by almost 10.2 W/m^2 at the top of the atmosphere. This is a major source of energy striking the earth's surface and not recognized in the IPCC report. The other important point is that the highest amount of energy absorbed by the earth was in 1997–1998, the year of the most impressive El Niño recorded. Chart 5.3 shows the decline in reflectivity of about 10.5 percent (which shows a range of 3.2% on the insolation at a 31% basic Albedo) and the related change in W/m² from their EOS article in January 2006.

In the May 6, 2005 issue of *Science* magazine, three articles were published that agreed that the earth's Albedo did change. Two of the articles supported, in general terms, the Earthshine data from Big Bear observatory in California. There was a change in the amount of energy absorbed. The article referred to earlier by Martin Wild, et al. [R4.3] agreed with the trend, but did not provide any data confirmation. An article by Dr. Pinker, et al., "Do Satellites Detect Trends in Surface Solar Radiation?" [R5.8] showed a similar range of energy change as the Earthshine data. Another report in that same issue showed that from 2000 to 2004

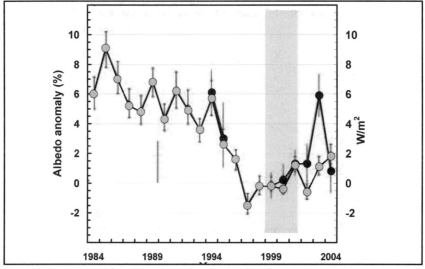

Chart 5.3: Reconstructed from: "Can the earth's Albedo and surface temperatures increase together?", E. Pallé, P.R. Goode, P. Montañés-Rodríguez, S.E. Koonin, EOS, Vol. 87, No. 4, 24 January, 2006.

the trend was to a higher absorption of energy from the sun, not a decline, but agreed that there was a 2 W/m² change. [R5.9]

Confirming these findings, the five additional datasets that show trends in the reflectivity of the earth (Albedo) were compared to the Earthshine data in a letter: "A multi-data comparison of shortwave climate forcing changes," *E. Palle, P. Montanes-Rodriguez, P.R. Goode, S.E. Koonin, M. Wild, S. Casadio,* Geophysical Research Letters, Vol. 32, No. 21, L21702, 10.1029/2005GL023847, 2005. [R5.10] The Earthshine team added data for 2004. Here is a replicated version of the Earthshine chart with comparable data from five other sources. The updated 2004 EOS data are included in Chart 5.4. Note that 2003 Earthshine data have been adjusted to reflect the article's authors' indication that the Earthshine data are probably too high due to sampling limitations.

Four agree in direction. Two agree in magnitude and are direct measurements of Albedo. One, presented by Dr. Wild, called the SBSRN, is a direct measurement from the surface and OBTsGOME, is a direct measurement from a European satellite. Of the two that agree in direction but do not agree in magnitude, one, ERBE, is derived by computer model from this satellite's data that measures the tropics only and the other, SMOD, is derived from a computer model of satellite data that estimate cloud totals only but does not estimate actual Albedo.

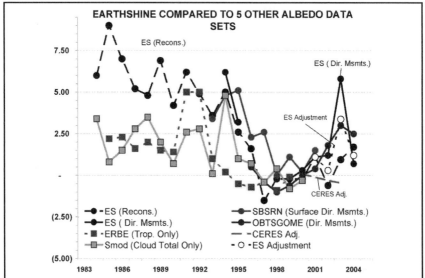

Chart 5.4: Replicated version of the Earthshine chart with comparable data from five other sources from "A multi-data comparison of shortwave climate forcing changes", E. Palle, P. Montanes-Rodriguez, P.R. Goode, S.E. Koonin, M. Wild, S. Casadio, Geophysical Research Letters, Vol. 32, No. 21, L21702, 10.1029/2005GL023847, 2005.. The updated 2004 EOS article data are included from Chart 5.3.

Thus, the Earthshine team gains support for their basic measurements from two direct measurement datasets and directional support from two additional datasets. The most important support is that the Albedo changed direction in 1997–1998. More solar energy is being reflected now than during that period.

One dataset developed from a computer model of satellite data from the CERES satellite was adjusted due to calibration issues identified by the original authors. After adjustments, it shows a slight downward trend for the period 2001–2003.

When we average those datasets that are direct measurements as well as average the two datasets that are computer-model datasets but support the direction of the Earthshine data, we have the chart 5.4a. This makes it easier to see the relative agreement between datasets. The CERES computer model dataset is certainly contrary to the rest of the datasets without resolution.

The Earthshine team has also revealed that the total SW, or short-wave, W/m^2 is only a portion of the effects of changes in clouds. There is a cooling effect in the LW, or long-wave, range that is difficult to measure. This cooling effect is estimated to be about half of the total change in the SW measurement. Thus the 6.8 W/m² is reduced by 50% in subsequent charts to best define the Albedo impacts. For a developed example of this "cooling" effect, see Appendix A.

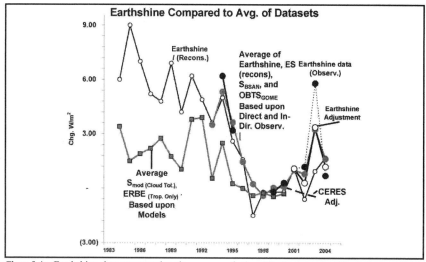

Chart 5.4a: Earthshine data compared to the average of other Albedo datasets. Calculations available at the website referred to in Appendix C.

How do we relate these changes in reflectivity to solar and other forces? The relationship to solar sunspots and solar magnetic flux was found by the Drs. Marsh and Svensmark as well as by Dr. Palle and the Earthshine team. They also identified a relationship to CR from the Climax data. We will test these approaches. There are data from the IPCC report regarding the number of W/m² that are available from GHG. CO_2 is in the Infra-red range not measured by the Earthshine data. Other GHG are probably in the visible range measured by the Earthshine data (see Chapter 7). We will need to add the CO_2 W/m² to the results of the regression fit to Earthshine which will include other GHG.

Chart 5.5 demonstrates that when we use an index of Total Solar Irradiance (TSI) and CR (cosmic rays as measured by the Climax Neutron collector), major ENSO events (+/- 0.9) and other GHG at 25% of CO_2 that we can describe 79% of the changes in the Earthshine data as measured at the surface. This surface measurement is based upon the Earthshine data relating to changes in reflectivity at the 154 W/m² surface. This level is a small difference from the IPCC report. The 154 W/m² on the surface is 45% of the top of the atmosphere (after adjusting for a geometric factor and Albedo). The regression is used to forecast 2005 and 2006.

A regression fit with the AA Index and Sun Spot Count substituted for Comax has a slightly higher statistically significant fit of 86% R². This alternative will be reviewed in Chart 5.9 and in the next chapter.

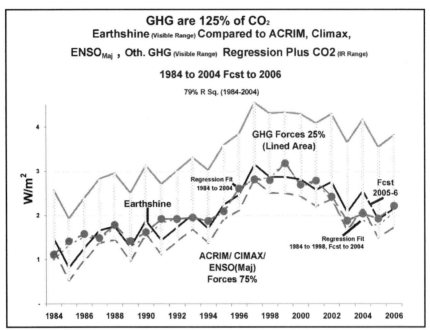

Chart 5.5: Earthshine as measured at the surface. Formula in Appendix A with comparisons to other options discussed in the chapter. Calculations are found in the website referred to in Appendix C.

The Chart 5.5 model is stable as demonstrated by a Hindcast repeatability test. The data from 1984 to 1998 were used to develop a similar regression fit and was forecast to 2006. It follows very closely the actual data and the regression fit that was developed using data from 1984 to 2004.

The regression fit has been established according to the levels of change at the surface. The surface W/m^2 as measured by the SBRN data is 14 W/m^2 lower than the IPCC report. The regression also demonstrates that the Albedo changes importantly over time. Chart 5.5a shows the differences between the IPCC report and the Earthshine regression fit. (See Appendices A and B.) Notice that CO_2 does not change much during the same period.

The Albedo or reflected short-wave and long-wave radiation occurs within the atmosphere as well as from the surface. The relatively flat line of the radiation at the top of the atmosphere does include the changes from solar radiation. The larger change is in reflectivity over this period of time.

Only 45% of the energy at the top of the atmosphere (after adjusting for the geometric factor averaged over 24 hours), and Albedo (reflection) actually strikes the surface directly or indirectly reduced by cloud cooling and precipitation. Of the total Albedo (reflectivity) change of 5.1 W/m^2, only 2.4 W/m^2 reached the surface.

Chart 5.5 uses the ACRIM TSI. The Max Planck solar regression does not provide a valid fit to Earthshine, and also does not provide a regression fit to

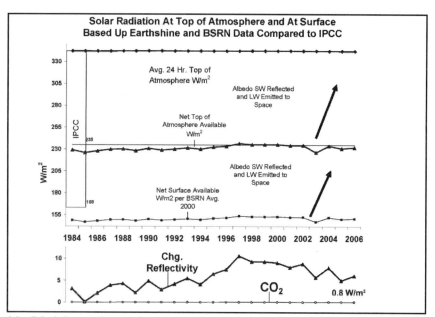

5.5a: Calculations are found in the web site referred to in Appendix C. LW is long wave (Infra-red) and SW is short wave (light and ultra-violet).

temperature that is valid. ACRIM is used for the remainder of the charts. (Appendix A provides a comparison of this model to the others models discussed in this chapter.)

Since we do not have actual measurements for the reflectivity of the earth prior to 1984, we will have to use the relationship between the Earthshine data and other datasets to create the probable reflectivity (Albedo) changes that occurred in prior years, possibly back to 1868.

There are two options for this forecast of high energy particles (CR). One regression fit is at the same levels as Climax and another at a higher, but surprising statistically significant level. Both options use the same ACRIM Solar TSI and GHG. Chart 5.6 is the projection of Earthshine Data from 1984 to 1868 showing both levels of CR.

If we compare the change in solar, natural-occurring Albedo (from CR at the same level of Climax) and GHG shown in the Earthshine regression fit to surface temperature changes, we have the results in Charts 5.8a and 5.8.

These regression fits support the following factors that change temperature:
1. The GHG energy absorbed appears influential in changes in 25% of total combined Albedo changes plus infra-red GHG.
2. The regression requires about the same cooling effects as the IPCC aerosols. Recent research from NASA has shown that 40% of the energy from increases in GHG forces is absorbed in the heat sink provided by the oceans. [R5.3b] The

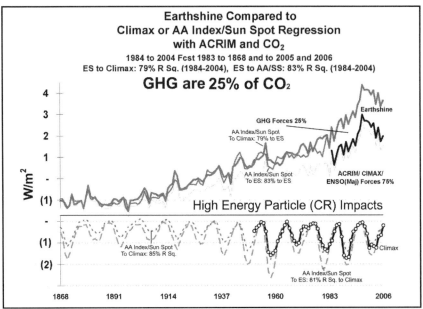

Chart 5.6 : Earthshine data as measured at the surface. The 79% R2 is the amount of the change in Earthshine data explained by the regression relationships of ACRIM solar impacts on cloud Albedo, Climax data and Other GHG from Chart 5.5. The CR impacts from Climax and two levels of forecasts from 1983 to 1868 are also shown. AA Index from: ftp://ftp.ngdc.noaa.gov/ STP/SOLAR_DATA/RELATED_INDICES/AA_INDEX/Aa_month. Sun Spot Number from: ftp://ftp.ngdc.noaa.gov/STP/SOLAR_DATA/SUNSPOT_NUMBERS/YEARLY. Formula in Appendix A. Calculations are found on the website referred to in Appendix C.

regression fit also finds that 40% of the watts associated with GHG could be absorbed by the oceans (or other cooling processes). This ocean effect represents 53% of the total aerosols in the IPCC report. If true, the absorption of these W/m^2 would most likely come from solar shorter wave-length sources. The reason is that long waves do not penetrate the oceans to any depth as they are rapidly absorbed. Determining whether the oceans are absorbing or other cooling processes are active are undetermined at this time, since the effects of this absorption will take many years to realize as the oceans have a great heat capacity.

a.   More research work is needed to understand how the ocean absorption of energy converts ultimately into surface temperature changes. This research could possibly help improve these regressions. Appendix B proposes an analysis of the impacts of the physical reality that long waves in the CO_2 range have a very limited impact upon the ocean's temperature. The analysis was able to establish a valid regression fit with 30% less GHG W/m^2 than Chart 5.8. Appendix B also provides a comparison of this model to the others models discussed in this chapter.)

b.   If true, the energy retained in the heat sink of the oceans must of course be

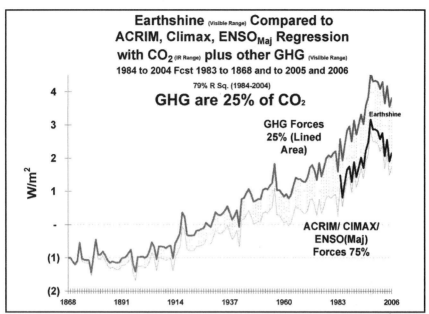

Above: Chart 5.7; Lower level of CR similar to Climax data.. Below: Chart 5.8a. The 96% R^2 is the amount of the change in global temperature explained by the regression relationships from the Earthshine data (of ACRIM solar impacts on cloud Albedo, Climax data, ENSO, Volcano, and GHG). Formula found in Appendix B. Calculations are found in the website referred to in Appendix C.

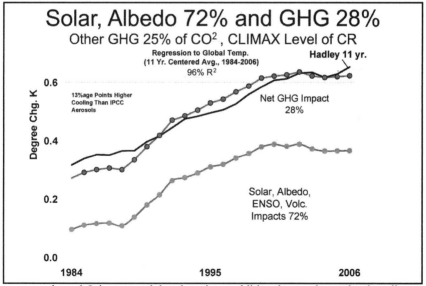

released. It is assumed that there is an additional natural, net cloud cooling at higher levels than our initial estimates that are canceling this energy source.

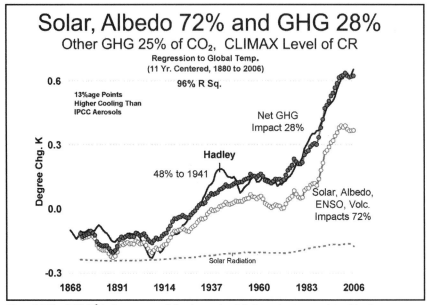

Chart 5.8 The 96% R^2 is the amount of the change in global temperature explained by the regression relationships from the Earthshine data (of ACRIM solar impacts on cloud Albedo, Climax data, ENSO, Volcano, and GHG). Calculations are found in the website referred to in Appendix C

3. The number of degrees of temperature changed by a watt of energy appears to be at a 0.24 K/W/m² as identified by Peter Dietze (Chart 5.1b).

Another research focus would be to verify that energy retransmitted to space by aerosols is as large as defined in the IPCC report.

However, when we compare Chart 5.8a, and 5.8, the impacts of GHG and other atmospheric factors such as Albedo seems to be represented within the Earthshine data as the regression results describe 96% of the changes in temperature when using this data. For these regressions about the same aerosol or cloud cooling impacts as the IPCC report are needed. (Appendix B provides a comparison of this model to the others models discussed in this chapter.)

Here is the regression result for higher levels of CR in the Earthshine Regression. These higher CR impacts support a 100% Solar regression explaining 98% of the change in temperature from 1880 to 2006 (Chart 5.9). In this chart, about the same cooling as the IPCC aerosols is needed to explain the changes.

There are questions regarding these regression fits. They do not quite follow the upward curve from 1938 to 1955 perfectly, and they do not quite follow the trend to 2006. This might be related to the effects of the ocean releasing some of the energy stored from prior years or data inaccuracies.

What have we learned so far?

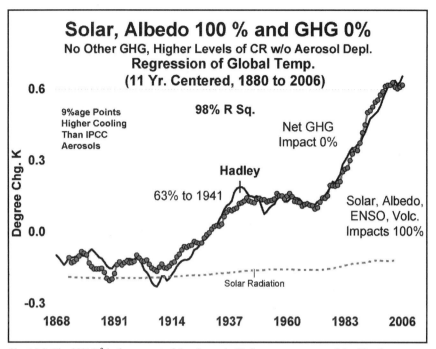

Chart 5.9: The 98% R^2 is the amount of the change in Hadley temperature explained by the regression relationships from the Earthshine data (of ACRIM solar impacts on cloud Albedo, Sun Spot/AA Index estimate of CR data, ENSO, volcano, and GHG). Formula found in Appendix B. Calculations found in the website referred to in Appendix C.

1. The temperature record has four alternative views that are not reconciled. However, the unadjusted NOAA surface data as well as the satellite data are similar to the changes in the Hadley. The Hadley has demonostrted a strong relationship to direct mesasured changes in the Earth's reflectivity (Albedo). Thus we are using the Hadley, but will test the other temperature datasets to determine whether they improve this strong relationship.
2. The solar irradiance record has two alternative views that are not reconciled, though ACRIM provides the only statistically valid relationships to the Earthshine data and temperature record.
   a. The Max Planck record, which shows relatively minor changes in solar irradiance since 1979.
   b. The ACRIM record, which shows increasing solar irradiance since 1979.
3. The sensitivity rate from watts of energy to degree changes in temperature have two alternative un-reconciled views:
   a. The IPCC report shows a range of sensitivity rates from 0.48 K/W/m^2 to 0.75 K/W/m^2.

     b. A Stefan Boltzmann factor of 0.24 K/W/m^2 for energy near the surface with a net emissivity of 77% has been proposed by Peter Dietze. This factor supports valid fits to the temperature record.

4. Two alternative views of the reflectivity of the atmosphere and surface have been proposed.

     a. The IPCC report assumes that reflectivity does not change over time and thus does not have any impact upon temperature.

     b. Six datasets from direct measurement sources demonstrate that the Albedo has changed dramatically since 1984. Four datasets demonstrate that the Albedo changes have reversed direction since 1997–1998.

        i. The Earthshine data constitute the longest dataset. As explained above, the data were adjusted for a 50% cloud cooling effect. It demonstrates a good regression fit to (1) ACRIM TSI, (2) changes in sunsports and solar magnetic flux (field) and solar dependent major ENSO events, and (3) other GHG as calculated in the IPCC report with no cooling from aerosols.

        ii. The best regression fits utilize ACRIM solar interpretation and suggest that over the period from 1984 to 2004, 25% of the changes in temperature are related to GHG and 75% are related to solar impacts on cloud Albedo and ENSO. Because the Albedo data demonstrate large changes in energy from 1984 to 2004, there is difficulty in relating varying watts of energy to static IPCC assumptions on an annual basis. (Appendices A and B provide a comparison of these model to the others models discussed in this chapter.)

5. When we related the impacts from GHG (at 125% of CO_2) and solar forces from the Earthshine data, the regressions demonstrate a strong relationship to both temperature records.

     a. Over 96% and 98% of the Global Surface changes in temperature since 1868 have been explained using the Earthshine regression relationships. One shows Solar 72% and GHG 28% impacts on temperature changes. The second excludes the GHG from the Earthshine regression and shows solar 100% and GHG 0% is a better fit to the temperature history. The temperature sensitivity factor of 0.24 deg. K/W/m^2 is also supported.

     b. Both regression fits demonstrated that the cooling levels from the IPCC report are all that is needed to balance these regressions.

     c. Additionally, IPCC proponents suggest that 40% of the GHG energy was absorbed in the heat sinks offered by the oceans in addition to the cooling from aerosols. These models only require the original cooling from the 2001 IPCC report. While the IPCC report has not been adjusted, it is apparent that the report must be adjusted to reconcile the apparent conflict.

Let's evaluate the results so far.

Chapter 6

Evaluating the Results

In order to understand these results and how they relate to other points of view, we need to use a scientific approach to keep our emotions from defining our outcomes. "Reality is" is a stark quote from St. Thomas Aquinas about truth. As we attempt to understand what "is" true, we need a method to protect us from constructing what we "wish" to be true. We need to let the truth speak to us. In the words of Albert Einstein, said as he struggled with discovering the truth: "Raffiniert ist der Herrgott, aber boshaft ist er nicht" ("God is subtle, but he is not malicious"). This quote is on a plaque at Fine Hall of Princeton University. [R6.1] If we stand detached using our scientific methods, the truth about the climate will have a chance of being revealed.

It is important that we understand all possibilities to find out if we have the "best" model for explaining the change in temperature since 1880. One way to make sure we are looking at all the possibilities is to use scientific principles to evaluate our efforts so far.

Here is one way to check our results. (Chart 6.1, below)

	YES	NO
1 Many Variables	☐	☐
2 Requires a Model	☐	☐
3 Uncompromised Data (No Gaps or Corruption)	☐	☐
4 Let the Data Choose the Model – "Best Fit"	☐	☐
4A If one Model is not the Only Possibility, Develop a Range of Outcomes that can Lead to Actionable Steps and Aid in Future Research.	☐	☐
5 Key Climate Forces Used In the Model Demonstrate that Temperature Follows (Dependent upon) Their Changes	☐	☐
5A Test to Determine that the Model "Forecasts History" Repeatably, Especially During Changes in Data Direction	☐	☐

Question 1: Yes, there is the possibility for many energy sources (or variables) to be driving the change in temperature.

Question 2:   Since the number of variables could be large, yes, a model will be necessary to evaluate which are important.

Question 3:   Are we able to work with uncompromised data, meaning no gaps or possibilities for corruption? This is a real and complex issue, but we need to be assured that we know what we are trying to explain. The answer is no, and we will have to be sure that the models we develop take the range of answers into account.

Question 4:   Yes, we are letting the data choose the model, with an approach that finds the "best fit." If we are not open to using mathematics to define the results, we will be open to emotional influences that might impair our ability to know the truth.

Question 4a: Yes, if one model is not the only possibility, we should be prepared to develop a range of possible outcomes that can lead to actionable steps and aid in future research. This point also keeps us open to the possibility of failure to get to the exact truth, but appreciative of getting closer to the truth than we were before. We might also be able to determine which opinions about reality are beyond the possibility of being correct.

Question 5:   Yes, since we are working with many variables, we must know that the key climate forcings, which mathematicians call the key variables, are independent of temperature and that they drive the change in temperature.

The major danger is to think that we have found a climate force that is driving temperature when we have actually found a set of data that seems to change in the same direction as temperature but it is actually driven by temperature or is completely unrelated to temperature.

A classic example of data that are interrelated would be to consider that there are more cases of cancer in the world and there are more people in the world. Both numbers are moving together and are highly statistically related. If we drew a conclusion from this statistical relationship, we might say that in order to eliminate cancer we need to eliminate people, but obviously we would not be truly curing cancer.

We might also consider a situation where the datasets are unrelated. For example the number of whales in the world has increased since 1980, and cancer has increased also. If we drew a strong statistical conclusion from this, we might say that we need to eliminate the whales to eliminate cancer, though the two are unrelated.

The history of science has many examples of these errors in methodology. Peter Dietze shared that even the early studies in global warming had difficulties with cause and effect. The original studies into Ice Age ice cores showed that CO_2 had increased. The original calculations used linear functions, not logarithmic, overstating the changes by a factor of 20. Additionally, the original cause and effect relationship cited was reversed, saying that CO_2 changed temperature. However, humans did not increase CO_2 during the Ice Age. The increases were caused by solar warming or cooling and changes in decay of vegetation.

All researchers are concerned to avoid these traps. In our case of trying to find an explanation for temperature change, there are only a few variables, and we can be assured that those we are considering are measured by scientists because they have important differences from each other.

If we look down the list in Chart 6.1, we will find that this last point has not been tested so far. We must realize that the atmosphere essentially is a large analogue computer. The changing forces of energy directly effect measured outputs from the atmosphere, such as temperature. In order to sort out the correct relationship between the temperature and the energy sources forcing the temperature change, we need to demonstrate to ourselves that the shape of the energy changes we select, once converted to the effects on temperature are as close as possible to the actual measured temperature measured changes. An almost identical relationship demonstrates the cause and effect connection we need in order to be certain of our conclusions. The best test we could use to make sure that we are using the correct data (or variables) that force temperature change is to test to see how well the models we create are capable of "forecasting history" repeatably as we did when we tested the regression fits for the Earthshine data.

To answer Question 5A accurately, we need to use the actual temperature data from 1880 to 1960 to develop a model. Then we can use this model to forecast the temperatures from 1961 to 2006 and check the estimated temperature against the known temperature. We would also need to develop the same relationships for 1880 to 1940, to 1950, to 1980, and to 1990. Each would be forecast to 2006. Chart 6.2 shows the results of that test for 1880 to 1960 as well as the results from tests from 1880 to 1940, 1950, 1980, and 1990. Notice that each of the regressions does forecast temperature very closely to the actual temperature line and overlaps the other forecasts.

It appears that the regression of 72% solar energy and 28% GHG. Climax level of CR is forcing the global temperature to change and is very reliable when related to global surface temperatures. If on the other hand, the forecasts for each model diverged from the actual temperature record, we would be accurate in saying that temperature does not follow the changes in the energy sources as modeled.

Another test to determine how closely the forcing energy sources as modeled demonstrate that temperature follows their influence is shown in Chart 6.2. Here we compare the regression from 1880 to 2006 to other regressions using recent years from 1940, 1950, 1960, and 1974 to 2006 projecting back to 1880. The Hindcasts overlap each other and the regression forecasts 2100 change in temperature at 0.26°K. If only GHG increase and solar forces remain the same.

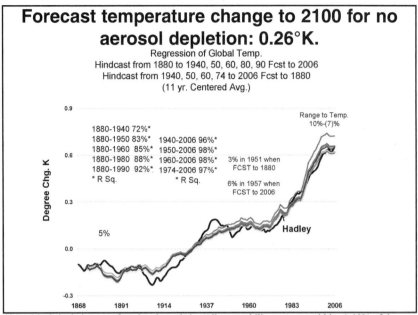

Chart 6.2: Calculations are found at the website. All repeatability tests are within +\-10% of the 2006 temperature.

Chart 6.3 shows the results from "forecasting history" (Hindcast for repeatability) of the 100% Solar and 0% GHG, Higher Level CR dataset. This regression is also reliable as predictors of temperature because the forecasts of history are close together, and do not exceed +/-10%, the range that can normally be expected. If one test predicted temperatures wider than + or -10% from the actual data, we might have questioned the importance of these forces in determining this temperature record. The Hindcast test for the periods of 1940, 1950, 1960, and 1974 to 2006 forecast to 1880 are also very close to each other. They show on a combined basis a close fit to the temperature history and forecast no temperature change to 2100.

We can safely say that we have demonstrated that the Earthshine data regression fit to the ACRIM TSI solar data, the Climax high-energy solar particles or high-level CR datasets, the IPCC levels of GHG watts, and El Niño is a direct forcing relationship.

The relationship of the Earthshine data strong fit to the temperature history found in the Hadley also demonstrates this same forcing relationship. It is additionally important to note that the Dietze-recommended Stefan Boltzmann physics law of 0.24 deg. $K/W/m^2$ is necessary to make this model successful. Another important statistical test is satisfactory. The pluses and minuses of the regression fit (residuals) when compared to the actual data are equally distributed

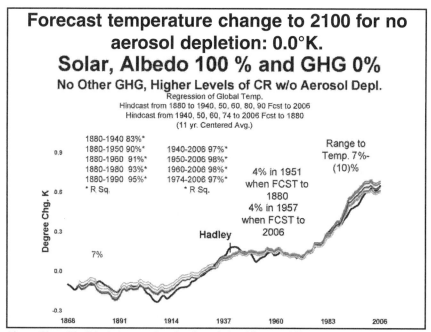

Above: Chart 6.3: Calculations are found at the website. All repeatability tests are within +/-10% of the 2006 regression.

and do not trend higher or lower than the temperature data. However, the periods from 1939 to 1955 and from 1880 to 1902 have the least precise fit to the historic temperature through the higher level of CR have the best fit during this period.

There are several speculative points regarding these periods that require more research.

a. The Climax Neutron Counter data on solar high-energy particle activity was available only from 1951 to 2006. The forecast of CR using AAIndex/Sun Spot Number have two levels, but do not explain the gap from 1939 to 1955 and during the 1880 to 1902 period. Appendix A discusses the relationship of the Climax data to Solar TSI. There is also a quantification of the missing data that might explain the gaps.

b. The estimates used to adjust temperature datasets, Solar TSI, or other energy sources have random errors that might explain these differences, given the level of uncertainty about historic datasets.

c. The heat sink of the oceans might have been releasing its energy during these periods. However, the fit in the current period do not leave much evidence for additional heat coming from the oceans.

d. These are, possibly, periods in which aerosols were depleted from the atmosphere at higher rates than other periods. This last point is highly speculative since the data on human-created aerosols focuses upon the period after

1960. The two primary periods in question are prior to 1960. Again, the fit to the current period does not leave much evidence of high aerosol depletion as expected in the IPCC report.

The above regression fits of the Earthshine datasets to the Hadley are not the only possibilities that can best optimize the limited data available. This approach was used on the temperature datasets of the NOAA Global Surface, the Satellite-Land-Ocean, and well as the Land-Ocean Index with no valid relationships developed to the Earthshine data at the Climax level of CR or the higher CR levels. A Satellite-Hadley temperature dataset did have valid relationships similar to the current. Additionally, it is important to note also that the Max Planck solar dataset did not create any fits that passed the Hindcast repeatability tests. The Max Planck solar data will be used only for the IPCC regression fits in Chapter 7. (See

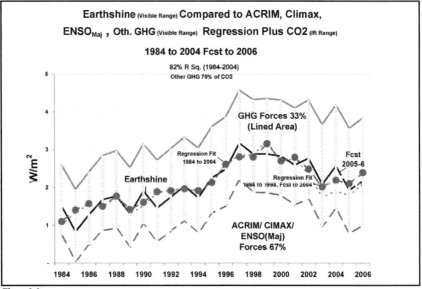

Chart 6.4.

Appendix B for details.) There are, though, three other options with enhanced GHG at higher levels than the above model. GHG at 70% enhanced levels produces an 82% R squared to the Earthshine data (Chart 6.4). The regression fits with GHG at 70% enhanced levels that are without or with IPCC levels of accelerted aerosol depletion assumptions pass the Hindcast (repeatability) test when using the ACRIM solar data, but are no different from each other as both forecast a change in 2100 of 0.36°K without aerosol depletion and 0.32°K with aerosol depletion, assuming no change in solar intensity. (Chart 6.5 and 6.5a for IPCC aerosol depletion.)

High aerosol depletion at 70% Enh. GHG is capable of passing the Hindcast test and is shown in Chart 6.6 and Chart 6.6a. The regression fit forecasts 2100

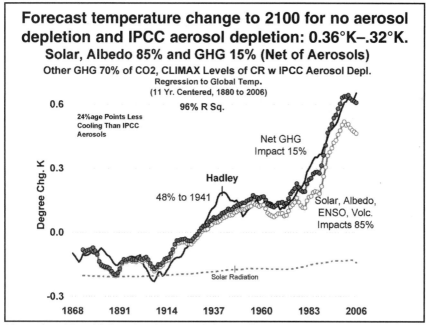

Above: chart 6.5, and, below, chart 6.5a.. Calculations are found at the website.

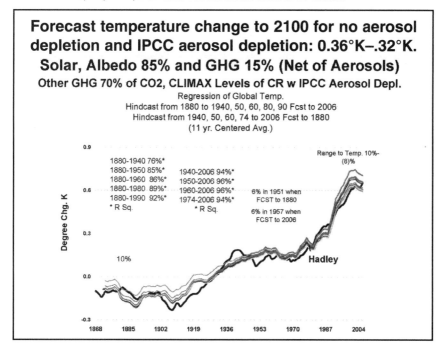

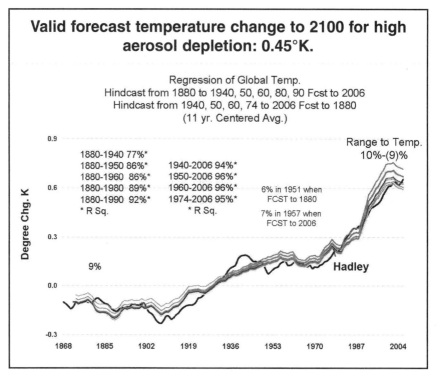

Chart 6.6 (above) and Chart 6.6a (below): Calculations are found at the website.

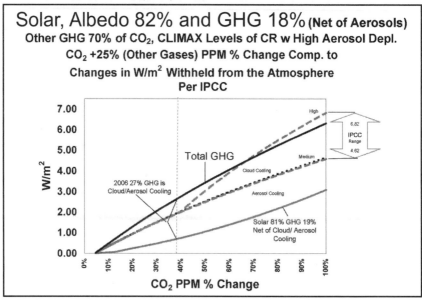

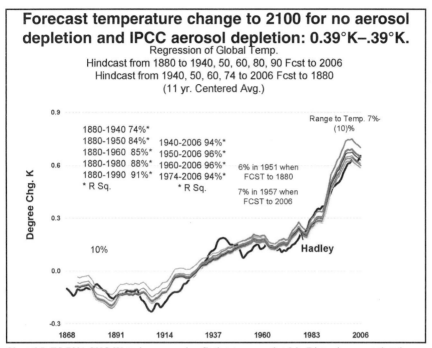

Chart 6.7: ES 70% GHG Watts is a regression fit that assumes that Mr. Dietze is correct that the IPCC GHG absorbed watts are overstated. The explanation can be found in the next chapter. Additional scenarios were reviewed and are available in Appendix B.

temperature to 0.45°K. To understand the concept that aerosols are "cloaking" the true warming effects of GHG, Chart 6.6a shows the relative levels of GHG assumed in the forecast compared to the IPCC range. It also shows the cooling from clouds and aerosols. Warming increases after 2006 at an increasing rate as the aerosols are more rapidly depleted from the atmosphere verses GHG. The same chart, with lower numbers, would show a similar increasing trend. (This chart is also available through the website.) However, it is not possible to discriminate between a 70% other GHG with or without rapid depletion of aerosols as both forecast about the same increase in temperature to 2100. Chart 6.6 with 70% Enh.GHG/high aerosol depletion forecasts a higher temperature in 2100 by 0.09°.

A case for other GHG at 85% without aerosol depletion does produce a valid fit, and it forecasts 0.39°K change to 2100, only six-hundredths of a degree different from the 70% Enh. GHG/high aerosol depletion in the assumptions. (Chart 6.7 compared to Chart 6.6) On the other hand, high aerosol depletion at the 85% level, produces an *invalid* forecast of 0.57°K. (Chart 6.8) Thus it is very questionable whether a case can be developed that substantiates the extraordinary increases in temperature of double digits that the IPCC report suggests because the temperature is also being forced to change from solar generated natural causes.

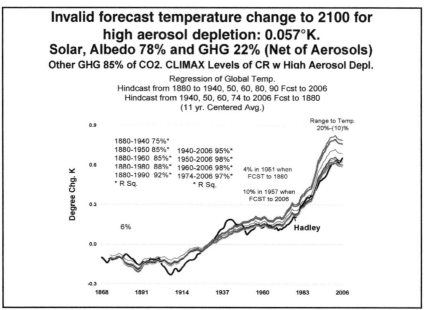

Above: Chart 6.8; below: Chart 6.9.

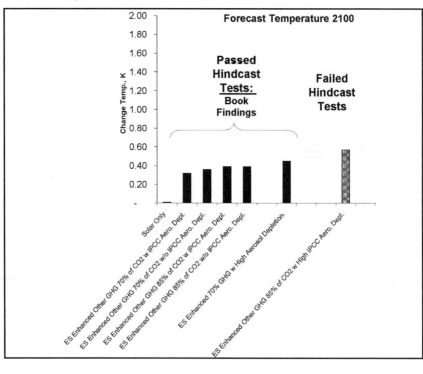

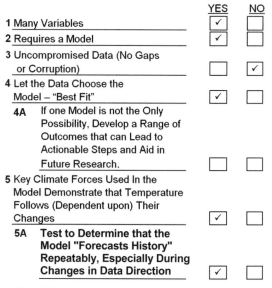

Chart 6.10.

If we summarize the results of these tests, we see that there are several major possible forecasts for the year 2100. None of them comes close to the double-digit changes that the IPCC report contains. Those that are the highest cannot pass a Hindcast (repeatability or forecast of history) test. The failures are quite large especially when we tried to develop regressions with 85% enhanced GHG and rapid depletion of aerosols. Chart 6.9 summarizes the results.

Since we have completed all the items on our checklist that we can do for these variables, let's fill out the checklist: with the previous responses and a "Yes" in 5A. (Chart 6.10)

This is a very good result for determining the driving forces for the Hadley. However, we know there are other views about the key energy sources that force temperature change, and we know that the model we developed is not "perfect."

It is in our best interest to understand those other views to make sure we are not missing something. We will not check question 4A until we have reviewed the other perspectives.

We also can use this checklist to evaluate the other points of view to determine if there is something that we should add to our point of view. On the other hand, if we find limitations with the other points of view, we will have a way to define the issues we discover. That way, we will not be telling someone we don't like their point of view; we will be able to discuss the deficiencies we find in those results, separate from the person. A lot of protracted arguments have been avoided by this type of detachment and is one of the centerpieces to the success of the scientific method.

Chapter 7

Alternative View by IPCC

The IPCC report has the view that the change in global surface temperature can be explained by the increase in absorption of irradiated energy by CO_2 and other "greenhouse" gases (GHG). There are other sources of absorbed energy and some gases that are cooling. To represent the changes in energy absorbed, the IPCC report developed the following bar chart (Chart 7.1a).

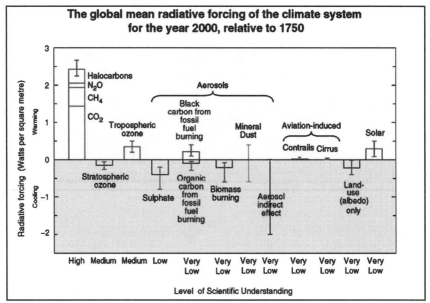

Chart 7.1a: IPCC report bar chart of energy changes from 1750 to 2000 found at: http://www.grida.no/climate/ipcc_tar/wg1/006.htm.

As we read across the bar chart for the changes from 1750 to 2000, it becomes very obvious that there are three areas of interest (Chart 7.1b). The first area is the increased energy absorption from not only CO_2 but from other GHG. The second area has a very low scientific understanding and has important levels of cooling from something called "aerosols." Highlighted atmospheric agents in this category are sulfur dioxides from burning coal and oil plus the effect of clouds. The last area of interest is that the solar force is only the change in radiation, and it is quite small, about 0.3 W/m^2 not the 0.5 from our model in Chapter 5. The effects from the 4.6 W/m^2 at the surface changes in reflectivity, called the Albedo, are missing.

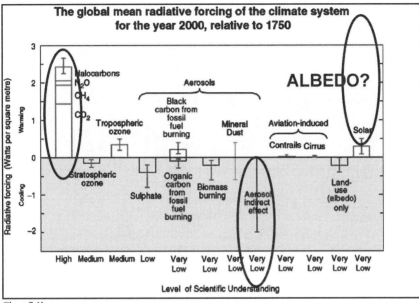

Chart 7.1b.

Of interest should be the rating of the level of scientific understanding. Only the GHG bar is listed as being high. All others, including the solar, are listed as being very low.

When we add the total positives and negatives from this bar chart, the total is 0.83 W/m^2. Temperature has increased about 0.6° K. This is a very high 0.76° K per Watt ratio. Another chart put together by a Dr. Hansen of NASA [R7.1] totals to 2.0 W/m^2 for a temperature change of 0.6° K, and a ratio of 0.34. This chart also does not recognize the change in Albedo (reflectivity of the earth) that was very important to the results of our first model. It is clear that the sensitivity factor is not very consistent.

In a different article referred to in Chapter 4, [R5.2] Dr. Hansen said that the sensitivity for CO_2 is 0.75° K/W/m^2; most recently, the sensitivity was adjusted to 0.67° K/W/m^2 [R5.3a].

Let's understand the reason that the Chart 7.1 Level of Scientific Understanding for GHG is listed as being "high." Researchers have been working on the absorption of various gases in the atmosphere for almost a century. They have developed the data shown in Chart 7.2 of the average absorption of the sun's irradiation for the full radiation spectrum from the sun. The bands of absorption of light by different gases are developed from spectroscopes. This chart should be treated as a representation because there are differing charts available. For our purposes, it is sufficiently accurate.

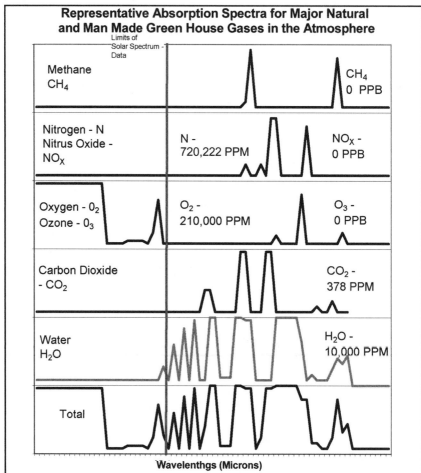

Chart 7.2: Adapted from spectroscopes charts. PPM refers to parts per million and PPB is parts per billion.

The critical "greenhouse gases" are listed in Chart 7.2 with the bands of infrared that they absorb. Also listed is the amount of these gases found in the atmosphere. Each spike indicates the light band that the gas absorbs. There are only a few key bands that are related to GHG.

The effective bands that are related to CO_2, ozone, and methane are shown in Chart 7.3. The primary CO_2 middle band is clipped by water vapor about 30%.

Quite a lot of news has referred to the GHG. Please note that *water vapor is the primary GHG* and that it interferes with methane, NO_x, and CO_2. The gaps in

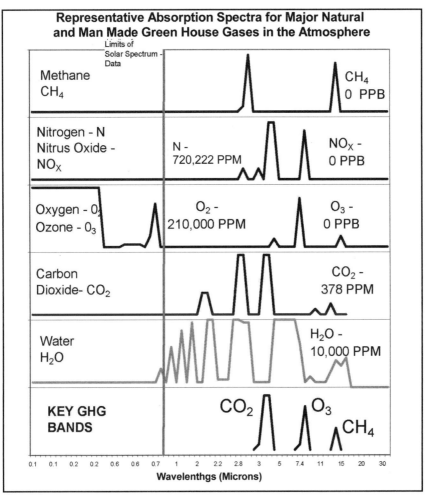

Chart 7.3.

the water-vapor absorption spectrum allow part of one of the CO_2 bands, one of the ozone, and one of the methane bands to absorb without interaction with changes in water vapor.

When we look at Chart 7.4, which is the average IR emission spectrum of the Earth for clear-sky conditions, measured by satellite, we see the CO_2 funnel. The total mean global emissions under the saw-toothed line are 240 W/m^2 when we include the absorption of CO_2, O_3, CH_4, and H_2O.

The amount of absorbed radiation by CO_2 is about 74 W/m^2, but 50% is retransmitted to space; thus 37 W/m^2 is available to the atmosphere in the IPCC report at 360 ppm. The IPCC report did not take into consideration any water vapor overlap. If this overlap had been taken into consideration, the number would have been 27 W/m².

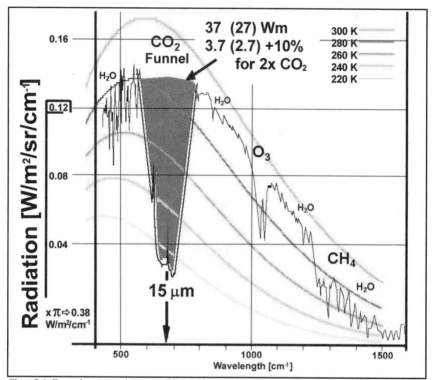

Chart 7.4: From the personal papers of Peter Dietze, this chart is based upon satellite images and is found at http://www.john-daly.com/forcing/ moderr.htm, Funnel calculations by Peter Dietze, printed with permission.

Now for the interesting part. The change in the amount of CO_2 has increased since 1750 from a base level of 270 ppm to 378 ppm in 2004, according to the observatory at Mauna Loa. Those scientists who are interested in the absorption of CO_2 have calculated what would happen if the CO_2 increased to twice the beginning amount of 270 ppm. The 2005 and 2006 data have not been published.

The 270 ppm is considered the beginning of the industrial era. Any increase in the CO_2 or other GHG is considered to be caused by humans. If the CO_2 doubles, increasing to 540 ppm, the calculations would indicate an increase in the W/m² by about 10%. That is the small line (arrow) outside the funnel, which shows the 10% increase. If we follow the concepts developed by the IPCC report, that there is no water vapor overlap in these CO_2 bands, then the W/m² would increase by 3.7. If water vapor overlap is considered, the W/m² would increase by 2.7.

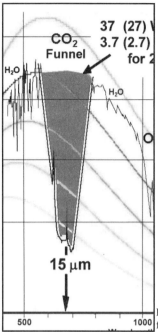

37 (27)
CO_2 3.7 (2.7)
Funnel for 2
H_2O
H_2O
O
15 µm
500 1000

The accompanying chart is an "average" generated from a blending of the results from sites at various latitudes. There is a striking difference between the Arctic and the equator.

If we superimpose the Arctic and tropical charts over the "average," the breadth of differences will be more obvious and will help us understand the difficulty in developing an "average." This average is from the MODTRAN Infrared Radiation Code at the University of Chicago, produced by Dr. D. and Mrs. J. Archer (Chart 7.5).

There is a negligible difference between the two average lines from Charts 7.4 and 7.5.

Chart 7.4 was completed to show you that there is a component of the CO_2 band that is also responsive to water. The IPCC 1994 report assumed no water vapor absorbing in the CO_2 bands and is not charted in the 2001 report (Chart 7.6).

Left: Chart 7.4 detail. Below: Chart 7.5: Source MODTRAN from http://geosci.uchicago.edu/~archer/cgimodels/radiation.html.

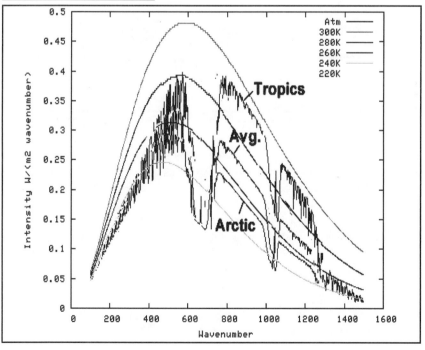

Tropics
Avg.
Arctic

Atm ———
300K ———
280K ———
260K ———
240K ———
220K ———

Intensity W/(m2 wavenumber)

Wavenumber

You probably have realized that we have moved to almost 40% of the doubling number (118 ppm since the industrial era began divided by 270 at the beginning of the industrial era). Notice anything unusual when you look outside, other than the weather forecasts are wrong 50% of the time, though showing signs of getting better? Now we will have to discuss another critical point.

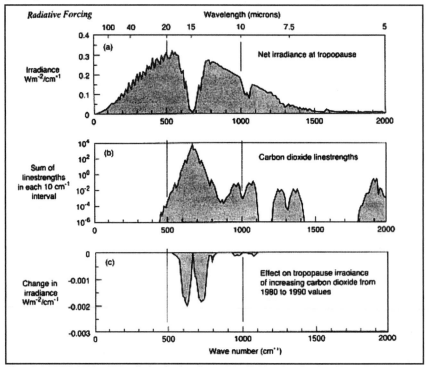

Chart 7.6: IPCC 1994 p.175 radiative forcing figure 4.1.gif. Also found at http://www.john-daly.com/forcing/moderr.htm.

The rise in CO_2 is not a straight-line relationship to the number of watts/m² that is withheld. The absorption curve for increasing CO_2 follows a decreasing (i.e., logarithmic) rate of change.

The formula is contained in the following excerpt from the IPCC report (Chart 7.7): For CO_2 doubling from 270 to 540 ppm, the absorbed W/m² increased by 7.4 W/m², but 50% (less an additional 30% for water vapor overlap) or 2.7 W/m² is withheld from forcing changes in the climate. The next doubling from 540 to 1080 is two times the 270 ppm or 200% increase, but only yields 3.7 W/m² or 137% additional forcing, if we assume no higher amounts of water vapor overlap these frequencies.

A chart showing this absorption of infrared energy is shown in Chart 7.8. This is anticipated to hold true for O_3, and CH_4.

Table 6.2: *Simplified expressions for calculation of radiative forcing due to CO_2, CH_4, N_2O, and halocarbons. The first row for CO_2 lists an expression with a form similar to IPCC (1990) but with newer values of the constants. The second row for CO_2 is a more complete and updated expression similar in form to that of Shi (1992). The third row expression for CO_2 is from WMO (1999), based in turn on Hansen et al. (1988).*

Trace gas	Simplified expression Radiative forcing, ΔF (Wm^{-2})	Constants
CO_2	$\Delta F = \alpha \ln(C/C_0)$	$\alpha = 5.35$
	$\Delta F = \alpha \ln(C/C_0) + \beta (\sqrt{C} - \sqrt{C_0})$	$\alpha = 4.841$, $\beta = 0.0906$
	$\Delta F = \alpha (g(C) - g(C_0))$ where $g(C) = \ln(1 + 1.2C + 0.005C^2 + 1.4 \times 10^{-6}C^3)$	$\alpha = 3.35$

Chart 7.7: From the IPCC report.

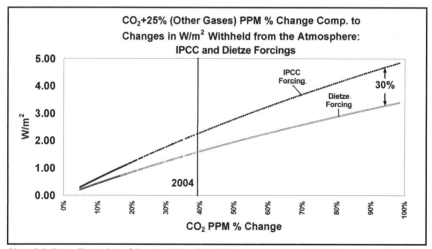

Chart 7.8: For a discussion of the actual data for 1950 to present, go to http://cdiac.esd.ornl.gov/trends/co2/sio-mlo.htm. Actual CO2 data from 1950 to 2003 is available from: ftp://cdiac.esd.ornl.gov/pub/maunaloa-co2/maunaloa.co2.

Before concluding the discussion on the energy sources, we need to discuss large countervailing forces at work that have kept the temperature under control according to the IPCC report as shown in Chart 7.1. The most important one has been the aerosols (sulfur from burning coal and oil). While the increase in CO_2

has some large impacts, according to the IPCC report, the aerosols have partly balanced their impact, thus were used to make up for the non-observed but asserted high-temperature increments.

It is interesting that the IPCC report does not recommend increasing sulfur-dioxide emissions as a means of controlling temperature, since in the reports' authors' minds this is a scientifically justified approach. The issue of our health could certainly be a reasonable defense of not raising this point. This is not said for any other purpose than to say that the IPCC report has other ways to solve the problem.

The next real issue is the forecast for CO_2. To be able to understand this issue, we need to be able to calculate the amount of CO_2 that is in the atmosphere from the emissions that the IPCC report calls "anthropogenic," or caused by human activities (Chart 7.9).

This is another area where the IPCC report has important confusion. But we need to begin with the basics. The parts per million (ppm) levels for CO_2 in 1880 are thought to be 280 ppm. There are some historic ice-core samples that show a level of CO_2 between 240 and 280. The emissions of CO_2 from various sources

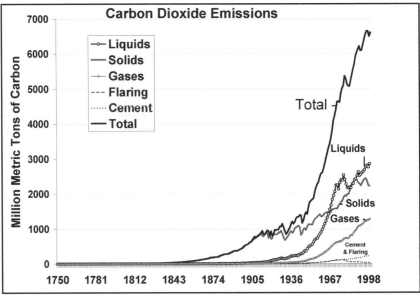

Chart 7.9 Data plotted from: http://cdiac.esd.ornl.gov/ftp/fossilfuel-co2-emissions/global.1751_2004.ems.

are shown in Chart 7.9. The five sources are solids (coal), liquids (gas, diesel), gases, flaring (from oil wells, pipelines, and sewage/land-fill sites), and cement plants.

An additional source is the natural sources from bio-decay and forest fires, which have their own line in this dataset starting in 1880, though a very low amount, which does not show on the chart below. There are no numbers for the tons of emissions from natural sources prior to 1880. This should also be of concern because so much, literally, is dependent upon these numbers.

Now, how do you calculate the ppm these gigatons of emission create over time? We will have to develop a way to understand the process of the leaching of CO_2 from the air to the sea and bio-mass (plants and trees).

The important point is to understand how long CO_2 stays in the atmosphere. The IPCC report has a calculation that seems to indicate that CO_2 remains in the atmosphere for over 500 years, though the discussion from the document asserts 120 years.

Peter Dietze developed a model using the principles from the half-life decay of radioactive materials, defining the time the CO_2 remains in the atmosphere in half lives. He calculates the number to be closer to 50% being leached from the atmosphere in 38 years. For those who wish to calculate this number for themselves, please go to the book's website and download the spreadsheet titled "Emissions.xls." In general, the formula is an exponential calculation. Another method similar to Peter Dietze's was developed by this author. The model found that 50% of the CO_2 Emissions from a specific year are leached from the atmosphere in 52 years. This model was used to estimate how much naturally occurring CO_2 had to be emitted during the pre-industrial era to realize the ppm numbers for those years. The model then is used to calculate the ppm that will occur if the

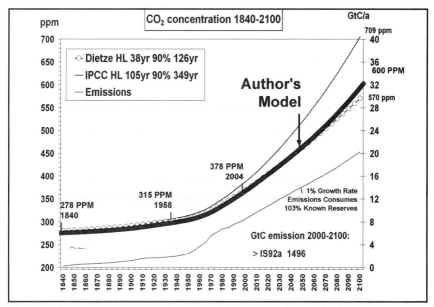

Chart 7.10: from Peter Dietze personal papers reprinted with permission. Also found at http://www.john-daly.com/dietze/cmodcalc.htm. Author's model calculations available at website.

assumptions of the IPCC report are correct. The same method was used to evaluate the high ppm numbers forecast in the IPCC report.

In Chart 7.10 we have plotted how the 1840–2004 historic and 2005–2100 forecast CO_2 emission has been related to the resulting ppm of CO_2 in the atmosphere. The historic and forecast from the above model is marked.

The actual data result for 1840–1880 are about 280 ppm; the actual data result for 1958, the first year of the Mauna Loa CO_2 dataset is 315 ppm. And the recently released data for 2004 are 378 ppm. The interesting point is that the historic calculations by Peter Dietze, as a reviewer of the IPCC report in 2001 and the author's model are both lower than the IPCC report and match history closely.

If the author's model is used to forecast the IPCC levels, in order for this forecast to reach the levels in the charts, the IPCC levels of atmospheric CO_2 would have to be 398 ppm in 2004, eleven years ahead of the Dietze and author's model. The IPCC report forecast assumptions do not reproduce historic levels (Chart 7.11).

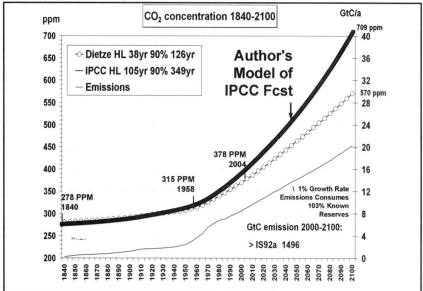

Chart 7.11 from Peter Dietze personal papers reprinted with permission. Also found at http://www.john-daly.com/dietze/cmodcalc.htm Author's model calculations available at website.

In Chart 7.12 we see the comparison for the years 1955 to 2020.

The point that is most compelling is that this IPCC forecast of emissions is 1492 GtC, 103% of the known fossil fuel reserves left on the earth over the next 100 years. Given the emissions that the report forecasts, the expected residual CO_2 ppm is overstated by more than 70% the change from 2004 of a realistic ppm estimate.

Furthermore, the forecast emissions are growing at 1% per year in the above

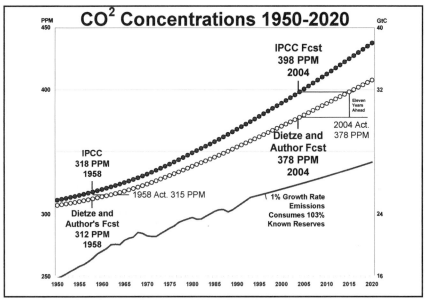

Above: Chart 7.12 is Chart 7.11 for 1955 to 2020. Below: Chart 7.13.

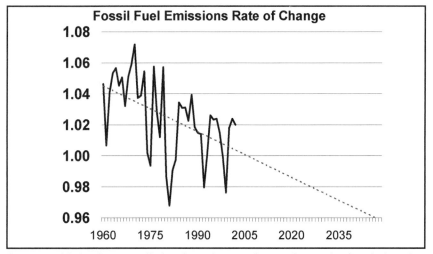

forecast. This is also unrealistic, since the actual rate of growth of emissions has been declining since 1960. Chart 7.13 has the actual rates of growth.

The reason the rate of growth has been declining is that the world manufacturers and transportation vehicles are becoming more efficient. The total per-capita usage of fossil fuels has been level for quite a few years at 1.8% in the 1970s to 1.2% per year now. (Chart 7.14). What is the correct amount of emissions to forecast?

Recent increases in gasoline prices and the resulting decrease in demand demonstrate that the use of fossil fuels will decline as the price increases. A better forecast, though aggressive, would be an annual increase rate of 0.5% shown in Chart 7.15.

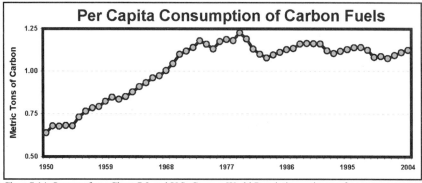

Chart 7.14: Sources from Chart 7.9 and U.S. Census, World Population estimates from http://www.census.gov/ipc/prod/wp02/tabA-01.csv.

This rate is probably too high in the later years because increased prices that will take place as reserves are depleted will support changes to other sources. The reduced forecast achieves 13 GtC/a from a base of 8 GtC/a as opposed to the IPCC forecast of 20 GtC/a. The IPCC report overstates the probable worst case emissions

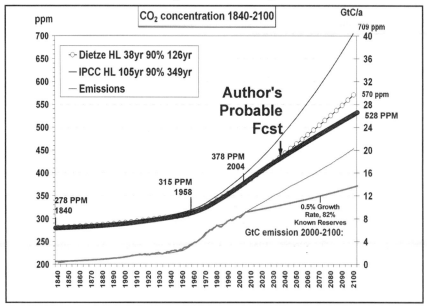

Chart 7.15 Author's model calculations available at website.

by 2.5 times. The IPCC report also overstates the likely worst case change in ppm by 2 times when compared to forecasts that closely follow historic changes.

Emissions will forecast an atmospheric accumulation of about 528 ppm, and for forecast purposes, we should grant perhaps a doubling of CO_2 from 1750 levels to 540 ppm. This consumes 82% of the known fossil fuel reserves. The Dietze and IPCC models have not been changed for comparison purposes (Chart 7.15).

Three fundamental concerns arise in understanding the IPCC report regarding emissions of CO_2:

1. The IPCC report does not match the actual historic ppm, exceeding the historic experience by 11 years when forecasting the first four years from 2000 to 2004.
2. Since the IPCC models do not match history, the forecast worst-case ppm is too high by 30% when compared to models that do match history.
3. The forecast of emissions is very aggressive, predicting the consumption of a large portion of total reserves in the next 100 years, when the actual rate of consumption has been declining. The IPCC report forecasts increases in worst-case emissions that are probably overstated by 60%.

In order to understand the meaning of these results, we need to review the forecasts for emissions and the resulting increases in CO_2 ppm from the IPCC report (Chart 7.16).

Since Dietze's and the author's forecasts of the probable GHG ppm are lower than the lowest forecast in the IPCC report, this means all of the high forecasts for Forcing Watts from the IPCC report are unlikely (Chart 7.17).

And since the extraordinary Forcing Watts are unlikely, none of these forecasts for temperature are probable (Chart 7.18).

How well does this temperature forecast match history? The IPCC historic models have divided the energy sources for temperature change into two groups. The first group is the naturally occurring changes in energy (or forces in the language of climate scientists) here shown in Chart 7.19. The lines around the temperature line are the various models of different natural sources of energy. The Hadley 11-year centered average global surface temperature is plotted over this temperature line. The 11-year centered averages of solar irradiance, ENSO (El Niño) index, and volcano impacts from the model listed below are also plotted over this group of IPCC model lines.

The difference between the IPCC lines and the data used in the model from Chapters 5 and 6 appears only to be in the years from 1980 to the present. The data used in the models in this book appear to have a slight upward trend vs. the IPCC models, which appear to be trending slightly downward. It is difficult to determine how much difference there is because the band of possible IPCC lines is quite wide. The most that the book's data exceed the range in the IPCC data is about 0.05° K.

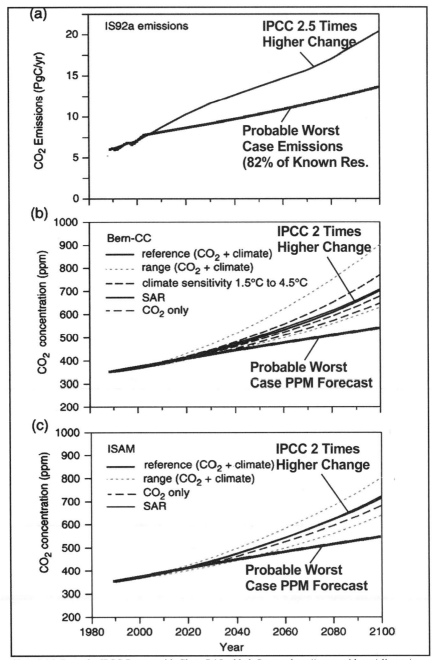

Chart 7.16: From the IPCC Report with Chart 7.15 added. Source: http://www.grida.no/climate/ipcc_tar/wg1/122.htm.

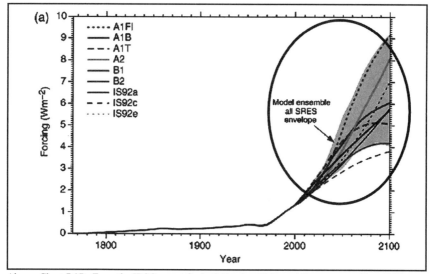

Above: Chart 7.17: From the IPCC report for both Forcing Watts and Temperature, Chart 7.17: http://www.grida.no/climate/ipcc_tar/wg1/353.htm. Below: Chart 7.18.

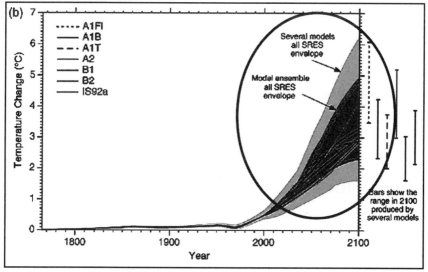

The GHG models from the IPCC report are shown in Chart 7.20. The same temperature line is also plotted over the IPCC lines. The GHG model that uses the formula from the IPCC report is plotted over the IPCC lines. This line is a net number that takes into effect the increases in energy from GHG absorption as well as the net cooling from aerosols. It appears to remain within the bands of the IPCC report.

When these two sets of data are combined by the IPCC and the book's model, the two appear to coincide, as we see in Chart 7.21. Notice, though, that the model changes direction with the temperature record from 1998 to 2006.

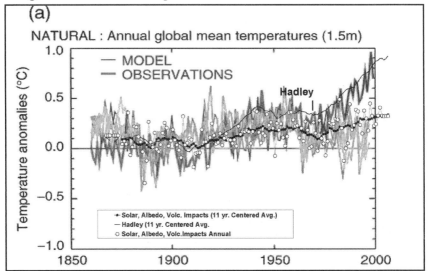

Above: Chart 7.19: Charts 7.19 to 7.21 are from the IPCC report at: http://www.grida.no/climate/ipcc_tar/wg1/450.htm#fig127. The regression formula is in the appendix. Calculations are available at the website. Below: Chart 7.20.

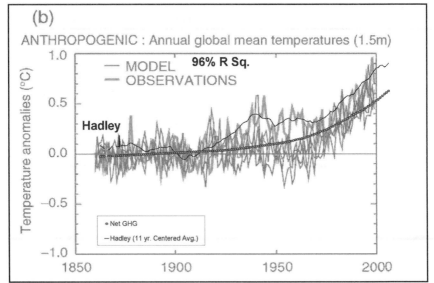

The same question arises when we attempt to use CO_2 to forecast a direction change in temperature. There are no dips in the historic data for the GHG, as seen

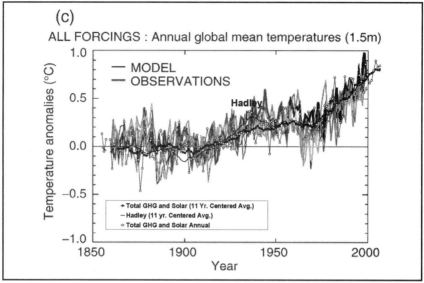

Chart 7.21 Plotted similarly to the IPCC report.

in Chart 7.20. Therefore, the model can't follow history. This raises a central issue. In order to predict temperature, the energy drivers have to demonstrate that the changes in temperature follow their changes, or there is a serious question with the model that is used. We saw that global temperatures followed our solar and GHG regressions "very" well, especially during turns in the temperature history. This demonstrates that solar forcings are the main drivers of temperature change.

Conversely, GHG history *cannot* demonstrate that it is the key driver of temperature change, since temperature does not seem to change *direction* as it changes. The models using GHG can give interesting statistical relationship to the data, but the "visual fit" has important gaps as one can see in Charts 7.22, 7.23, and 7.23a.

The best way to demonstrate the fact that GHG do not primarily drive temperature is to test how well the model forecasts history. Chart 7.22 can only explain 38% of the change in 1941. Chart 7.23 shows that several of the forecasts are extraordinarily higher forecasts than actual and appear to be "hockey sticks." These abrupt departures from the actual temperature demonstrate that there is a poor relationship between GHG and temperature, since temperature does not follow the changes of GHG. In fact, the change in temperature should be 1.03° K if the forecast were correct, not the 0.65° K of today.

Similarly, when we compare the results from Chart 5.8 or Chart 5.9 to the IPCC fit with 2006 estimates, notice that the global-warming forecast (in Chart 7.24) does not change directions as does the Chart 5.8 or Chart 5.9 using the Earthshine data.

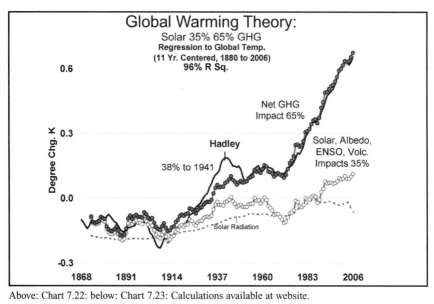

Above: Chart 7.22: below: Chart 7.23: Calculations available at website.

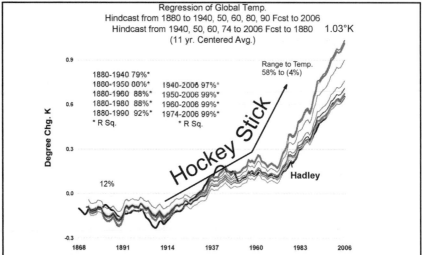

As we forecast forward with these models, Chart 7.24 shows that the other IPCC high forecasts are probably based upon invalid statistical relationships.

It is evident that there has not been a large increase in the temperature. We have experienced hail and snow close to the latest dates in history in some places during May 2005. Two men attempted a trek across the Arctic Sea on May 10, 2005, to bring attention to global warming, but canceled the trip on June 3, 2005, because of the severe ice and snow conditions, according to a spokesperson from

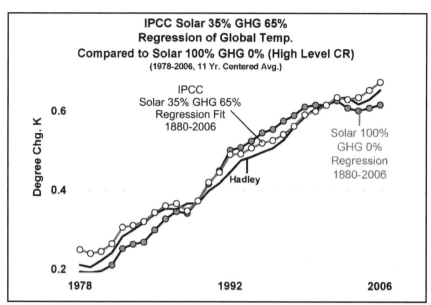

Chart 7.23a: Calculations available at website.

Greenpeace, which co-sponsored the trip. [R7.2] Alaska had record low temperatures in November and December 2005. February 2006 also had record lows in Houston, Texas.

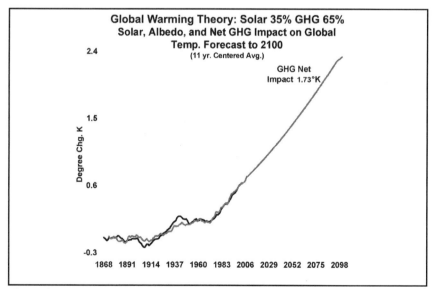

Above: Chart 7.24: Author's model calculations available at website.

Implicit in the forecast is an accentuation of the temperature increase because of the rapid depletion of aerosols when compared to GHG, as shown in Chart 7.24a. Of interest are the small amounts of change due to the rapid depletion of aerosols. The number is large in relationship to GHG, but when compared to the 11.2 W/m^2 total cooling from natural and human aerosols found in the Earthshine data, the changes are minor.

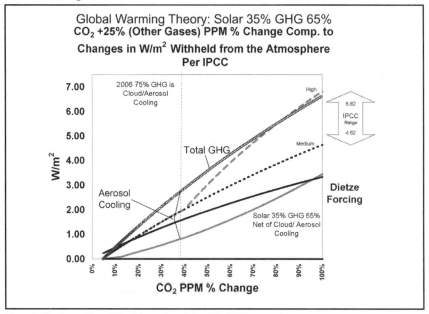

Chart 7.24a: From Chart 7.8 with results of the 67% GHG regression.

Here is this invalid global-warming forecast from Chart 7.24 in comparison to others in the IPCC report. (Chart 7.25.)

Perhaps you are wondering about the possibility that while the IPCC report might need to be adjusted, the increase in GHG primarily is causing the changes in the Albedo (or reflectivity) by affecting cloud formations. *While this point of view is quite scientifically unfounded, we still can test its validity from a statistical point of view.* A lower statistical relationship can be developed with the Earthshine Albedo changes, as seen in Chart 7.26. However, it should be noted that the model does not show a decline from 1998 to 2006. The only change in direction in this regression fit comes from the naturally occurring solar changes in CR.

This GHG Earthshine model is similar to the solar Earthshine model used in Chapters 5 and 6, with GHG substituted for Solar TSI. The model has the same credibility concerns as direct GHG, including extraordinarily over-forecasts of history and not fitting to the temperature data. (Chart 7.27)

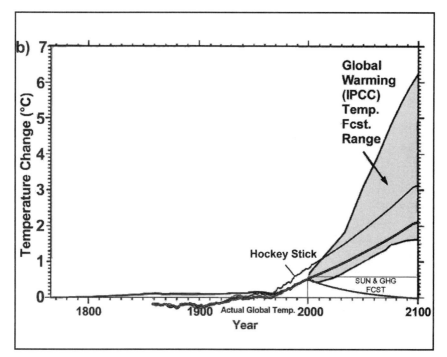

Above: Chart 7.25: combination of 7.18 and 7.24. Below: Chart 7.26: GHG substituted for Solar

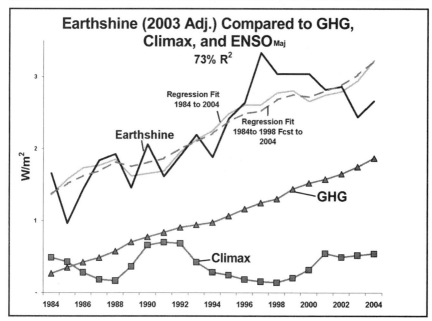

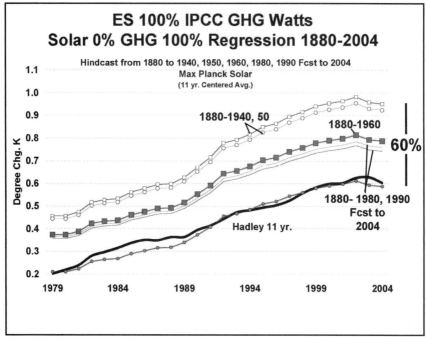

Chart 7.27: GHG substituted for Solar TSI.

In principle, then, the IPCC report demonstrates that:

1. Temperature does *not* follow the GHG radiative forces as modeled, especially during recent years when the impact of GHG was at its peak. The regressions also demonstrate statistical reliability problems that should have been readily observed by the IPCC researchers.

    a   The model does not match historic changes in temperature, especially during the period from 1930 to 1970. (Chart 7.22)

    b.   The 1880 to 1940, 1950, 1960, 1980, and 1990 regression fits are a "hockey stick," forecasting above the historic temperature record by a significant error factor. (Chart 7.23)

    c.   The model does not change directions after 1998 to reflect the downturn in temperature. (Chart 7.23b)

2   Global-warming models do *not* demonstrate a careful analysis of fit of GHG to historic data in:

    a. CO_2 absorption is overstated by 30% because it does not take into consideration the water vapor overlap. (Chart 7.11)

   b. CO_2 emissions sensitivity to worst-case ppm is overstated by 2 times
       when compared to models that do match history.

   c, Other GHG are assumed to follow CO_2 and thus have the failures of the
       above two points.

   d. Forecasts of worst-case emissions are probably overstated by 2.5 times.
       (Chart 7.15)

3. The assumptions made about aerosols are at best guesses. This may have
    diverted attention away from other radiative sources that can demonstrate a
    high degree of fit to historic data and thus reliability.

   a. All of the extraordinary forecasts assume that the aerosols will be
       depleted from the atmosphere at much faster rates than GHG. As we
       have proven in Chapter 6, all the regression fits that included High accel-
       erated depletion of aerosols proved to fail the Hindcast repeatability tests
       and could show no difference to models without accelerated aerosol
       depletion nor forecast the IPCC double-digit temperature changes in

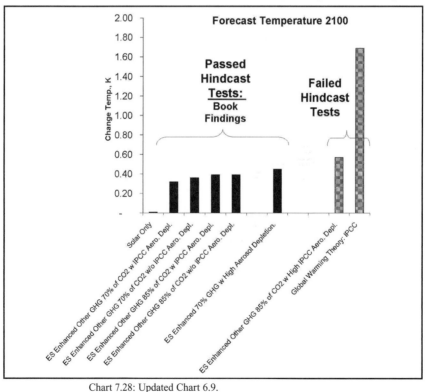

Chart 7.28: Updated Chart 6.9.

2100. Similarly, the global-warming models from this chapter have also failed these same Hindcast tests. (Updated here in Chart 7.28.) Additionally, these model show that the aerosol estimates are overstated. The fits do not require different assumptions about the amount of watts from GHG being canceled by aerosols. Furthermore, the changes in GHG would not better match the decline in temperature since 1998 if the aerosols were being leached from the atmosphere at a faster rate than GHG. Quite the opposite would be predicted – greater increases in temperature would be expected, not less.

b. To summarize the results from the Earthshine data, it is apparent that the reflectivity of the earth has changed over the past 125 years. The total change of 11.2 W/m^2 must be reduced by 86% for cloud and aerosol cooling. An additional loss of energy to the heat sink of the oceans is probable either as a latent heat source or a mixture of latent heat source and increased cooling losses from clouds and/or aerosols. The total losses are about 86%. Determining whether there is large influence from rapid aerosol depletion certainly is not supported by the data. Minor changes less than 0.5 watts are difficult to discern because there are significant uncertainties regarding the temperature record and the actual data on energy sources. The best models in Chart 5.9, Chart 5.8, and Chart 6.7 have explained almost all the changes in the past 125 years and therefore the influence of other energy sources is not likely or not evident.

	YES	NO
1 Many Variables	✓	
2 Requires a Model	✓	
3 Uncompromised Data (No Gaps or Corruption)		✓
4 Let the Data Choose the Model – "Best Fit"		✓
4A If one Model is not the Only Possibility, Develop a Range of Outcomes that can Lead to Actionable Steps and Aid in Future Research.		✓
5 Key Climate Forces Used In the Model Demonstrate that Temperature Follows (Dependent upon) Their Changes		✓
5A Test to Determine that the Model "Forecasts History" Repeatably, Especially During Changes in Data Direction		✓

Chart 7.29.

4. The overall conclusions are dependent upon assumptions that infer the need for action that are in fact unsubstantiated.

5. The IPCC report discounted solar forces and models that had better documented assumptions than the selected energy sources.

    Let's evaluate this IPCC effort against the checklist (Chart 7.29).

Chapter 8

Alternative View by
Peter Dietze, IPCC Reviewer

Early in the IPCC effort, Peter Dietze was selected as a reviewer of the 2001 report. In the mid-1990s he and a group of scientists and engineers began an effort to evaluate the direction that the IPCC report group was taking. For many years, they have presented broader views of the natural-occurring irradiative forces behind the changes in temperature. Their key differences with the IPCC report centered around four points.

The *first* point was that the main forces for temperature change were due to the changes in the sun's radiation and its influence on the levels of cloud cover. This was demonstrated by Drs. Posmentier, Soon, and Baliunas in 1998 [R8.1], based upon the work of Drs. Marsh and Svensmark [R4.5]. The data presented in this chapter support their view with more recent data.

The *second* point as discussed in Chapter 4 was that there were important differences in the sensitivity rate of degrees k/W/m^2. Using the physics understanding of absorption of an object such as the earth, called a "black body," they found that the response of the earth should be about 0.24 times the radiative force as a sensitivity factor to temperature change. This factor is based upon the principles of Stefan Boltzmann and is a factor of a third to a half less than the assumptions used in the IPCC report shown in Chart 5.1a and 5.1b.

The *third* point was that the forecasts for GHG emissions and the quantities that will reside in the atmosphere are overstated by 2.5 times, as we have shown in the previous chapter in Chart 7.15

The *fourth* and most important point is that the equilibrium climate sensitivity for CO_2 doubling is not 2.8° K as found in the IPCC report. It is only 0.7° K. This difference is based upon a combination of the above points. The IPCC overestimates temperature increments up to 600% higher based upon exaggerated assumptions.

Also, the current estimated 381 ppm is 45% of the doubling 540 ppm when we use the change in W/m^2. This leaves 55% for the GHG total of 0.92° K or 0.51° K for a doubling from 2006.

The Dietze model would be different from the IPCC report. Here are those areas where it is different. GHG levels are below the IPCC report. Earth's reflectivity

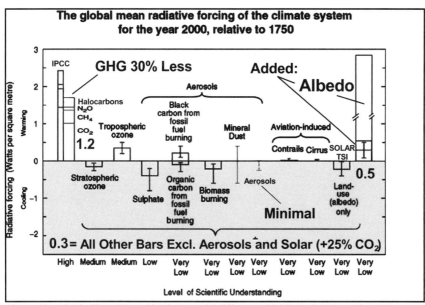

Above: Chart 8.1 is Chart 7.1a. with Dietze model differences highlighted. Below: Chart 8.2 Calculations available at website.

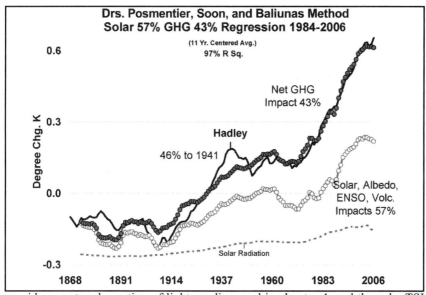

provides greater absorption of light, as discussed in chapter 4, and the solar TSI is higher. Notice also that the aerosol numbers are lower (Chart 8.1).

When we include the GHG along with solar energy sources, there are several levels that GHG improve the regression fit. The highest level of GHG that improves the regression fit is 43%. Here is how the regression result is charted with the GHG included in Chart 8.2. Notice that the model does better than the Chapter 7 regression fits in the 1928 to 1948 period, but not as well as Chart 5.9.

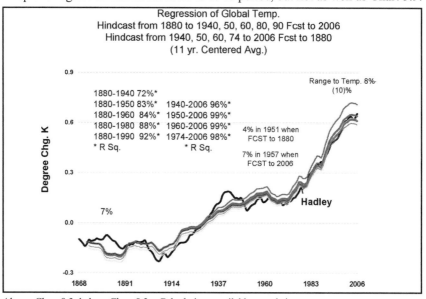

Above: Chart 8.3; below: Chart 8.3a: Calculations available at website

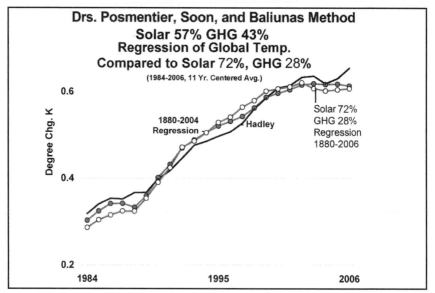

The model passes the Hindcast test because it fits the temperature history as well as Chart 5.8, as we see in Chart 8.3a.

We have seen that the 65% GHG, which can include or exclude accelerated depletion of aerosols, shows extraordinary "hockey stick" forecasts of temperature and cannot pass Hindcast repeatability tests. Dr. Posmentier, et al.'s method passes the Hindcast test and does not have extraordinary "hockey stick" characteristics. It is also important to point out that Mr. Dietze's and Dr. Posmentier, et al.'s forecasts were available to the global-warming community and the IPCC group at the time of the 2001 IPCC report. They were published on the web and through Mr. Dietze's status as a 2001 IPCC reviewer. The accuracy of this forecast is quite interesting, especially given the apparent problems with the Global Warming Theory.

The Dietze alternative in Chart 8.2 shows an increase of 0.44° K and the results from Chart 6.7 show a possible increase of about 0.45° K. These two approaches suggest that the worst case for GHG is about 0.45° K in 2100. Chart 8.4a shows the amount of additional energy that will probably be absorbed in the atmosphere if the global community consumes 83% of global reserves by 2100 that supports this forecast.

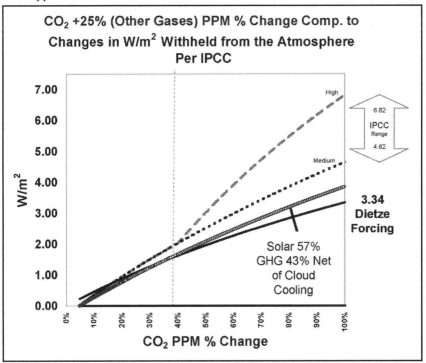

Chart 8.4a: From Chart 6.8 with results of the Solar 53%, GHG 43% regression from chart 8.2. The results of the Solar 72%, GHG 28% regression from Chart 5.8 are similar.

Since we recognize that the highest valid regression forecast for 2100 is the Chart 6.6 of 0.45° K, we will use it as the worst case for Chart 8.4.

The reverse worst case would be Chart 5.9, that there is no net GHG effect, while the solar activity returns to the 1929–30 levels, though historic mini-ice ages may also be possible in this period of time. When we plot these two worst cases, we see that we have a very good forecast range of possibilities that are reliable. (Chart 8.4)

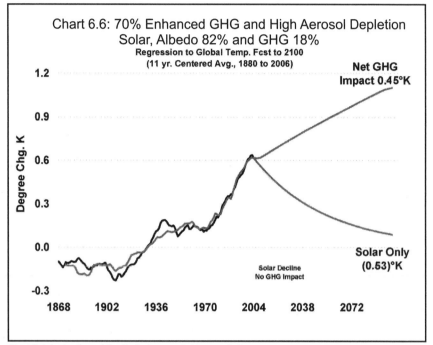

Chart 8.4 Author's model calculations available at website.

A complete review of the different options regarding solar- or global-warming shows a definite conclusion. The Global Warming Theory is statistically not valid. On the other hand, those models that utilize the Earthshine data with up to Solar 62% GHG 38% have been proven to be statistically valid. Higher levels of GHG with and without accelerated depletion of aerosols have not been proven valid. Also, there is no evidence that accelerated depletion of aerosols is taking place. In essence, the Global Warming Theory is statistically not valid, while the Solar Warming Theory is statistically valid. Chart 8.5 represents all the cases we have studied.

Therefore, we have completed our efforts to understand historic changes in temperature and have reliable forecasts. Now we need the future to demonstrate the accuracy of the forecasts.

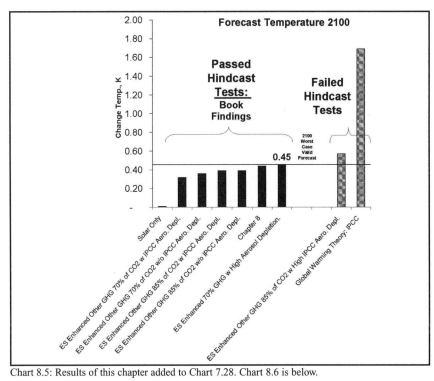

Chart 8.5: Results of this chapter added to Chart 7.28. Chart 8.6 is below.

	YES	NO
1 Many Variables	✓	
2 Requires a Model	✓	
3 Uncompromised Data (No Gaps or Corruption)		✓
4 Let the Data Choose the Model – "Best Fit"	✓	
4A If one Model is not the Only Possibility, Develop a Range of Outcomes that can Lead to Actionable Steps and Aid in Future Research.	✓	
5 Key Climate Forces Used In the Model Demonstrate that Temperature Follows (Dependent upon) Their Changes	✓	
5A **Test to Determine that the Model "Forecasts History" Repeatably, Especially During Changes in Data Direction**	✓	

If we complete our checklist, we find a very good result.

Since the results from Chart 6.6 are statistically the worst cases, we will use them to construct this chart to show the difference in our models versus the IPCC models. (Chart 8.7)

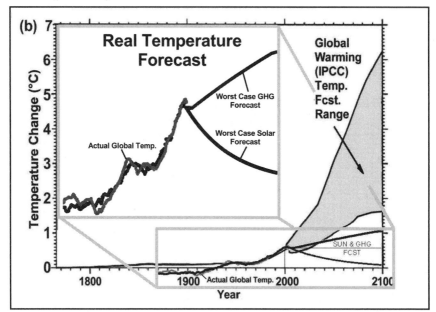

Chart 8.7 Real temperature forecast developed as a worst case in this book compared to the IPCC forecasts of expected temperature increases.

Chapter 9

Other Issues

Other issues have been raised in the IPCC report. The information on each item is presented for you so that you will have the opportunity to decide for yourself whether the issues are important.

1. The rise in the sea from melting ice caps will inundate major cities on the globe.
2. Hurricanes and tornados will increase.
3. Tropical diseases will attack northern countries.
4. The ecosystem will be destroyed because of the reduction in the ozone layer.

Rising Sea

Key bits of information are important to keep in mind. Ice does melt at 32° F and melts rapidly at 58° F, the temperature of the pre-industrial world. The oceans have been rising because the temperature of the pre-industrial world was significantly above freezing. The question is, how rapidly is it rising now that temperatures are at higher levels by about 1° F?

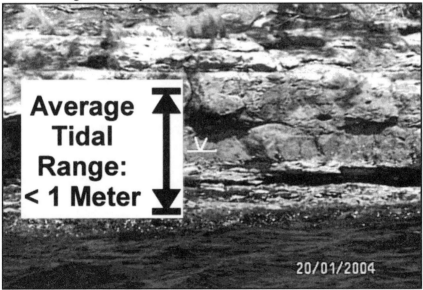

Chart 9.1: Picture by John L Daly with permission from www.john-daly.com. The horizontal line is 50 cm long.

John L. Daly of Tasmania took this picture at low tide on January 20, 2004. It is the average tide mark placed there in 1864. The normal sea rise since that time has taken place. The average tidal range is less than a meter in this region. Notice that it is hard to tell if the ocean's surface has risen in the past 142 years. The IPCC report also shows Chart 9.2, regarding measurements of the sea height changes vs. sea surface temperature changes. The peak is during the 1998 El Niño, and the level declines as the temperature declines after the event. In the chart, the increase was 10 mm (.4 inches) in 6 years with some decline or 16.6 mm (0.65 inches) per decade (0.7 feet, 6.5 inches) per century. That is well below the decadal average from historic records.

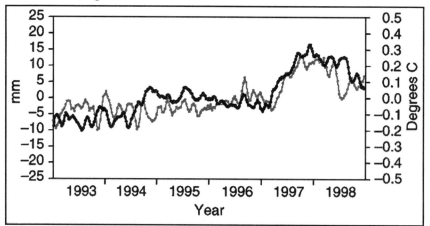

Chart 9.2 IPCC Report ttp://www.grida.no/climate/ipcc_tar/wg1/424.htm.

Even at the peak, which was the change in 1997–1998 of 0.74° K in the satellite dataset, the change in rate is 10 mm per year or 100 mm (4 inches) per decade. A century would be 3.3 feet. In the worst-case scenario from Chapter 7, the increase would be 0.47°/0.74° or 64%, possibly 2 ft.

The data on sea levels are not very reliable. On page 92 is another historic record from the IPCC report (Chart 9.3). The information is from Sweden. It doesn't seem to be extraordinary.

One would expect much better data to be presented to support catastrophic forecasts.

Hurricanes and Tornadoes

There has been a significant amount of controversy over the statement that hurricanes and tornados would increase dramatically in number and severity with higher temperatures. The controversy came to crisis levels when the IPCC chair for this portion of the report stated that the committee unequivocally agreed with the extraordinary forecasts contained in the report.

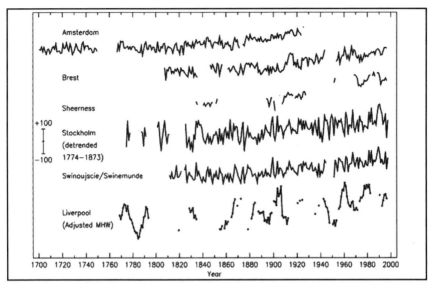

Above: Chart 9.3: IPCC Report www.grida.no/climate/ipcc_tar/wg1/013.htm#b4. Below: Chart 9.4 IPCC Report www.grida.no/climate/ipcc_tar/wg1/092.htm.

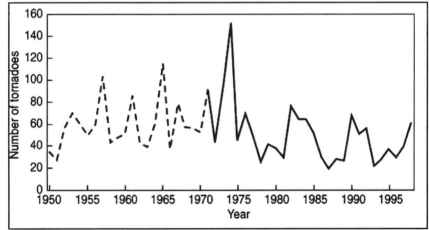

Within several weeks of this statement, the following resignation letter was publicly submitted by a key contributor to the IPCC report. It was submitted to protest that the organization was politicized. The full text is in [R9.1], but the central scientific analysis is contained in this paragraph from that letter which states:

> "Moreover, the evidence is quite strong and supported by the most recent credible studies that any *impact in the future from global warming upon hurricanes will likely be quite small.*" [emphasis added] – Dr. Chris Landsea, NOAA Dir. Of Hurricane and Tornado Studies.

Here are the charts from the actual IPCC report to which Dr. Landsea had helped contribute. Do you notice any increase in tornadoes during the period of increased temperatures from 1980 to 2000? (See Chart 9.4.)

Did you notice any increasing trend in major hurricanes during the period of 1980 to 2000? (See Chart 9.5.)

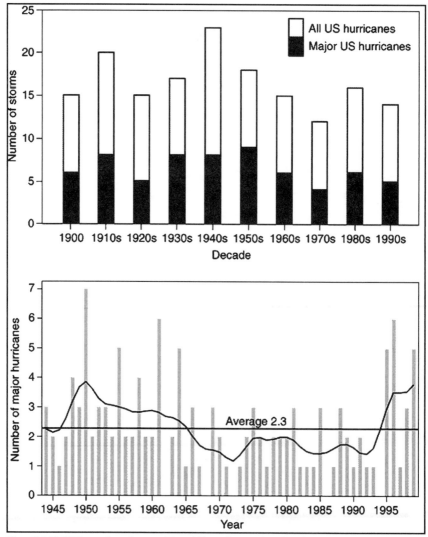

Chart 9.5: IPCC Report http://www.grida.no/climate/ipcc_tar/wg1/091.htm#2731.

Do you understand his point now?

He is still commenting on information regarding tornadoes and hurricanes.

In July 2005, the AP reported on a MIT group that stated historic data confirmed that hurricane intensity should be increasing with global warming. Dr. Landsea was also quoted. He made the point that the study had a "large bias removal" [eliminated major hurricanes – *author*] from its study because of what the research group defined as "questionable" data. Dr. Landsea stated that this "bias was greater than the global warming signal itself." If they had included the excluded hurricane data, they would not have been able to arrive at their conclusions [R9.1a]. One of the nation's leading hurricane forecasters, Dr. William Gray of Colorado State University, said the MIT conclusions were based on imprecise information about the strength of hurricanes, especially in past decades [R9.1b]. Dr. Gray has also resigned from the IPCC.

The latest research release in March 2007 has shown that Drs. Landsea and Gray are correct in their skepticism. Dr. Kossin et al.in the *Geophysical Research Letters,* found that while storm intensity has increased in the North Atlantic during their research period, however, no major trends in the global averages were detected. [R9.1c]

Tropical Diseases
There have been a lot of anecdotal reports of diseases found in the tropics migrating north, with the potential of creating pandemics or other dire outcomes. For the record, Florida has always had malaria and yellow fever. The author of this book has lived in jungle areas. Malaria was there as well as yellow fever and a lot of other diseases we did not see in Chicago unless we traveled to Florida or further south. A very large number of people live quite well with these threats as long as public-health authorities manage the mosquito population and provide other normal protective services they perform in Florida.

By the way, not many people are aware that the Black Plague has been found in rural squirrels in California for over a century. Forest-service and public-health officials manage their populations quite successfully. Antibiotics have so far been successful at curing the few people who are bitten by the fleas from these squirrels.

West Nile Fever was introduced to the U.S. from mosquitoes that probably arrived by plane and not as a result of rising temperatures. Mosquito populations are managed by public health, though the spread of this disease has not been successfully stopped. It is important to note also that West Nile fever from Egypt flourishes in a latitude equal to Washington D.C.

Ozone Hole
Much has been discussed about the ozone hole in the Antarctic. When first discovered, there were a lot of dire forecasts about ultra-violent light (UV) causing skin cancer once the ozone layer had disappeared, caused by human sources of chlorofluorocarbons, or CFCs. That was the first global treaty on the environment and caused us all to have to change to "green," less-efficient gases for refrigera-

tion. France was the only nation not to join the treaty, and the French are now the sole suppliers to the world of CFCs for so-called ozone depleting refrigerants.

The website identified in Chart 9.6 was set up to monitor the ozone hole. As you will note in Chart 9.6 the hole, as of December 2005, is smaller than it was in 2003, and 2004 was smaller than the average for the limited number of years of the study; 2006 appears about the same level as 2003.

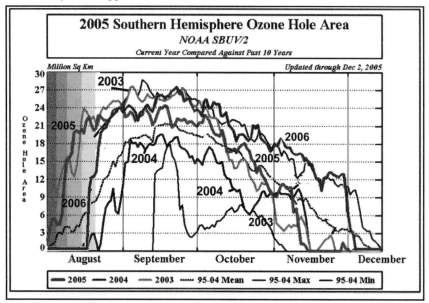

Chart 9.6: From NOAA/National Weather Service, National Centers for Environmental Prediction found at www.cpc.ncep.noaa.gov/products/stratosphere/polar/gif_files/ozone_hole_plot.png.

There seems to be some large fluctuations in the size of the hole. By October or early November, the ozone hole disappears each year, according to NOAA.

NASA Goddard also reported in 2001 that solar storms increase the ozone hole. [R9.2]

Recent articles have indicated that bromine salts (which act chemically similar to chlorine and CFCs) from seawater have been found in upper altitudes from normally occurring wind vortexes. They apparently account for part of the winter ozone-hole changes in the southern latitudes. [R9.3]

Chapter 10

Summary

The temperature and solar irradiation levels were reviewed. The temperature history from the British Hadley and MSU satellite sources showed a difference to the NOAA surface data. An attempt by NOAA to adjust for known problems from sea-surface data required creating a NOAA Land-Sea Index from their land-surface data and the sea data from the MSU satellite data. This new index did not resolve all of the differences. However, after removing human adjustment factors from the NOAA data, the differences appeared to be minimal between the various sources. We decided that since the Hadley and MSU data were close to each other and the NOAA data had known problems, we could safely use the Hadley to test temperature change. Most importantly, the global surface temperature reached a peak in 1998 and has been flat to down since then.

The solar energy measurements presented from several sources were compared. The NASA ACRIM dataset has some differences from the Max Planck dataset used by the IPCC report. We also compared the sensitivity rates of the number of degrees of temperature change that would have to take place by an increase in irradiative energy from any source as measured by W/m^2. We found that a much lower sensitivity rate of 0.24 for irradiative forces conversion factor to temperature was the most appropriate factor to explain the changes in temperature. This factor is two to three times lower than the factor used in the IPCC 2001 report.

We then reviewed the changes in solar forces as measured by high-energy particles (cosmic rays) from the sun, and related them to measurements of reflectivity (Albedo) of the earth. The directly measured data from the Earthshine project represented the visible light portion of the Albedo change. After cloud cooling, the change in net reflectivity showed a total of 2.4 W/m^2 at the surface for the period from 1984 to 2004, with the peak in 1998. GHG only provide up to 33% of the Earthshine energy over the same period.

This gave us a clear understanding of the probability that the sun's changes in activity could provide the majority of the energy to explain the change in global surface and satellite temperature changes. We verified this through valid regression fits to historic temperature data as shown in Charts 5.8, 5.9, and 6.6, and 6.7. These valid regression fits to the historic temperature data were only possible using the NASA ACRIM solar dataset. The period from 1938 to 1955 is not matched perfectly, though a solar-only regression fit this period best.

We did verify that the changes in direction of temperature closely followed the changes in direction of the energy forcings from the sun. The models forecast history very well and passed Hindcast repeatability tests. Using data from 1880 to 1940, we could forecast the temperature in 2006 within a few percentage points. This was also true using the data from 1880 to 1950, or 1960, and 1970 or later. The forecast of temperature change from these valid regressions to 2100 would support a 0.0° K to 0.45° K increase.

We also found no evidence for valid regressions (after failing Hindcast tests) using the Earthshine data with GHG and accelerated depletion of aerosols that showed significant differences to valid regressions without accelerated depletion of aerosols. Only invalid regressions could support the double-digit increases in the forecast 2100 temperature as reported by the IPCC. The highest 2100 valid forecast with accelerated depletion of aerosols was 0.06°K higher than cases with no accelerated depletion of aerosols. The worst-case forecast temperature increases to 2100 were 0.45° K.

We explored other views, first the Global Warming Theory supported by the IPCC 2001 report. After reviewing the sensitivity of fossil-fuel emissions and forecasts, it was apparent that the forecasts by the IPCC 2001 report beyond 2000 overstated the possible atmospheric concentrations of GHG that could be predicted from human sources. The very high forecasts of temperature change are also based upon assumptions that do not "forecast history" well. The IPCC forecasts created in 2000 within four years are probably eleven to twelve years ahead of actual data in 2004, a miss of extraordinary magnitude.

Another discovery was that the historic temperature record did not follow the changes in the GHG, especially since 1998. The IPCC report identifies these gases as being the key sources of energy-changing temperature and that rapid aerosol depletion will accentuate temperature changes. The statistical validity problems associated with using GHG with rapid aerosol depletion as the primary variable to predict temperature changes created forecasts from 1940 or 1950 to 2006 that were up to 49% higher than the actual temperatures we experienced. We realized that the reliability of these models was statistically unsound, as they could not pass Hindcast repeatability tests to demonstrate that the shape of the GHG energy data matched the changes in temperature.

We developed four findings from reviewing the Global Warming Theory from the IPCC 2001 report. The first finding was that we verified that *(1) the sensitivity rate used to derive temperature changes is above scientifically plausible levels by a factor of 2 to 3.*

After reviewing the results of the successful regression fits from the Earthshine data linking solar and GHG influences upon changes in the atmosphere's reflectivity (Albedo, or amount of light energy absorbed by the atmosphere), we discovered that *(2) the Global Warming Theory does not recognize any changes in the earth's reflectivity. This is a major concern because we confirmed that six recently published directly measured data sources also showed changes in reflectivity* while one of these sources, published by Marsh and Svensmark, was ignored in the IPCC 2001 report.

Next we found that *(3) it was improbable that future atmospheric concentrations of GHG would reach the levels forecast by the IPCC 2001 report. And, rapid depletion of aerosols is not supported by statistically valid regression fits.* As a result, the theory that the cooling-effects aerosols would deplete from the atmosphere more rapidly than GHG, so creating an accentuation of temperature change was not conceivable. Together these improbable forecasts raised doubts about the extraordinary temperature forecasts found in the report.

The final finding was *(4) that the GHG models could not produce statistically valid regressions, and they could not even fit the historic temperature data, especially from 1939 to 1955.*

As a result of these four findings, the expected high temperature forecasts must be considered implausible.

Then we reviewed an alternative option by Peter Dietze, an IPCC reviewer who published at the time of the 2001 IPCC report. He recommended a lower sensitivity rate of energy to temperature and a view that a combination of sun-related energy sources and GHG are the best explanation for the change in temperature.

Mr. Dietze's and Dr. Posmentier et. al.'s regression passed the validity tests. We found that their model of up to 57% solar and 43% GHG irradiative forces was a better model than the 2001 IPCC report's models. The information Mr. Dietze presented was available to the global-warming community and the IPCC group prior to the 2001 report, both on public websites and through personal contact because of his status as an IPCC reviewer. His models were obviously ignored, as there is no mention of this approach in that IPCC document. His updated forecast increase to 2100 was only 0.44° K.

Since Chart 6.6 is the highest we can validly use for an upper worst-case scenario, our worst-case future expectations are for a 0.45° K increase shown in Chart 8.7, much below the most minimal of the global-warming theory's invalid forecasts. This increase is the expected temperature increase from a doubling of CO^2 concentrations from 270 ppm to 540 ppm. The level in 2006 was 381 ppm, or 45% of the expected change from a doubling. The remaining 55% of this change is 0.46° K. We additionally included an assumption from the Solar 100%, GHG 0% valid regression from Chart 5.9. This assumes the sun's irradiation returns to 1929–30 lows as a possible minimum scenario. Mini-ice ages have occurred historically that might question whether this is the lowest worst case within the next 94 years.

As a result of these findings, it is clear that there is no need to spend uncounted amounts of money on reducing GHG to solve the risks of global warming. *Solar warming is not a probable threat as even the worst-case forecast is below the levels the Global Warming Theory deems as being important considerations.*

When we reviewed the other claims of the IPCC report that human impacts upon the climate would cause major devastation, we found no basis for these claims. The report said major cities would be inundated from the rising sea; hurricanes and tornadoes would dramatically increase in number and severity; tropical diseases would move north, causing pandemics; and the ozone hole would increase, causing a collapse of the ecosystem. We found no evidence from U.S. government sources and the IPCC report itself to support those claims. If anything, we found data and information that refutes these IPCC report claims.

Furthermore, we found a resignation from the IPCC by an important participant because the scientific integrity of the organization was becoming "politicized." *Recent research has shown skepticism about hurricane intensity to be scientifically supported.*

There is, then, we must conclude, no scientific basis or other reasons to spend money on decreasing GHG emissions.

References

Website with excel models available at www.itsthesunnotyoursuv.com. This site will maintain updated sites for the book's references in the case that a web master changes a location of the relevant site.

Chapter 1

[R1.1]: "Climate Conference Hears Degree of Danger," Paul Brown, environment correspondent, Thursday February 3, 2005, *The Guardian* from: http://education.guardian.co.uk/higher/sciences/story/0,12243,1404455,00.html.

> Dr Andrei Illarionov, economic adviser to the Russian president, told the Guardian: "President Putin was under great pressure to sign the Kyoto protocol, and Russia did so because we like to be friends with Europe, not because we believe in the science of climate change."

[R 1.2]: "Germany's Wind Farms Blowing out of Control," by Rod Myer, February 2, 2005, *The Age* at: http://www.theage.com.au/news/Business/Germanys-wind-farms-blowing-out-of-control/2005/02/01/1107228697876.html?oneclick=true.

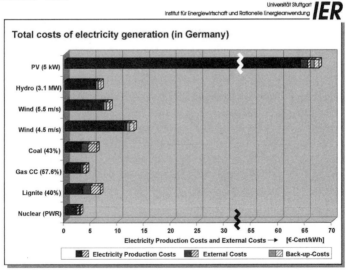

Note: "PV" is Photovoltaic

[R 1.2a]: Chart (see p. 99) is provided courtesy of: Institut für Energiewirtschaft und Rationelle Energieanwendung, Universität Stuttgart, Heßbrühlstr., 49a, D-70565, Stuttgart, Tel.: 49 (0711) 78061 11, FAX: 49(0711) 78061 822, e-mail: alfred.voss@ier.uni-stuttgart.de.

[R1.3]: "New ENSO Forecasts Based on Solar Model" by Dr. Theodor Landscheidt (22 Dec 2003), Schroeter Institute for Research in Cycles of Solar Activity, Waldmuenchen, Germany found at http://www.john-daly.comtheodor/new-enso.htm.

Chapter 3

[R3.1]: For more detail on space suit temperatures see: http://www1.jsc.nasa.gov/er/seh/suitnasa.html.

Chart 3.1: The data comes from the National Oceanographic and Atmospheric Agency (NOAA). The data site is located at: http://www.giss.nasa.gov/data/update/gistemp/graphs/, then click on your choice of chart or data file.

Sea-surface temperatures from NOAA at:
www.ncdc.noaa.gov/oa/climate/research/1998/anomalies/annual_ocean.ts. 2001-2006 not currently available.

Hadley Global temperature is from: http://www.cru.uea.ac.uk/ftpdata/tavegl2v.dat from 1854 to 2005. Change in http://www.cru.uea.ac.uk/cru/data/temperature/hadcrut3vgl.txt from 2005 to 2006 added to above data for 2006.

Chart 3.2: From IPCC 2001 report http://www.grida.no/climate/ipcc_tar/wg1/054.htm; the stations represented are non-urban stations only. All stations are not available in the report.

Chart 3.3: In IPCC 2001 Report and available at: http://www.ncdc.noaa.gov/img/climate/research/ushcn/ts.ushcn_anom25_diffs_urb-raw_pg.gif.

[R3.2]: Some Convergence of Global Warming Estimates by Roy Spencer, August 11, 2005, online at: http://www.techcentralstation.com/081105RS.html.

The key clarification of the differences between the two approaches comes from the UAH team. Here is their quote in this article:

> While their criticism of the UAH diurnal cycle adjustment method is somewhat speculative, Mears & Wentz were additionally able to demonstrate to us, privately, that there is an error that arises from our implementation of the UAH technique. *This very convincing demonstration, which is based upon simple algebra and was discovered too*

late to make it into their published report, made it obvious to us that the UAH diurnal correction method had a bias that needed to be corrected.

Since we (UAH) had already been working on a new diurnal adjustment technique, based upon the newer and more powerful AMSUs that have been flying since 1998, we rushed our new method to completion recently, and implemented new corrections. As a result, the UAH global temperature trends for the period 1979 to the present have increased from +0.09 to +0.12 deg. C/decade – still below the RSS estimate of +0.19° C/decade. (emphasis added)

Our new AMSU-based (observed) diurnal cycle adjustments end up being very similar to RSS's climate model (theoretical) adjustments. So why the remaining difference between the trends produced by the two groups? While this needs to be studied further, it looks like the reason is the same as that determined for the discrepancy in deep-tropospheric satellite estimates between the two groups: the way in which successive satellites in the long satellite time series are intercalibrated. There has been a continuing, honest difference of opinion between UAH and RSS about how this should best be done." quote opening?

Chart 3.4: Satellite Global Troposphere Temperatures from http://www. nsstc. uah.edu/data/msu/t2lt/uahncdc.lt. then copy and edit out spaces and place into a spreadsheet.

Charts 3.5 and 3.6: Map of Satellite Global Troposphere Temperatures from: http://wwwghcc.msfc.nasa.gov/temperature completed here? currently not available. Trend data offered at: ww.climate.uah.edu.

Chart 3.7: A combination of datasets from Charts 3.1b, 3.3, and 3.4.

Chart 3.8: A combination of datasets from Charts 3.1b, and 3.7.

Chart 3.9: A combination of datasets from Charts 3.1b 3.4 and 3.2. The calculations are available at the website.

[R3.3]: "Disparity of tropospheric and surface temperature trends: New Evidence," D. Douglass, B. Pearson, S. Singer, P. Knappenberger, and P. Michaels, *Geophysical Research Letters*, Vol. 31, L13207, doi:10.1029/2004GL020212, 2004.

Chart 3.10: All the data come from the dataset used for Chart 3.4 http://www.nsstc.uah.edu/data/msu/t2lt/uahncdc.lt.

Chart 3.11: The data are from NOAA at: http://www.giss.nasa.gov/data/ update/gistemp/graphs/, then click on your choice of chart or data file.

Chart 3.12: A combination from Charts 3.1, 3.3, 3.4, and 3.11.

Chart 3.13: Weather Balloon data from: http://cdiac.esd.ornl.gov/ftp/trends/temp /angell/global.dat.

[R3.4]: Sherwood, S., J. Lanzante, and C. Meyer, 2005: Radiosonde daytime biases and late 20th century warming. August 11. Online at http://www.scienceexpress.org.

Chart 3.14: Data from Charts 3.1b, 3.3, and 3.4.

Chapter 4

Chart 4.1: Data from NOAA at: ftp://ftp.ncdc.noaa.gov/pub/data/paleo/climate_ forcing/solar_variability/bard_ irradiance.txt.
   The calculation for the temperature in 1146 is at the website. It comes from the model for 100% Solar that explains 98% of the change in Global Surface Temperature from 1880 to 2006.

[R4.1]: Abstract from: ftp://ftp.ncdc.noaa.gov/pub/data/paleo/climate_forcing/ solar_variability/bard_irradiance.txt.

Based on a quantitative study of the common fluctuations of 14C and 10Be production rates, we have derived a time series of the solar magnetic variability over the last 1200 years. This record is converted into irradiance variations by linear scaling based on previous studies of sun-like stars and of the Sun's behavior over the last few centuries. The new solar irradiance record exhibits low values during the well-known solar minima centered about 1900, 1810 (Dalton), and 1690 AD (Maunder). Further back in time, a rather long period between 1450 and 1750 AD is characterized by low irradiance values. A shorter period is centered about 1200 AD, with irradiance slightly higher or similar to present day values. It is tempting to correlate these periods with the so-called "little ice age" and "medieval warm period," respectively. An accurate quantification of the climatic impact of this new irradiance record requires the use of coupled atmosphere-ocean general circulation models (GCMs). Nevertheless, our record is already compatible with a global cooling of about 0.5–1 C during the "little ice age," and with a general cooling trend during the past millennium followed by global warming during the 20th century (Mann et al. 1999).

[R4.2]: "The Hockey Stick Debate: Lessons in Disclosure and Due Diligence," S. McIntyre, R. McKitrick, Published by Marshall Institute, May 11, 2005 at: http://www.marshall.org/article.php?id=293.

Chart 4.2: From IPCC Report at: http://www.grida.no/climate/ipcc_tar/wg1/fig6.8.htm.

Chart 4.3: Adapted from earlier version of Mauna Loa chart currently available from: http://www.mlo.noaa.gov/programs/esrl/solar/img/img_solar_radiation_transmission.jpg.

[R4.3]: "From Dimming to Brightening: Decadal Changes in Solar Radiation at Earth's Surface," M. Wild, H. Gilgen, A. Roesch, A. Ohmura, C. Long, E. Dutton, B. Forgan, A. Kallis, V. Russak, A. Tsvetkov, *Science*, vol .308, Issue 5723, 847–850, 6 May 2005, [DOI: 10.1126/science.1103215].

Chart 4.4: From the IPCC report at: http://www.grida.no/climate/ipcc_tar/wg1/244.htm.

Chart 4.5: Adapted from the ACRIM website at: http://www.acrim.com/RESULTS/Earth%20Observatory/earth_obs_fig26.pdf.

Chart 4.6: Lean 2000 from: ftp://ftp.ncdc.noaa.gov/pub/data/paleo/climate_forcing/solar_variability/lean2000_irradiance.txt. This data are used from 1860 to 1969. The Max Planck estimates from http://www.mps.mpg.de/projects/sun-climate/papers/ iscs2003.pdf, Figure 6 is used from 1980 to 2006, and the ACRIM data is from chart 4.5 from 1984 to 2006. The actual datasets are available at the website referred to in Appendix C.

[R4.4]: "SOLAR TOTAL AND SPECTRAL IRRADIANCE: MODELLING AND A POSSIBLE IMPACT ON CLIMATE", N. A. Krivova and S. K. Solanki, from http://www.mps.mpg.de/projects/sun-climate/papers/iscs2003.pdf.

Chapter 5

[R5.1]: 1.2.1 Natural Forcing of the Climate System

The Sun and the global energy balance

The ultimate source of energy that drives the climate system is radiation from the Sun. About half of the radiation is in the visible short-wave part of the electromagnetic spectrum. The other half is mostly in the near-infrared part, with some in the ultraviolet part of the spectrum. Each square metre of the Earth's spherical surface outside the atmosphere receives an average throughout the year of 342 Watts of solar radiation, 31% of which is immediately reflected back into space by clouds, by the atmosphere, and by the Earth's surface. The remaining 235 Wm^{-2} is partly absorbed by the atmosphere but most (168 Wm^{-2}) warms the Earth's surface: the land and the ocean. The Earth's surface returns that heat to the atmosphere, partly as infrared radiation, partly as sensible heat and as water vapor which releases its heat when it condenses higher up in the atmosphere. This exchange of energy between surface and atmosphere maintains under present conditions a global mean temperature near the surface of 14°C, decreasing rapidly with height and reaching a mean temperature of –58°C at the top of the troposphere." This is from the IPCC report at: http://www.grida.no/climate/ipcc_tar/ wg1/041.htm.

[R5.2]: "Can We Defuse The Global Warming Time Bomb?," Dr. J. Hansen, NASA Goddard Institute for Space Studies, and Columbia University Earth Institute, *naturalSCIENCE*, ISSN 1206–940X Copyright © 1997/2003, Heron Publishing, Victoria, Canada. Found at http://naturalscience.com/ns/articles/ 01–16/ns_jeh.html.

Chart 5.1a: Data are developed from dividing the temperature change in degrees for B2 by the watts per square meter for B2 as found in Charts 7.14 and 7.15. http://www.grida.no/climate/ipcc_tar/wg1/353.htm. Calculations are available at the website.

[R5.3a]: "James Hansen increasingly insensitive," posted April 28, 2005 from http://www.worldclimatereport.com/index.php/category/climate-politics/page/2/.

[R5.3b]: "A Lag in Global Warming," Dr. J. Hansen, *Science* 3 June 2005; 308: 1373 [DOI: 10.1126/science.308.5727.1373b].

Chart 5.1b: Stefan-Boltzmann factor explained at http://www.john-daly.com/ forcing/moderr.htm.

Chart 5.2: Using the factors from Chart 5.1b. Calculations available at the website.

[R5.4]: For a more complete explanation of how cosmic rays are measured, consult: http://ulysses.sr.unh.edu/NeutronMonitor/background.html.

[R5.5]: "Low Cloud Properties Influenced by Cosmic Rays," by N. Marsh and H. Svensmark, Danish Space Research Institute, Copenhaven, Denmark, Physical Review Letters PACS numbers 92.60.Nv, 92.70.Gt, 96.40.Kk, Copyright 2000 The American Physical Society.

[R5.6]: 6.11.2.2 Cosmic rays and clouds

Svensmark and Friis-Christensen (1997) demonstrated a high degree of correlation between total cloud cover, from the ISCCP C2 dataset, and cosmic ray flux between 1984 and 1991. Changes in the heliosphere arising from fluctuations in the Sun's magnetic field mean that galactic cosmic rays (GCRs) are less able to reach the Earth when the Sun is more active so the cosmic ray flux is inversely related to solar activity. Svensmark and Friis-Christensen analyzed monthly mean data of total cloud using only data over the oceans between 60°S and 60°N from geostationary satellites. They found an increase in cloudiness of 3 to 4% from solar maximum to minimum and speculated that (a) increased GCR flux causes an increase in total cloud and that (b) the increase in total cloud causes a cooling of climate. Svensmark and Friis-Christensen (1997) also extended this analysis to cover the years 1980 to 1996 using cloud data from the DMSP and Nimbus-7 satellites and showed that the high correlation with GCR flux is maintained. However, it was not possible to inter-calibrate the different datasets so the validity of the extended dataset as a measure of variations in absolute total cloudiness is open to question.

Svensmark (1998) showed that, at least for the limited period of this study, total cloud varies more closely with GCRs than with the 10.7 cm solar activity index over the past solar cycle. On longer timescales he also demonstrated that Northern Hemisphere surface temperatures between 1937 and 1994 follow variations in cosmic ray flux and solar cycle length more closely than total irradiance or sunspot number. There has been a long-term decrease in cosmic ray flux since the late 17th century, as evidenced by the ^{10}Be and ^{14}C cosmogenic isotope records (Stuiver and Reimer, 1993; Beer et al., 1994), and this mirrors the long-term increase in TSI. However, the TSI reconstruction of Hoyt and Schatten (1993), which is based on solar cycle lengths, does not appear to track the cosmogenic isotope records any more closely than that of Lean et al. (1995), which is based on sunspot cycle amplitude (Lean and Rind, 1998). Such use of different solar indices may help to identify which physical mechanisms, if any, are responsible for the apparent meteorological responses to solar activity.

Kuang et al. (1998) have repeated Svensmark and Friis-Christensen's analysis of ISCCP data and showed high correlations with an El Niño-Southern Oscillation (ENSO) index difficult to distinguish from the GCR flux. Farrar (2000) showed that the pattern of change in cloudiness over that period, particularly in the Pacific Ocean, corresponds to what would be expected for the atmospheric circulation changes characteristic of El Niño. Kernthaler et al. (1999) have also studied the ISCCP dataset, using both geostationary and polar orbiter data and suggested that the correlation with cosmic ray flux is reduced if high-latitude data are included. This would not be expected if cosmic rays were directly inducing increases in cloudiness, as cosmic ray flux is greatest at high latitudes. Kernthaler et al. (1999), Jørgensen and Hansen (2000), and Gierens and Ponater (1999), also noted that a mechanism whereby cosmic rays resulted in greater cloud cover would be most likely to affect high cloud as ionisation is greatest at these altitudes. Even if high cloud did respond to cosmic rays, it is not clear that this would cause global cooling as for thin high cloud the long-wave warming effects dominate the short-wave cooling effect. Kristjánsson and Kristiansen (2000) have additionally analysed the ISCCP D2 dataset, 1989 to 1993, and found little statistical evidence of a relationship between GCRs and cloud cover with the possible exception of low marine clouds in mid-latitudes. They also noted that there was no correlation between outgoing long-wave radiation, as represented in ERBE data, and GCRs. Thus the evidence for a cosmic ray impact on cloudiness remains unproven.

A further consideration must be potential physical mechanisms whereby cosmic rays might enhance cloudiness. Cosmic rays are the principal source of ionisation in the free troposphere. Furthermore, ionisation rates and atmospheric conductivity are observed to vary with solar activity. Svensmark and Friis-Christensen (1997) propose that the correlation between cosmic rays and cloud cover that they observed is due to an increase in efficiency of charged particles, over uncharged ones, in acting as cloud condensation nuclei. There is evidence for this occurring in thunderstorms (Pruppacher and Klett, 1997) but it is not clear to what extent this affects cloud development. There is also evidence that ions are sometimes critical in gas-to-particle sensitivity but again there is no evidence that this has any impact on cloud formation.

In a series of papers, Brian Tinsley has developed a more detailed mechanism for a link between cosmic rays and cloudiness (e.g., Tinsley, 1996). This is based on the premise that aerosols ionised by cosmic rays are more effective as ice nuclei and cause freezing of supercooled water in clouds. In clouds that are likely to cause precipitation the latent heat thus released then causes enhanced convection which promotes cyclonic development and hence increased storminess. There is some laboratory evidence to suggest that charging increases ice nucleation efficiency (Pruppacher, 1973) although there is no observational evidence of this process taking place in the atmosphere. Furthermore, only a small proportion of aerosol particles are capable of acting as ice nuclei, depending on chemical composition or shape. There are also laboratory studies (Abbas and Latham, 1969) which indicate the existence of "electrofreezing," but again no evidence in the real atmosphere. Thus Tinsley's mechanism is plausible but requires further observational and modeling studies to establish whether or not it could be of sufficient magnitude to result in the claimed effects (Harrison and Shine, 1999).

We conclude that mechanisms for the amplification of solar forcing are not well established. Variations in ultraviolet and solar-induced changes in O_3 may have a small effect on radiative forcing but additionally may affect climate through changing the distribution of solar heating and thus indirectly through a dynamical response. At present there is insufficient evidence to confirm that cloud cover responds to solar variability."

From the IPCC at www.grida.no/climate/ipcc_tar/wg1/246.htm.

[R5.7a]: "Changes in the Earth's reflectance over the past two decades," Drs. E. Palle, P.R. Goode, P. Montañes Rodriguez and S.E. Koonin (*Science*, 28 May 2004). Reprinted Fig. 3 with permission from Palle et al, SCIENCE 304:1299–1301 (28 May 2004). Copyright 2004 AAAS. [DOI: 10.1126/science.1094070].

[R5.7b] and Chart 5.3: Reconstructed from: "Can the earth's albedo and surface temperatures increase together?" E. Pallé, P.R. Goode, P. Montañés-Rodríguez, S.E. Koonin, EOS, Vol. 87, No. 4, 24 January, 2006. Figure 2 is basis of Chart 5.3.

[R5.8]: "Do Satellites Detect Trends in Surface Solar Radiation?," R. T. Pinker,[1]

B. Zhang,[2] E. G. Dutton, *Science*, Vol. 308, Issue 5723, 850–854, 6 May 2005, [DOI: 10.1126/science.1103159].

[R5.9]: "Changes in Earth's Albedo Measured by Satellite," B. Wielicki, T. Wong, N. Loeb, P. Minnis, K. Priestley, R Kandel, *Science*, vol. 308, Issue 5723, 825, 6 May 2005, [DOI: 10.1126/science.1106484].

[R5.10]: "A multi-data comparison of shortwave climate forcing changes," E. Palle, P. Montanes-Rodriguez, P.R. Goode, S.E. Koonin, M. Wild, S. Casadio, Geophysical Research Letters, Vol. 32, No. 21, L21702, 10.1029/2005GL023847, 2005.

Chart 5.4 & 5.4a: Replicated version of the Earthshine chart with comparable data from five other sources from "A multi-data comparison of shortwave climate forcing changes", E. Palle, P. Montanes-Rodriguez, P.R. Goode, S.E. Koonin, M. Wild, S. Casadio, Geophysical Research Letters, Vol. 32, No. 21, L21702, 10.1029/2005GL023847, 2005. The updated 2004 EOS article data are included from Chart 5.3.

Charts 5.5 and 5.5a: Calculations are found in the website.

Chart 5.6: Earthshine data as measured at the surface. The 79% R2 is the amount of the change in Earthshine data explained by the regression relationships of ACRIM solar impacts on cloud Albedo, Climax data and Other GHG from Chart 5.5. The CR impacts from Climax and two levels of forecasts from 1983 to 1868 are also shown. AA Index from: ftp://ftp.ngdc.noaa.gov/STP/SOLAR_DATA/ RELATED_INDICES/AA_INDEX/Aa_month. Sun Spot Number from: ftp://ftp. ngdc.noaa.gov/STP/SOLAR_DATA/SUNSPOT_NUMBERS/YEARLY. Formula in Appendix A. Calculations are found on the website referred to in Appendix C.

Chart 5.7: Lower level of CR similar to Climax data.

Chart 5.8b: The 96 R^2 is the amount of the change in global temperature, and is explained by the regression relationships from the Earthshine data (of ACRIM solar, Climax data, ENSO, volcano, and GHG). Calculations are found in the website.

Chart 5.8: The 96% R2 is the amount of the change in global temperature is explained by the regression relationships from the Earthshine data (of ACRIM solar impacts on cloud Albedo, Climax data, ENSO, Volcano, and GHG). Calculations are found in the website referred to in Appendix C.

Chart 5.9: The 98% R2 is the amount of the change in Hadley temperature is explained by the regression relationships from the Earthshine data (of ACRIM solar impacts on cloud Albedo, Sun Spot/AA Index estimate of CR data, ENSO, volcano, and GHG). Calculations found in the website referred to in Appendix C.

Chapter 6

[R6.1]: Inscribed in Fine Hall, Princeton University, found at: http://www.working-minds.com/AEquotes.htm.

Charts 6.2 to 6.9: Calculations are found at the website.

Chapter 7

Chart 7.1a and 7.1b: found at: http://www.grida.no/climate/ipcc_tar/wg1/006.htm.

[R7.1]: This chart was found at: http://www.met.tamu.edu/class/atom629/hansen.pdf, but has been taken off their website.

Charts 7.2 and 7.3: Adapted from spectroscope charts. PPM refers to parts per million and PPB is parts per billion.

Chart 7.4: From the personal papers of Peter Dietze, this chart is based upon satellite images and is found at http://www.john-daly.com/forcing/moderr.htm, Funnel calculations by Peter Dietze, printed with permission.

Chart 7.5: This average is from the MODTRAN Infrared Radiation Code at the University of Chicago, produced by Dr. D and Mrs. J Archer. Source MODTRAN found at: http://geosci.uchicago.edu/~archer/cgimodels/radiation.html.

Chart 7.6: IPCC 1994 p.175 radiative forcing figure 4.1.gif. Also found at http://www.john-daly.com/forcing/moderr.htm.

Chart 7.7: From IPCC report: http://www.grida.no/climate/ipcc_tar/wg1/222.htm#tab62.

Chart 7.8: For a discussion of the actual data for 1950 to present, go to http://cdiac.esd.ornl.gov/trends/co2/sio-mlo.htm.
Actual CO_2 data from 1950 to 2003 is available from ftp://cdiac.esd.ornl.gov/pub/maunaloa-co2/maunaloa.co2. end? 2004 data has been "published".

2005 to present available from http://www.esrl.noaa.gov/gmd/ccgg/trends/, but this government site is not "free" to use without permission. Model has accurately forecast present actual levels.

Chart 7.9: The Carbon Dioxide Information Analysis Center (CDIAC), which includes the World Data Center for Atmospheric Trace Gases, is the primary global-change data and information analysis center of the U.S. Department of Energy (DOE). Data plotted from: http://cdiac.esd.ornl.gov/ftp/fossilfuel-co2-emissions/global.1751_2004.ems.

Chart 7.10: From Peter Dietze's personal papers, reprinted with permission. Also found at http://www.john-daly.com/dietze/cmodcalc.htm. Author's model calculations available at website.

Chart 7.11: From Peter Dietze's personal papers, reprinted with permission. Also found at http://www.john-daly.com/dietze/cmodcalc.htm Author's model calculations available at website.

Chart 7.12 is Chart 7.11 for 1955 to 2020.

Chart 7.13 and Chart 7.14 are from the data source in Chart 7.9 and U.S. Census, World Population estimates from http://www.census.gov/ipc/prod/wp02/tabA-01.csv.

Chart 7.15: Author's model calculations available at website.

Chart 7.16: http://www.grida.no/climate/ipcc_tar/wg1/122.htm.

Chart 7.17 and Chart 7.18: for both Forcing Watts and Temperature, from: http://www.grida.no/climate/ipcc_tar/wg1/353.htm.

Charts 7.19 to 7.21: From the IPCC report at: http://www.grida.no/climate/ipcc_tar/wg1/450.htm#fig127. Author's model calculations available at website.

Chart 7.22 to 7.24a: Author's model calculations available at website.

[R7.2]: "Explorers abandon Arctic Ocean crossing" according to State Wire on June 3, 2005 which reports that "Two Minnesota men who planned to cross the Arctic Ocean to call attention to global warming have abandoned their trek because of unexpectedly heavy snow, wind, and ice," said "Greenpeace, which co-sponsored the trip." This is from: http://www.startribune.com/stories/468/

5438540.html [no longer available on web, but currently available at: http://www.outsidethebeltway.com/archives/2005/06/global_warming_trek_cancelled_due_to_snow/]

Chart 7.25 is a combination of 6.18 and 6.24.

Charts 7.26 and 7.27: CO_2 was substituted for Solar TSI. Model calculations are available at the website.

Chart 7.28: Updated chart 6.9.

Chapter 8

[R8.1]: Drs. Posmentier, Soon, and Baliunas multiple regression model from Peter Dietze personal papers also found at: http://www.john-daly.com/forcing/moderr.htm.

Chart 8.1 is Chart 6.1 with Dietze model super imposed.

Charts 8.2 to 8.4, and 8.6: Author's model calculations available at website.

Chart 8.5: Results of this chapter added to Chart 7.28

Chapter 9

Chart 9.1: Picture by John L Daly with permission from www.john-daly.com.

Chart 9.2: IPCC Report http://www.grida.no/climate/ipcc_tar/wg1/424.htm.

Chart 9.3: IPCC Report http://www.grida.no/climate/ipcc_tar/wg1/013.htm#b4.

[R9.1]: Dr. Landsea's Open Letter of Resignation from the IPCC posted at: http://sciencepolicy.colorado.edu/prometheus/archives/science_policy_general/000318chris_landsea_leaves.html.

January 17, 2005 Chris Landsea Leaves IPCC
This is an open letter to the community from Chris Landsea.

"Dear colleagues,

After some prolonged deliberation, I have decided to withdraw from participating in the Fourth Assessment Report of the Intergovernmental Panel on Climate Change (IPCC). I am withdrawing because I have come to view the part of the

IPCC to which my expertise is relevant as having become politicized. In addition, when I have raised my concerns to the IPCC leadership, their response was simply to dismiss my concerns.

With this open letter to the community, I wish to explain the basis for my decision and bring awareness to what I view as a problem in the IPCC process. The IPCC is a group of climate researchers from around the world that every few years summarize how climate is changing and how it may be altered in the future due to manmade global warming. I had served both as an author for the Observations chapter and a Reviewer for the 2nd Assessment Report in 1995 and the 3rd Assessment Report in 2001, primarily on the topic of tropical cyclones (hurricanes and typhoons). My work on hurricanes, and tropical cyclones more generally, has been widely cited by the IPCC. For the upcoming AR4, I was asked several weeks ago by the Observations chapter Lead Author – Dr. Kevin Trenberth – to provide the writeup for Atlantic hurricanes. As I had in the past, I agreed to assist the IPCC in what I thought was to be an important, and politically-neutral determination of what is happening with our climate.

Shortly after Dr. Trenberth requested that I draft the Atlantic hurricane section for the AR4's Observations chapter, Dr. Trenberth participated in a press conference organized by scientists at Harvard on the topic "Experts to warn global warming likely to continue spurring more outbreaks of intense hurricane activity" along with other media interviews on the topic. The result of this media interaction was widespread coverage that directly connected the very busy 2004 Atlantic hurricane season as being caused by anthropogenic greenhouse gas warming occurring today. Listening to and reading transcripts of this press conference and media interviews, it is apparent that Dr. Trenberth was being accurately quoted and summarized in such statements and was not being misrepresented in the media. These media sessions have potential to result in a widespread perception that global warming has made recent hurricane activity much more severe.

I found it a bit perplexing that the participants in the Harvard press conference had come to the conclusion that global warming was impacting hurricane activity today. To my knowledge, none of the participants in that press conference had performed any research on hurricane variability, nor were they reporting on any new work in the field. All previous and current research in the area of hurricane variability has shown no reliable, long-term trend up in the frequency or intensity of tropical cyclones, either in the Atlantic or any other basin. The IPCC assessments in 1995 and 2001 also concluded that there was no global warming signal found in the hurricane record.

Moreover, the evidence is quite strong and supported by the most recent credible studies that any impact in the future from global warming upon hurricane will likely be quite small. The latest results from the Geophysical Fluid Dynamics Laboratory (Knutson and Tuleya, Journal of Climate, 2004) suggest that by around 2080, hurricanes may have winds and rainfall about 5% more intense than today. It has been proposed that even this tiny change may be an exaggeration as to what may happen by the end of the 21st Century (Michaels, Knappenberger, and Landsea, Journal of Climate, 2005, submitted).

It is beyond me why my colleagues would utilize the media to push an unsupported agenda that recent hurricane activity has been due to global warming. Given Dr. Trenberth's role as the IPCC's Lead Author responsible for preparing the text on hurricanes, his public statements so far outside of current scientific understanding led me to concern that it would be very difficult for the IPCC process to proceed objectively with regards to the assessment on hurricane activity. My view is that when people identify themselves as being associated with the IPCC and then make pronouncements far outside current scientific understandings that this will harm the credibility of climate change science and will in the longer term diminish our role in public policy.

My concerns go beyond the actions of Dr. Trenberth and his colleagues to how he and other IPCC officials responded to my concerns. I did caution Dr. Trenberth before the media event and provided him a summary of the current understanding within the hurricane research community. I was disappointed when the IPCC leadership dismissed my concerns when I brought up the misrepresentation of climate science while invoking the authority of the IPCC. Specifically, the IPCC leadership said that Dr. Trenberth was speaking as an individual even though he was introduced in the press conference as an IPCC lead author; I was told that that the media was exaggerating or misrepresenting his words, even though the audio from the press conference and interview tells a different story (available on the web directly); and that Dr. Trenberth was accurately reflecting conclusions from the TAR, even though it is quite clear that the TAR stated that there was no connection between global warming and hurricane activity. The IPCC leadership saw nothing to be concerned with in Dr. Trenberth's unfounded pronouncements to the media, despite his supposedly impartial important role that he must undertake as a Lead Author on the upcoming AR4.

It is certainly true that "individual scientists can do what they wish in their own rights," as one of the folks in the IPCC leadership suggested. Differing conclusions and robust debates are certainly crucial to progress in climate science. However, this case is not an honest scientific discussion conducted at a meeting of climate researchers. Instead, a scientist with an important role in the IPCC represented himself as a Lead Author for the IPCC has used that position to promulgate to the media and general public his own opinion that the busy 2004 hurricane season was caused by global warming, which is in direct opposition to research written in the field and is counter to conclusions in the TAR. This becomes problematic when I am then asked to provide the draft about observed hurricane activity variations for the AR4 with, ironically, Dr. Trenberth as the Lead Author for this chapter. Because of Dr. Trenberth's pronouncements, the IPCC process on our assessment of these crucial extreme events in our climate system has been subverted and compromised, its neutrality lost. While no one can "tell" scientists what to say or not say (nor am I suggesting that), the IPCC did select Dr. Trenberth as a Lead Author and entrusted to him to carry out this duty in a non-biased, neutral point of view. When scientists hold press conferences and speak with the media, much care is needed not to reflect poorly upon the IPCC. It is of more than passing interest to note that Dr. Trenberth, while eager to share his views on global warming and hurricanes with the media, declined to do so at the Climate Variability and Change Conference in January where he made several presentations. Perhaps he was concerned that such speculation – though worthy in his mind of public pronouncements – would not stand up to the scrutiny of fellow climate scientists.

I personally cannot in good faith continue to contribute to a process that I view as both being motivated by pre-conceived agendas and being scientifically unsound. As the IPCC leadership has seen no wrong in Dr. Trenberth's actions and have retained him as a Lead Author for the AR4, I have decided to no longer participate in the IPCC AR4.

Sincerely, Chris Landsea

Attached are the correspondence between myself and key members of the IPCC FAR"

[Author: Consult the website to review].

Chart 9.4: IPCC Report http://www.grida.no/climate/ipcc_tar/wg1/092.htm.

Chart 9.5: IPCC Report http://www.grida.no/climate/ipcc_tar/wg1/ 091.htm #2731.

[R9.1a] Quote can be found at this site: http://www.nwcn.com/sharedcontent/ nationworld/nation/073105ccjrcwnatwarminghurricanes.2b37098b.html.

> But some scientists questioned Emanuel's methods. For example, the MIT researcher did not consider wind speed information from some powerful storms in the 1950s and 1960s because the details of those storms are inconsistent.
>
> Researchers are using new methods to analyze those storms and others going back as far as 1851. If early storms turn out to be more powerful than originally thought, Emmanuel's findings on global warming's influence on recent tropical storms might not hold up, they said.

"I'm not convinced that it's happening," said Christopher W. Landsea, another research meteorologist with NOAA, who works at a different lab, the Atlantic Oceanographic & Meteorological Laboratory in Miami. Landsea is a director of the historical hurricane reanalysis.

"His conclusions are contingent on a very large bias removal that is large or larger than the global warming signal itself," Landsea said.

[R9.1b]: Quote can be found at this site: http://www.boston.com/news/nation/articles/2005/08/01/hurricanes_more_powerful_study_says/.

One of the nation's leading hurricane forecasters, William Gray of Colorado State University, said Emanuel is leaping to conclusions based on imprecise information about the strength of hurricanes, especially in decades past. He said Emanuel's formula for calculating the energy released by hurricanes obscures the fact that no one directly measured the winds in many of the storms, roughly estimating speeds from satellite images instead.

"It's a terrible paper, one of the worst I've ever looked at," said Gray, who does not believe that cyclone intensity worldwide is increasing. He also questioned Emanuel's contention that human actions, such as the burning of oil and other fuels, have caused the surface of the ocean to warm. Gray said the ocean-temperature increase is natural."

[R9.1c] Kossin, J.P.; Knapp, K.R.; Vimont, D.J.; Murnane, R.J.; Harper, B.A., "A Globally Consistent Reanalysis of Hurricane Variability and Trends," *Geophys. Res. Lett.*, Vol. 34, No. 4, L04815 10.1029/2006GL028836 28 February 2007.

Chart 9.6: From NOAA/ National Weather Service, National Centers for Environmental Prediction found at: http://www.cpc.ncep.noaa.gov/products/stratosphere/polar/gif_files/ozone_hole_plot.png.

[R9.2] is from "Solar Storms Destroy Ozone, Study Reconfirms," NASA/Goddard Space Flight Center, 2001–08–02, Science Daily found at: http://www.sciencedaily.com/releases/2001/08/010802080620.htm.

[R9.3]: "The Antarctic atmosphere: barometer on a changing world," S. Wood, D. Lowe, B. Connor, K. Kreher, S. Nichol, G. Bodeker, Water & Atmosphere, NIWA, 11 2003 found at http://unidata.com.au/pubs/wa/11-3/barometer.

Appendix A

Evaluation of Forces that Drive Albedo Changes

The goal of this book is to establish the range of possible cause-and-effect climate forcings that can demnstrate statistically valid relationships to the historic temperature data. There are three sections.

Section 1: Earthshine Options

    A: Two levels of CR influences

    B: Speculation of gaps in CR data and temperature.

    C. Max Planck and GHG only fits to Earthshine data

Section 2: 1145 A.D. implications.

1.A.: Earthshine Options: Two levels of CR influences

The primary frequencies that CO_2 and other GHG absorb are the near infrared ranges, though Ozone and Methane are in the middle of the visible light range. As a result, the relationship of the visible light-range Earthshine data to the visible light range other GHG must be established. For our purposes, we have used the general ranges from the IPCC report to establish the high and low level. In principle, the low range would be 25% of CO_2 as Ozone and Methane comprise about 17% to 25% of the CO_2 estimates in the absorption chart (Chart 7.4). The next level would be 70% from the 2001 IPCC report most notably from Chart 7.1. There is some discussion in the 2001 IPCC report that other GHG might have greater impacts. As a result, we will attempt to use 85% of CO_2 and determine whether any of these levels can establish a valid fit to both the Earthshine data and the historic temperature data.

There is some concern regarding the mathematical increased uncertainty of only having 20 years of Earthshine data. The selection of one model over another is made more difficult. If the climate scientific community had recognized the need to measure the changes in reflectivity earlier, we would have more data even if the techniques used were those used by the Earthshine team at Big Bear, California. Observatories have been available long before satellites were built. Resolving the question of which regression model to select can best be determined by utilizing the regression fits to the 125+ years of data available from temperature records.

There are two levels of high-energy solar-particles (CR) fits to the Earthshine dataset that fit the historic temperature record well, though not perfectly. The two levels are related to the direct measurements from the Climax Neutron Counter or the fit to the two other solar datasets: the AA Index of the sun's magnetic force and the Sun Spot number. A lower level of CR impacts is the correlation between Climax and the Earthshine data. A higher level of CR impacts is found with the correlation of the AA Index and the Sun Spot Number.

There is an important point to address regarding the relationship between the Sun Spot and AA Index fit to the Climax data. The direct fit of these two indexes to the Earthshine data provides a slightly lower trend of the Climax data from 1868 to 1950 than a fit of these two indexes to the Climax data (Chart Appendix A.1).

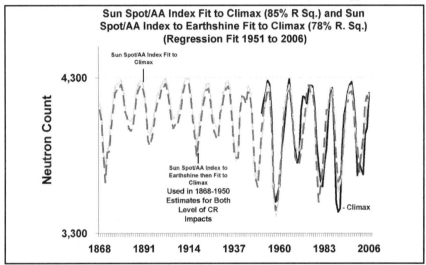

Chart Appendix A.1 (above) and Chart Appendix A.1a. Calculations at the website in Appendix C.

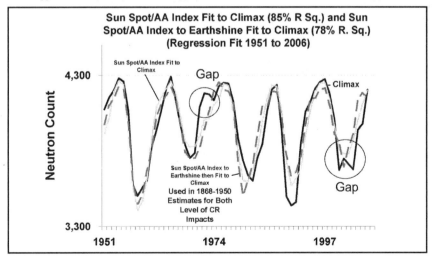

Additionally, the relationship between, especially, the Sun Spot Number and the Climax data produces gaps in 1971–1973 and 1998–2000. This has several speculative answers. First, the Sun Spot Number does not take into account the intensity of solar flares. For example, major solar flares take place after the peak in the solar TSI each 11 years. However, only a few of these flares cause disruptions to the electrical grids on the ground. It is assumed that the charge of the particles from the flares permits the earth's magnetic field to attract or repel these particles. Attracted particles are assumed to permit the particles to reach the surface, and thus to overload the electric grids, causing widespread power outages. These solar flares may account for the gaps in the Sun Spot data fit to the Climax data (Chart Appendix A.1a).

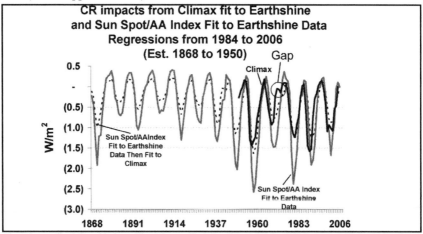

Chart Appendix A.2 and below: Chart Appendix A.2a: CR and Solar TSI Impacts with lower levels of CR fit to Earthshine with 17% other GHG to CO_2. Both can be found at the website in Appendix C.

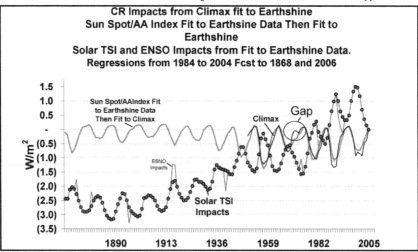

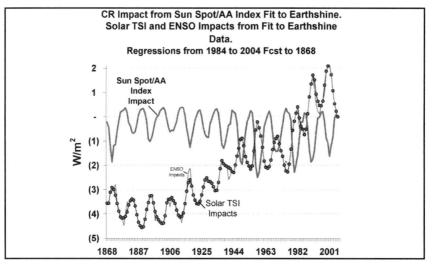

Above: Chart Appendix A.2b: CR and Solar TSI Impacts with higher levels of CR fit to Earthshine with 17% other GHG to CO_2.; below: Chart Appendix A.2c: Lower levels of CR fit to Earthshine with 25% other GHG to CO_2. Both can be found at the website in Appendix C.

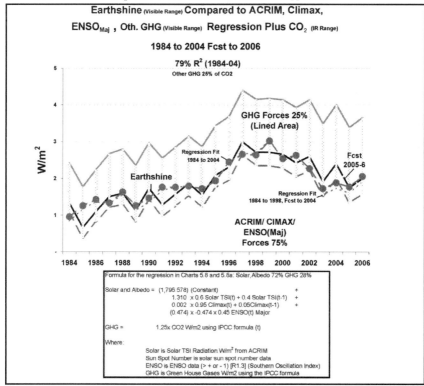

The difference between these two approaches is significant in the fit to Earthshine and to the temperature record. When we use the Climax data to establish the CR influences on clouds and thus upon changes in the earth's reflectivity, the W/m^2 are lower than a direct fit to the Earthshine data. The fit to the Earthshine data is better with the higher levels of CR, creating a 86% R sq. vs. a 79% R sq. for the lower levels of CR. Chart Appendix A.2 shows the comparison of the two approaches. Solar impacts are also shown in Charts Appendix A.2a and A.2b. The regression fits to Earthshine are shown in Charts Appendix A.2c and A.2d.

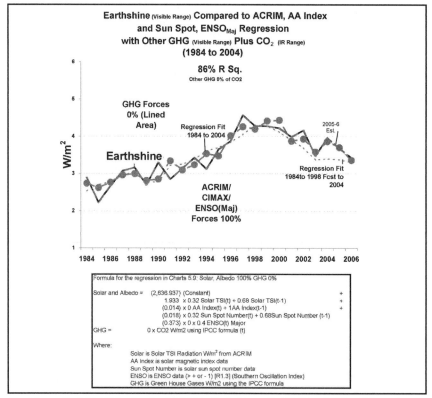

Chart Appendix A.2d: Higher levels of CR fit to Earthshine with 0% Other GHG to CO_2 can be found at the website in Appendix C.

The lower level CR impacts produces a 97% R^2 and support a valid Solar Only scenario. The higher CR influences shown in the wider spread of CR influences improves the temperature fit to 98% R^2. It also substantiates a valid Solar Only scenario but only has valid fits to temperature with GHG reduced to the surface levels similar to the reductions applied to the Earthshine data. Both do not fit 1935 to 1955 perfectly (Charts Appendix A.3 and Appendix A.3a). We will provide some speculations on the reasons that these two options do not fit this period perfectly later, when we address possible explanations for the gaps in the CR estimates in Section 1.B below.

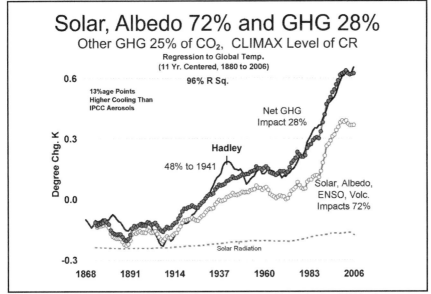

Above: Chart Appendix A.3 and Chart 5.8: Fit to temperature of lower levels of CR in the Earthshine data with 25% other GHG to CO_2; below: Chart Appendix A.3a and Chart 5.9: Fit to temperature of higher levels of CR fit to Earthshine with 25% other GHG to CO_2. Both can be found at the website in Appendix C.

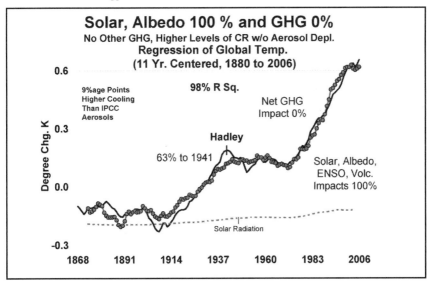

Section 1.B.: Earthshine Options: Speculation regarding gaps in CR data and temperature

There is a possible explanation for the gaps in the regression fits to the years 1935 to 1950. The lack of Climax data prior to 1951 creates a need to estimate the earlier periods using Sun Spot and AA Index data. These two fit very well to the Climax data, but they lack the ability to differentiate the intensity of CR levels that strike the earth. The major gap is during the period from 1971 to 1974. If we adjust this period for the apparent understated CR counts, we can also assume that the previous period understated was 31 years earlier, during 1940–1943, as there appears to be a cyclicality to this understatement (Chart Appendix A.4).

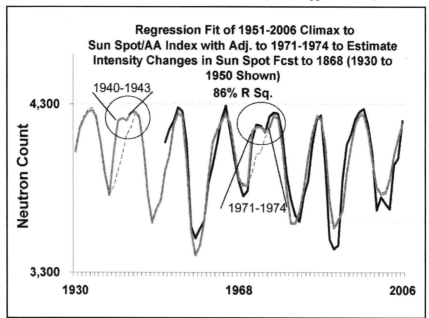

Chart Appendix A.4: Speculations regarding gaps in CR data vs. Sun Spot and AA Index fit to Climax data 1951 to 2006. Two gaps estimated: 1940–1943 and 1971–1974.

If we also speculate about the reasons that the regression fit in Chart 5.9 does not fit the earlier years from 1880 to 1913, we might substitute the Land-Ocean Index from NOAA for these years. They seem to fit the regression much closer. If we reestablish our regression fit, we have an improvement in the R^2 from 98% to 99%. Obviously, these speculations need further study to determine if they are reasonable (Chart Appendix A.4a).

Top of page 123: Chart Appendix A.4a: 99% R2 regression fits to Land-Ocean Index (1880–1913), Hadley (1914 to 2006), and adjusted gaps in CR data vs. Sun Spot and AA Index fit to Climax data 1951 to 2006. Two gaps estimated: 1940–1943 and 1971–1974.

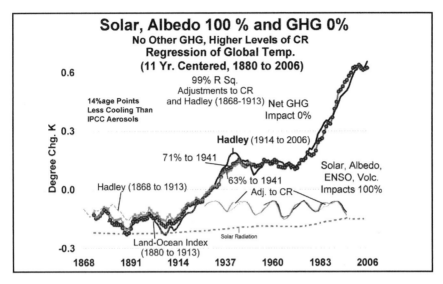

Section 1:C Earthshine Options: Max Planck and GHG only fits to Earthshine data

The Max Planck version of the regression fit to the Earthshine data is in Chart

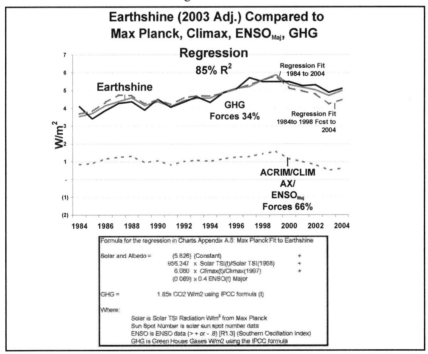

A.5 for the period 1984 to 2004. Visual fit to the Earthshine data raises questions. First, the fit assumes that all GHG (the visible range Other GHG plus the IR range CO_2) are needed to develop this regression, a point that defies scientific cause-and-effect support. Chart Appendix A.5 shows total GHG are 185% of CO_2.

Furthermore, the regression fits to the temperature record using the Max Planck data for solar TSI shows several issues when compared to the best fit using the ACRIM solar TSI. First, the model explains less of the changes in temperature and as stated in Chapters 2, 5, 6, and Appendix B could not produce a valid regression fit to temperature. More details are available at the website referred to in Appendix C.

Additionally, the regression fit to Earthshine with only Other GHG at 85% of CO_2 levels can only produce a 55% R^2. The R^2 declines as the Other GHG as a percentage of CO_2 declines. Additionally, this fit does not produce a valid regression (pass Hindcast repeatability tests) to the temperature record (Chart Appendix A. 6).

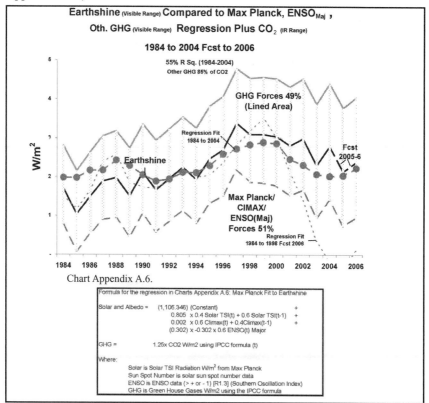

Chart Appendix A.6.

The regression fit substituting GHG in the place of ACRIM TSI is shown in Chart Appendix A.6a.

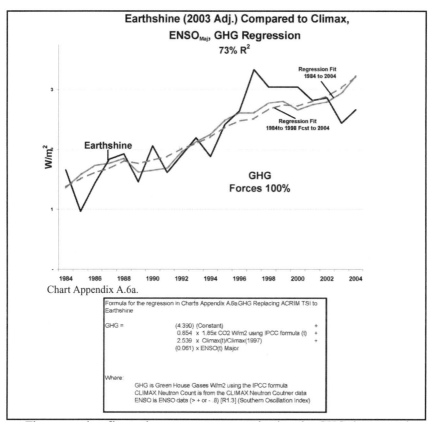

Chart Appendix A.6a.

The regression fits to the temperature record using the GHG data to replace solar TSI show several issues when compared to the best fit using the ACRIM

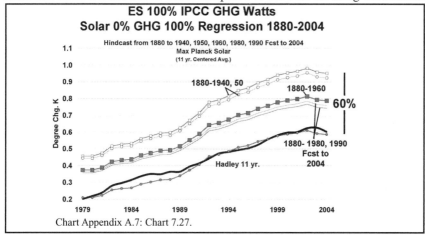

Chart Appendix A.7: Chart 7.27.

solar TSI. The model does not demonstrate the ability to pass Hindcast (repeatability) tests as shown in Appendix A.7 and Chart 7.27 as the IPCC regression models.

2. Implications for 1145 Temperatures

A possible model from the Earthshine Chart 6.3 Solar 100% and GHG 0% would predict a change in peak temperature in 1145 of 1.36° K. The regression fit from Chapter 8 of Solar 57% and GHG 43% would predict a change in peak temperature in 1145 of 0.38° K: This assumes that GHG are at historic natural levels (Appendix A Table.1 below).

Solar 100% GHG 0%	W/m^2	Chg. Temp. (from 1930)
Solar Chg.	0.37	0.09° K
ENSO	0.52	0.12° K
Albedo	4.79	1.15° K
	5.69	1.36° K

Solar 57% GHG 43%	W/m^2	Chg. Temp. (from 1930)
GHG (No Impact)	-	-
Solar Chg.	0.61	0.15° K
ENSO	0.52	0.12° K
Albedo	0.41	0.11° K
	1.54	0.38° K

Appendix B

Resolving Key Issues

There are 3 sections in this appendix:

Section 1: resolving the physics problem of infra-red absorption by oceans.

Section 2: volcano and other dust sources such as the Tunguska event of 1908.

Section 3: full tables of regression options developed:

Table 1: 1880 to 2006 High and Low CR using Earthshine, ACRIM, Other from 25% to 85% GHG

Table 2: 1880 to 2004 High and Low CR using Earthshine, ACRIM, Other from 25% to 85% GHG

Table 3: 1880 to 2004 Earthshine, Max Planck, GHG

Table 4: 1880 to 2006 High and Low CR using Earthshine, ACRIM, Other from 25% to 85% GHG with Hadley from 1880 to 1997 and Satellite from 1998 to 2006

Section 1: Resolving the Physics Problem of Infra-Red (CO_2 absorption frequencies) Absorption by Oceans

There is a physics problem related to the amount of infra-red energy that changes the temperature of the oceans. The current knowledge about these frequencies is that they are the primary CO_2 absorption frequencies. It is also true that the oceans absorb these frequencies rapidly, in the first few inches, when compared to the visible light frequencies, which impact to greater depths. It is assumed that as CO_2 increases in atmospheric concentration, the amount of energy retained into the atmosphere increases. It is also assumed that CO_2 re-emits this energy to the surface, adding to increases in temperature.

This theory then conflicts with the laws of physics when it is assumed that the re-emission of infra-red to the surface has the same sensitivity rate as other frequencies of light from the sun. To resolve this issue, the amount of energy that is absorbed at the ocean surface must be diminished by some factor that has not been defined to this point.

To address this issue, we need to reconsider our basic assumptions of the models from Chapter 5 and Chapter 6.

We utilized the factor that the Earthshine team defined for the amount of light energy they showed changed when they measured the earth's reflection on the Dark Side of the Moon. The total change from 1984 to 1998 was about 10.4

W/m². The amount has declined since 1998. The climate scientist community also holds, according to the Earthshine team that there is a cooling effect from cloud formation that reduces the amount of energy available near the surface. This factor was about 50% or greater.

We used that 50% factor for both infra-red (the primary frequencies associated with increased CO_2 ppm in the atmosphere) and for the other frequencies primarily in the visible light spectrum associated with natural occurring changes, though there are limited visibly light regions associated with other GHG.

If the energy absorbed by the ocean is primarily in the visible light frequencies associated with natural occurring changes in solar or Albedo, then the amount of cooling that would be applied to the natural occurring changes would need to be reduced and the amount of cloud cooling applied to CO_2 would have to be increased. The result then would be a higher amount of the change in temperature related to natural occurring changes in solar or Albedo and a commensurate decrease in the amount of change related to GHG.

What should that factor be? The best tool we have is to use the models from Chapters 5 and 6 and adjust the amount of energy we allocate to cloud cooling between the energy associated with natural sources and the amount we associate to GHG over the 71% of the planet that the oceans represent.

To resolve this issue, the ratio of cloud cooling associated with the additional energy being absorbed into the oceans was changed in the regression models. It was assumed that if we held the amount of additional cloud cooling factor the same from the best model, but changed the ratios, we could visually determine the probable limits to this adjustment. In other words, if the model did not change remarkably from the original best model, we could say that the impacts of this shift would probably be the reasonable limits that could be expected. We could also test to see how much of the energy over the oceans that was associated with GHG changes was affected. If this number was a much higher number, it would indicate that the impacts from the laws of physics were being represented, while not precise, but sufficiently accurate to have a comfort that the impact levels were within some range.

The changes that were made to Chart 5.8 regression as follows:

ITEM CHANGED:	
Original factor for cloud cooling for **all frequencies** in Chart 5.8 model.	46.3%
Additional cloud cooling or aerosol cooling needed for **increased Infra-Red Frequencies**	1.4%
Final cooling for lower absorption by CO_2 in the oceans	44.9%

The above chart shows that the original model required an assumption of cooling of 46.3% of the total energy to balance the regression. This was applied equally to infra-red and visible light frequencies. The factors were adjusted down for the visible-light frequencies to 85% while the CO_2 has no adjustment.

These changes realized a comparable model to the original as shown in Appendix B1.

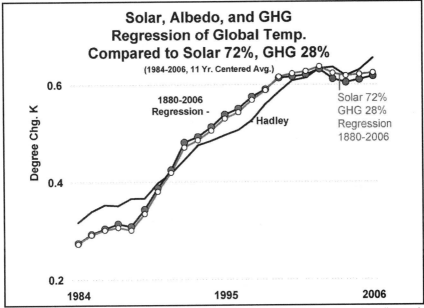

Above: Chart Appendix B.1: Compares Chart 5.8a to the corrections for CO_2 absorptions discussed above. Below: Chart Appendix B2: comparison of the results of Chart 5.8 and Appendix B1. Calculations and other options are available at the website referred to in Appendix C.

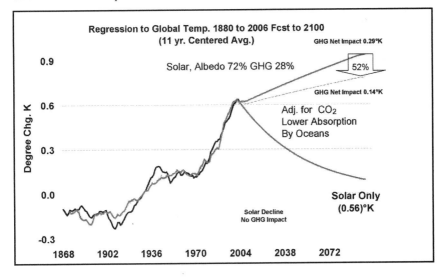

While the models appear very close in fit to the global temperature record called Hadley, the impact upon future expected temperature change is quite large. Chart Appendix B3 shows a 52% reduction in the expected temperature change with the same high level fit to the actual temperature data.

This decline is related to the increase in the cloud cooling factor by 1.4%. As we forecast into the future, it is apparent that if the laws of physics are correct, any fears about human influence upon global temperature should be further assuaged.

Section 2: resolving volcano and other dust sources such as the Tunguska event of 1908.

The data used for volcano and other dust sources is from the IPCC report. The dataset used is the Robock and Free series shown in this chart from the IPCC report.

There are two options offered, but the Sotos et al. dataset does not show the Tunguska event or the El Chichon and Pinatubo event as pronounced as the Robock and Free data. The Tunguska event was the high altitude explosion of a probable comet over this named area in Siberia that produced reported "bright nights" from the particles that remained in the upper atmosphere. The El Chichon and Pinatubo events are also documented in the Maui Data from Chart 4.3. Of interest is that the Robock and Free data set also greatly improved the Global Warming Theory: IPCC Hindcast (repeatability) tests.

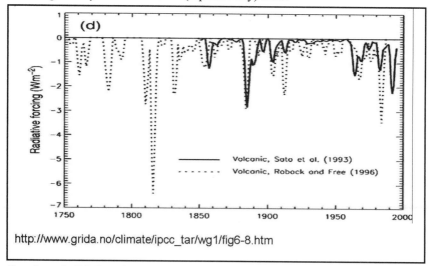

Chart Appendix B.3: From the IPCC report as cited.

Section 3: Full Tables of Regression Options Developed.

Table 1

ACRIM Solar Dataset

Hadley 1880-2006 Climax Levels of CR (Natural) Influence

	2100 Degree Change	Solar %	GHG %	R.Sq.	% of 2002	1984-2006 Hindcast to 1868 within 10%	1880-1940, 50, 60, 80, 90 Hindcast to 2006 within 10%	Rapid Aerosol Depletion
Solar Only	-	100%	0%	97%	101%	Yes 9%	Yes 10%	No
ES 70% GHG (Dietze) Enh. Oth. GHG 25% w/o Depl. & GHG Ocean Impacts	0.09	83%	17%	97%	100%	Yes 5%	Yes 9%	No
ES Enh. Other GHG 25% of CO2 w/o Depl. And GHG Ocean Impacts	0.16	77%	23%	97%	100%	Yes 8%	Yes 10%	No
ES 70% GHG Watts (Dietze) Enhanced Other GHG 25% w/o Depl.	0.17	78%	22%	97%	100%	Yes 6%	Yes 9%	No
ES Enh. Other GHG 17% of CO2 w/o Depl. And GHG Ocean Impacts	0.26	72%	28%	96%	100%	Yes 6%	Yes 10%	No
ES Enhanced GHG 70% of CO2 w/o IPCC Aero. Depl.	0.32	85%	15%	96%	102%	Yes 10%	Yes 10%	Yes
ES Enhanced Other GHG 70% of CO2 w/o IPCC Aero. Depl.	0.36	64%	36%	96%	100%	Yes 7%	Yes 10%	No
ES Enhanced Other GHG 85% of CO2 w IPCC Aero. Depl.	0.39	83%	17%	96%	101%	Yes 10%	Yes 10%	Yes
ES Enhanced Other GHG 85% of CO2 w/o IPCC Aero. Depl.	0.39	61%	39%	96%	100%	Yes 6%	Yes 10%	No
Chapter 8	0.44	57%	43%	97%	97%	Yes 7%	Yes 10%	No
ES Enhanced 70% GHG w High Aerosol Depletion.	0.45	82%	18%	96%	101%	Yes 9%	Yes 10%	Yes
ES Enhanced Other GHG 85% of CO2 w High IPCC Aero. Depl.	0.57	78%	22%	96%	100%	Yes 6%	No 21%	Yes
Global Warming Theory: IPCC	1.73	35%	65%	96%	100%	No 12%	No 49%	Yes

Hadley 1880-2006 High Levels CR (Natural) Influence

	2100 Degree Change	Solar %	GHG %	R.Sq.	% of 2002	1984-2006 Hindcast to 1868 within 10%	1880-1940, 50, 60, 80, 90 Hindcast to 2006 within 10%	Rapid Aerosol Depletion
Solar Only	-	100%	0%	98%	98%	Yes 6%	Yes 10%	No
ES Enh. Other GHG 17% of CO2 w/o Depl. And GHG Ocean Impacts	-	93%	7%	98%	97%	Yes 7%	Yes 9%	Yes
ES 70% GHG Watts (Dietze) Enhanced Other GHG 12% w/o Depl.	-	91%	9%	97%	94%	Yes 7%	Yes 9%	No
ES Enhanced Other GHG 6% of CO2 w IPCC Aero. Depl.	0.03	95%	5%	98%	98%	Yes 8%	Yes 7%	No
ES 70% GHG (Dietze) Enh. Oth. GHG 12% w/o Depl. & GHG Ocean Impacts	0.03	96%	4%	97%	93%	Yes 7%	Yes 9%	No
ES Enh. Other GHG 17% of CO2 w/o Depl. And GHG Ocean Impacts	0.06	88%	12%	98%	98%	Yes 7%	Yes 9%	No
ES Enhanced Other GHG 13% of CO2 w/o IPCC Aero. Depl.	0.06	94%	6%	98%	97%	Yes 7%	Yes 9%	No
ES Enhanced 6% GHG w High Aerosol Depletion.	0.08	94%	6%	98%	98%	Yes 8%	Yes 9%	Yes
ES Enhanced Other GHG 6% of CO2 w/o IPCC Aero. Depl.	0.10	85%	15%	97%	97%	Yes 8%	Yes 9%	No
ES Enhanced Other GHG 13% of CO2 w/o IPCC Aero. Depl.	0.11	84%	16%	98%	97%	Yes 5%	Yes 10%	No
ES Enhanced Other GHG 13% of CO2 w High IPCC Aero. Depl.	0.14	92%	8%	98%	98%	Yes 9%	Yes 10%	Yes
Chapter 8	0.44	57%	43%	97%	98%	Yes 7%	Yes 10%	No
Global Warming Theory: IPCC	1.73	35%	65%	96%	100%	No 12%	No 49%	Yes

Failed Hindcast Repeatability Test

ACRIM Solar Dataset

Table 2

Hadley 1880-2004 Climax Levels of CR (Natural) Influence

Solar Only	2100 Degree Change	Solar %	GHG %	R Sq.	% of 2002	1984-2006 Hindcast to 1868 within 10%		1880-1940, 50, 60, 80, 90 Hindcast to 2004 within 10%		Rapid Aerosol Depletion
	—	100%	0%	97%	101%	Yes	8%	Yes	10%	No
ES 70% GHG (Dietze) Enh. Oth. GHG 25% w/o Depl. & GHG Ocean Impacts	0.13	83%	17%	97%	100%	Yes	9%	No	15%	No
ES Enh. Other GHG 25% of CO_2 w/o Depl. And GHG Ocean Impacts	0.19	78%	22%	97%	100%	Yes	8%	No	11%	No
ES 70% GHG Watts (Dietze) Enhanced Other GHG 25% w/o Depl.	0.19	77%	23%	97%	99%	Yes	9%	No	14%	No
ES Enh. Other GHG 25% of CO_2 w/o Depl. And GHG Ocean Impacts	0.27	71%	29%	96%	98%	Yes	9%	No	13%	No
ES Enhanced Other GHG 70% of CO_2 w IPCC Aero. Depl.	0.34	84%	16%	97%	100%	Yes	9%	No	24%	Yes
ES Enhanced Other GHG 70% of CO_2 w/o IPCC Aero. Depl.	0.38	63%	37%	96%	98%	Yes	7%	No	23%	No
ES Enhanced Other GHG 85% of CO_2 w/o IPCC Aero. Depl.	0.40	60%	40%	97%	98%	Yes	7%	No	22%	No
Chapter 8	0.46	57%	43%	96%	97%	Yes	7%	No	12%	No
ES Enhanced 70% GHG w High Aerosol Depletion.	0.46	81%	19%	96%	100%	Yes	10%	No	27%	Yes
ES Enhanced Other GHG 85% of CO_2 w High IPCC Aero. Depl.	0.59	77%	23%	96%	97%	Yes	10%	No	32%	Yes
ES Enhanced Other GHG 85% of CO_2 w IPCC Aero. Depl.	0.39	83%	17%	97%	101%	No	11%	No	24%	Yes
Global Warming Theory: IPCC	1.73	35%	65%	96%	100%	No	14%	No	46%	Yes

Hadley 1880-2004 High Levels CR (Natural) Influence

Solar Only		Solar %	GHG %	R Sq.	% of 2002	Hindcast to 1868 within 10%		Hindcast to 2004 within 10%		Rapid Aerosol Depletion
	(0.08)	100%	0%	98%	98%	No	10%	Yes	10%	No
ES Enh. Other GHG 17% of CO_2 w/o Depl. And GHG Ocean Impacts	—	93%	7%	98%	97%	Yes	8%	Yes	10%	Yes
ES 70% GHG Watts (Dietze) Enhanced Other GHG 12% w/o Depl.	—	91%	9%	97%	94%	No	9%	Yes	9%	No
ES Enhanced Other GHG 6% of CO_2 w IPCC Aero. Depl.	0.03	95%	5%	98%	98%	No	9%	Yes	10%	No
ES 70% GHG (Dietze) Enh. Oth. GHG 12% w/o Depl. & GHG Ocean Impacts	0.03	96%	4%	97%	93%	No	11%	Yes	9%	No
ES Enh. Other GHG 17% of CO_2 w/o Depl. And GHG Ocean Impacts	0.06	88%	12%	98%	98%	Yes	8%	Yes	10%	No
ES Enhanced Other GHG 13% of CO2 w IPCC Aero. Depl.	0.06	94%	6%	98%	97%	No	9%	Yes	10%	No
ES Enhanced 6% GHG w High Aerosol Depletion.	0.08	94%	6%	98%	98%	Yes	9%	Yes	10%	Yes
ES Enhanced Other GHG 6% of CO_2 w/o IPCC Aero. Depl.	0.10	85%	15%	97%	97%	Yes	7%	Yes	10%	No
ES Enhanced Other GHG 13% of CO_2 w/o IPCC Aero. Depl.	0.11	84%	16%	98%	97%	Yes	7%	Yes	10%	No
ES Enhanced Other GHG 13% of CO_2 w High IPCC Aero. Depl.	0.14	92%	8%	98%	98%	Yes	7%	No	12%	Yes
Chapter 8	0.46	57%	43%	97%	98%	Yes	7%	No	12%	No
Global Warming Theory: IPCC	1.73	35%	65%	96%	100%	No	14%	No	46%	Yes

Failed Hindcast Repeatability Test

Max Planck Solar Dataset

Table 3
Hadley 1880-2004 Assuming CO₂ and other GHG influence Earthshine data

	2100 Degree Change	Solar %	GHG %	R.Sq.	% of 2002	1984-2006 Hindcast to 1868 within 10%		1880-1940, 50, 60, 80, 90 Hindcast to 2004 within 10%		Rapid Aerosol Depletion
3 ES 100% IPCC GHG Watts	0.33	68%	32%	96%	97%	Yes	5%	No	18%	No
# ES Enhanced 5% GHG w/o Aerosol Depletion	0.35	67%	33%	96%	97%	Yes	7%	No	16%	No
# ES Enhanced 20% GHG w/o Aerosol Depletion.	0.40	57%	43%	97%	97%	Yes	6%	No	17%	No
2 Dietze Chapter 8	0.46	57%	43%	96%	99%	Yes	8%	No	15%	No
# ES Enhanced 70% GHG w High Aerosol Depletion.	0.78	39%	61%	97%	102%	Yes	10%	No	24%	Yes
# ES Enhanced 70% GHG w/o Aerosol Depletion.	0.01	42%	58%	95%	91%	No	28%	No	24%	No
7 Solar Only	0.01	100%	0%	96%	89%	No	40%	No	23%	No
6 ES 70% (Dietze) Red. GHG Impact Oceans	0.09	88%	12%	97%	94%	No	23%	No	19%	No
4 ES 100% w Red. GHG Impact Oceans	0.14	85%	15%	95%	93%	No	22%	No	19%	No
5 ES 70% (Dietze) IPCC GHG Watts	0.22	68%	32%	96%	94%	No	15%	No	20%	No
8 ES Enhanced 70% GHG Red. GHG Impact Oceans	0.46	87%	13%	94%	93%	No	40%	No	36%	No
9 ES Enhanced 70% GHG w Aerosol Depletion	0.62	49%	51%	97%	98%	No	13%	No	11%	Yes
1 Global Warming - IPCC Chapter 7	1.96	36%	64%	95%	103%	No	12%	No	94%	Yes

Hadley 1880-2006 Both Climax and High Levels of CR (Natural) Influence

9 ES Enhanced Other GHG 85% of CO₂ w IPCC Aero. Depl.										
4 Enh. Other GHG 25% of CO₂ w/o Depl. And GHG Ocean Impacts										
7 Solar Only										
8 ES Enhanced Other GHG 85% of CO₂ w High IPCC Aero. Depl.										
6 ES 70% GHG (Dietze) Enh. Oth. GHG 25% w/o Depl. & GHG Ocean Impacts			Not Meaningful, Relationship to Earthshine is Below Statistically Valid Levels.							
5 ES 70% GHG Watts (Dietze) Enhanced Other GHG 25% w/o Depl.										
3 ES. Enh. Other GHG 17% of CO₂ w/o Depl. And GHG Ocean Impacts										
# ES Enhanced Other GHG 85% of CO₂ w/o IPCC Aero. Depl.										
# ES Enhanced Other GHG 70% of CO₂ w/o IPCC Aero. Depl.										
2 Chapter 8										
# ES Enhanced 70% GHG w High Aerosol Depletion.										
# ES Enhanced Other GHG 70% of CO₂ w IPCC Aero. Depl.										
1 Global Warming Theory: IPCC	1.73	30%	70%	95%	102%	Yes	3%	No	48%	Yes

Failed Hindcast Repeatability Test

ACRIM Solar Dataset

Table 4

Hadley 1880-1997, Satellite 1998-2006 Climax Levels of CR (Natural) Influence

	2100 Degree Change	Solar %	GHG %	R Sq.	% of 2002	1984-2006 Hindcast to 1868 within 10%		1880-1940, 50, 60, 80, 90 Hindcast to 2006 within 10%		Rapid Aerosol Depletion
7 Solar Only	-	100%	0%	97%	101%	Yes	10%	Yes	3%	No
6 ES 70% GHG (Dietze) Enh. Oth. GHG 25% w/o Depl. & GHG Ocean Impacts	0.13	83%	17%	97%	100%	Yes	6%	Yes	10%	No
4 ES Enh. Other GHG 25% of CO_2 w/o Depl. And GHG Ocean Impacts	0.19	78%	22%	97%	100%	Yes	9%	Yes	9%	No
5 ES 70% GHG Watts (Dietze) Enhanced Other GHG 25% w/o Depl.	0.19	77%	23%	97%	99%	Yes	5%	Yes	10%	No
3 ES Enh. Other GHG 17% of CO_2 w/o Depl. And GHG Ocean Impacts	0.29	71%	29%	96%	98%	Yes	9%	Yes	10%	No
# ES Enhanced Other GHG 70% of CO_2 w/IPCC Aero. Depl.	0.35	84%	16%	97%	100%	Yes	10%	Yes	10%	No
# ES Enhanced Other GHG 70% of CO_2 w/o IPCC Aero. Depl.	0.38	63%	37%	96%	98%	Yes	9%	Yes	10%	No
9 ES Enhanced Other GHG 85% of CO_2 w IPCC Aero. Depl.	0.39	83%	17%	97%	101%	Yes	10%	Yes	10%	No
# ES Enhanced Other GHG 85% of CO_2 w/o IPCC Aero. Depl.	0.41	60%	40%	97%	98%	Yes	7%	Yes	10%	No
2 Chapter 8	0.43	57%	43%	96%	97%	Yes	7%	Yes	10%	No
# ES Enhanced 70% GHG w High Aerosol Depletion.	0.45	81%	19%	96%	100%	Yes	9%	No	13%	Yes
8 ES Enhanced Other GHG 85% of CO_2 w High IPCC Aero. Depl.	0.58	77%	23%	96%	97%	Yes	6%	No	22%	Yes
1 Global Warming Theory: IPCC	1.69	35%	65%	96%	100%	No	11%	No	59%	Yes

Hadley 1880-1997, Satellite 1998-2006 High Levels of CR (Natural) Influence

	2100 Degree Change	Solar %	GHG %	R Sq.	% of 2002	1984-2006 Hindcast to 1868 within 10%		1880-1940, 50, 60, 80, 90 Hindcast to 2006 within 10%		Rapid Aerosol Depletion
7 Solar Only	-	100%	0%	98%	98%	Yes	9%	Yes	8%	No
# ES Enhanced Other GHG 6% of CO_2 w/IPCC Aero. Depl.	0.01	96%	4%	97%	93%	Yes	9%	Yes	10%	No
4 ES Enh. Other GHG 17% of CO_2 w/o Depl. And GHG Ocean Impacts	0.01	93%	7%	98%	97%	Yes	8%	Yes	9%	No
5 ES 70% GHG Watts (Dietze) Enhanced Other GHG 12% w/o Depl.	0.01	91%	9%	97%	94%	Yes	8%	Yes	8%	No
3 ES Enh. Other GHG 17% of CO_2 w/o Depl. And GHG Ocean Impacts	0.03	88%	12%	98%	98%	Yes	4%	Yes	10%	No
6 ES 70% GHG (Dietze) Enh. Oth. GHG 12% w/o Depl. & GHG Ocean Impacts	0.04	95%	5%	98%	98%	Yes	8%	Yes	9%	No
9 ES Enhanced Other GHG 13% of CO_2 w/IPCC Aero. Depl.	0.04	85%	15%	97%	97%	Yes	8%	Yes	10%	No
# ES Enhanced 6% GHG w High Aerosol Depletion.	0.06	94%	6%	98%	97%	Yes	8%	Yes	10%	No
# ES Enhanced Other GHG 6% of CO_2 w/o IPCC Aero. Depl.	0.08	84%	16%	98%	97%	Yes	9%	Yes	8%	No
# ES Enhanced Other GHG 13% of CO_2 w/o IPCC Aero. Depl.	0.09	57%	43%	97%	98%	Yes	6%	Yes	9%	No
8 ES Enhanced Other GHG 13% of CO_2 w High IPCC Aero. Depl.	0.13	94%	6%	98%	98%	Yes	10%	Yes	9%	No
2 Chapter 8	0.43	92%	8%	98%	98%	Yes	7%	Yes	9%	No
1 Global Warming Theory: IPCC	1.69	35%	65%	96%	100%	No	11%	No	59%	Yes

Failed Hindcast Repeatability Test

Appendix C

Website Instruction

The Excel™ spreadsheets that were used to generate the results and charts for this book are available from the website: **www.itsthesunnotyoursuv.com**.

The website requests that you send an e-mail to the web manager requesting the 2003 Excel™ spreadsheets you desire. *In order to receive these spreadsheets, it is required that you include your name and address. The data will not be used for any other purpose than to identify you.* There are no instructions at the website. The instructions to request the datasets are only available in this appendix.

The spreadsheets are protected in key parts to avoid unintentional changes. You can make your own adjustments to the models. If you wish to make changes to the basic calculations, you will be able to copy and paste the primary spreadsheets to a new spreadsheet.

To review the models, you should begin with the primary models that are located in the files with the name Climatemodel…xls. On the worksheet titled: "Model Inputs and Charts" provides a cell at B4 for you to make your choices of possible options you would like to review. Those options are listed from J4 to V4. There is also a column in W4 for you to make changes to the factors that are used in the model. Lower on the worksheet are self-identified charts that correspond to the various chapters in the book or the unpublished equivalents.

The worksheet titled "Yearly Numbers" contains the primary calculations. This spreadsheet is important to review if you would like to check calculations. The worksheet titled "Earthshine" holds the calculations for the basic Earthshine data. The spreadsheet is quite complex because of all the options within the spreadsheet. Good programming skills and knowledge of Excel™ functions are needed to understand the formulas. Other worksheet names are explained in the "Read Me" tab.

The 2003 Excel™ spreadsheets (3 mbts each) that are available are as follows:

1. Climatemodel06.xls contains 1880 to 2006 regression fits to the Hadley temperature record using the ACRIM Solar TSI dataset and Climax level CR.

2. Climatemodelaasp06.xls contains 1880 to 2006 regression fits to the Hadley temperature record using the ACRIM Solar TSI dataset and Higher Level CR.

3. Climatemodel04.xls contains 1880 to 2004 regression fits to the Hadley temperature record using the ACRIM Solar TSI dataset and Climax level CR.

4. Climatemodelaasp04.xls contains 1880 to 2004 regression fits to the Hadley temperature record using the ACRIM Solar TSI dataset and High level CR.

5. Climatemodel06MaxPlanck.xls contains 1880 to 2006 regression fits to the Hadley temperature record using the Max Planck Solar TSI dataset.

6. ClimatemodelGHG.xls contains 1880 to 2004 regression fits to the Hadley temperature record substituting GHG for the ACRIM Solar TSI in the Earthshine regression and uses the Max Planck Solar TSI dataset within the Climate model.

7. Emissions.xls contains the 1880 to 2100 review of probable fossil fuel emissions and their conversions to atmospheric CO_2 ppm.

Index